THE FLYING ADVENTURES OF CHARLES GREEN

THE FLYING ADVENTURES OF CHARLES GREEN

THE EXTRAORDINARY AIRMAN WHO REVOLUTIONISED 19TH CENTURY AERONAUTICS

ALASTAIR GOODRUM

Pen & Sword
AVIATION

First published in Great Britain in 2025 by
PEN AND SWORD AVIATION
An imprint of
Pen & Sword Books Limited
Yorkshire – Philadelphia

Copyright © Alastair Goodrum, 2025

ISBN 978 1 03611 330 8

The right of Alastair Goodrum to be identified as Author
of this work has been asserted by him in accordance with the Copyright,
Designs and Patents Act 1988.

A CIP catalogue record for this book is available from the British Library.

All rights reserved. No part of this book may be reproduced, transmitted,
downloaded, decompiled or reverse engineered in any form or by any means,
electronic or mechanical including photocopying, recording or by any information
storage and retrieval system, without permission from the Publisher in writing.
No part of this book may be used or reproduced in any manner for the purpose of
training artificial intelligence technologies or systems.

Typeset in Ehrhardt 10/13 by
SJmagic DESIGN SERVICES, India.
Printed and bound in the UK by CPI Group (UK) Ltd, Croydon, CR0 4YY.

The Publisher's authorised representative in the EU for product safety is
Authorised Rep Compliance Ltd., Ground Floor, 71 Lower Baggot Street, Dublin
D02 P593, Ireland.
www.arccompliance.com

For a complete list of Pen & Sword titles please contact
PEN & SWORD BOOKS LIMITED
George House, Units 12 & 13, Beevor Street, Off Pontefract Road,
Barnsley, South Yorkshire, S71 1HN, England
E-mail: enquiries@pen-and-sword.co.uk
Website: www.pen-and-sword.co.uk

or

PEN AND SWORD BOOKS
1950 Lawrence Rd, Havertown, PA 19083, USA
E-mail: uspen-and-sword@casematepublishers.com
Website: www.penandswordbooks.com

Contents

Acknowledgements		vi
Conversion Table		vii
Chapter 1	The Hatter's Son	1
Chapter 2	Crowning Glory	12
Chapter 3	Ditching, Dutchmen and Dastardly Deeds	21
Chapter 4	Flying Tours	34
Chapter 5	Sophia, The Girl Who Fell to Earth	49
Chapter 6	Another Balloon Lost	62
Chapter 7	The Eagle & The Horse	71
Chapter 8	Log-Book Puzzles	86
Chapter 9	A Mysterious Disappearance	97
Chapter 10	Foreign Expeditions	108
Chapter 11	Parachute Disaster	129
Chapter 12	Adventures with *Albion*	140
Chapter 13	Bombs Away! & The Brunswick Escapade	158
Chapter 14	Happy Landings	172
Appendix 1	List of Claimed and Verifiable Ascents by Charles Green	182
Appendix 2	Charles Green's Passenger List	194
Endnotes		217
Bibliography		219
Index		221

Acknowledgements

The author gratefully acknowledges the information and images, received variously from the archives of the Wellcome Collection; the US Library of Congress; the Linda Hall Library of Science, Engineering & Technology, Kansas City, USA and the British Newspaper Library, London. Thanks also to Islington Local History Centre, Finsbury Library, London and the Camden Local Studies and Archives Centre, Holborn Library, London. Special thanks to the artist Peter Woodward of 3details Art & Design and to Stephanie Hemmings of the British Balloon and Airship Club for permission to use images from their respective websites. The author is most grateful to Jonathan Wright, Charlotte Mitchell and Harriet Fielding of Pen & Sword, for their help in getting Charles Green's amazing story off the ground.

Conversion Table

1 inch	25.400 millimetres
1 foot (12 inches)	0.305 metre
1 yard (3 feet)	0.914 metre
1 mile (1,760 yards)	1.604 kilometres
1 cubic-foot	0.283 cubic-metre
1 square-yard	0.836 square-metre
1 acre	0.405 hectare
1 pint	0.568 litre
1 gallon (8 pints)	4.546 litres
1 grain	0.065 gramme
1 ounce	28.350 grammes
1 pound [lb] (16 ounces)	0.453 kilogram

To convert temperatures from Fahrenheit to Centigrade: subtract 32, multiply by 5, divide by 9.

Freezing point = 32 degrees Fahrenheit; 0 degrees Centigrade.

British pre-decimal currency (£-s-d): £1 = 20 shillings (s); 1 shilling = 12 pence (d). 1 guinea = 21 shillings.

Chapter 1

The Hatter's Son

With a flying career spanning thirty-five years, Charles Green (1785-1870) strode the sky like a Colossus; his adventures in the air eclipsing those who went before him and those who followed.

When presenting aeronautical history there is a tendency to overlook its first one hundred years. What follows in this book, however, will help remind readers of an era that was nonetheless challenging, exciting and dangerous for participants and observers alike.

Coal, that black gold and fuel of the Industrial Revolution, helped usher in the factory age of the early 1800s. In addition to providing the basis of steam propulsion for railways, ships and machinery, its other by-product - coal gas - made it possible to illuminate homes, streets and work places in the towns and cities of England and new gas works companies proliferated. It was this development that was to facilitate the use of coal gas in the world of ballooning - but it needed someone to initiate the change.

The science of aerostation (ballooning) had been responsible for conveying men and women into the air since 1783 - but its shine had worn off. The aeronaut, astronomer and lecturer, John Mackenzie Bacon MA FRAS (1846-1904) summed up the decline of aeronautics in the second decade of the nineteenth century:

> 'As a mere exhibition the novelty of a balloon ascent had much worn off. No experimentalist was ready with any new departure in the art. No fresh adventure presented itself to the minds of the more enterprising spirits; and, whereas a few years previously ballooning exploits crowded into every summer season and were not neglected even in winter months, there is now for a while little to chronicle, either abroad or in our own country.
>
> But the fame of any aeronaut [prior to 1820], must inevitably pale before the dawning light shed by Charles Green in England. [Green] who has been well styled the "Father of English Aeronautics," now entered on a long and honoured career of so great importance and success that we must reserve for him a separate and special chapter.
>
> The balloon, which had gradually been dropping out of favour, had now been virtually laid aside, and, to all appearance, might have continued so, when, as if by chance concurrence of events, there

arrived both the hour and the man to restore it to the world, and to invest it with a new practicability and importance. The coronation of George the Fourth was at hand, and this became a befitting occasion for the rare genius [of Charles Green] to put in practice a new method of balloon management and inflation, the entire credit of which must be accorded to him alone.'[1]

While Charles Green's entry into this field was relatively late, his contribution was nevertheless highly significant and exceedingly influential. His unique contribution to aeronautics is that he was the first person to exploit the ability of coal gas to be used as a practical load-lifting agent and then, in 1821, the first to employ coal gas to inflate a balloon large enough to carry himself into the air. Green burst into prominence in nineteenth century balloon aeronautics in a way that was destined to keep him at its forefront for the next thirty-five years and his technique to remain in use, unaltered, for a century. Furthermore, he was astute enough to recognise the business potential of the spectacle of ballooning and took the gamble on himself, his apparatus and his business acumen to make ballooning his livelihood. Charles Green would become the first aeronaut to carry large groups of paying passengers on what, in modern times, are called 'joy-rides.' Following on from this, he made the concept of public travel by air a reality.

He was self-taught in both his experiments with coal gas and hydrogen and indeed as an aeronaut. From a humble, working-class background, this man became the outstanding aeronaut of the Georgian and Victorian eras and well and truly imprinted the science of ballooning in the minds of the people the length and breadth of the kingdom and beyond. In doing so, Charles Green endeared himself to their hearts to such an extent that in his hey-day his name became a by-word for all things aeronautical. His contribution to the public promotion of aeronautics would be equalled only by exploits of men such as Sir Alan Cobham, a hundred years later.

Some historians have suggested that Charles Green was uneducated or was not a 'scientific aeronaut' but, in the light of what Green achieved, such remarks are surely unwarranted. Consider, for example, the opinion of Theodosius Purland MA PhD (1805-1881) a surgeon-dentist practising in London, widely acknowledged in his time as a prolific society-commentator, literary collector and antiquarian. He claimed the Green family was well-known to him, having been taken aloft (probably on 'tethered' ascents) by Charles Green on at least five occasions at The Royal Gardens, Vauxhall.

'All his family were exceedingly illiterate and vulgar and yet, for all his vulgarity, the instant he touched the balloon in Vauxhall Gardens, or anywhere else, he became the gentleman and the man of science. The transformation was complete!'[2]

Charles Green was not and never claimed to be, a scientist in the mould of Henry Cavendish, Joseph Black or Joseph Gay-Lussac, for example, but he deserves great credit for discovering the qualities of coal gas that could be applied to aeronautics and furthermore, what it took to venture into the air efficiently and return to earth safely, time after time, in all weathers. He was certainly neither uneducated nor illiterate, as the many articulate accounts of his journeys; theories; letters and lectures will testify. As for 'vulgar' i.e. 'lacking sophistication or good taste,' that seems to be Purland's pretentious, self-opinionated view of this blunt, working-class aeronaut. The scientific value of Green's self-taught observations, though initially lacking some procedural finesse, was praised by the Royal Institution of Great Britain which, with just three ascents to his name, offered the following encouragement after the second of his two flights from Portsea in 1821.

'It is to be hoped that Mr Green will be enabled to persevere in his exertions, as a continuation of such observations cannot fail to be of the utmost use to science.'

Green also introduced a number of technical innovations to balloon operations that, to some, were merely practical rather than scientific, but that view could - in that age of technical discovery that was the nineteenth century - be regarded as a matter of semantics. For example, he developed and used a glue product that was used very effectively to cement and seal fabric seams during balloon manufacture. The balloon fabric envelopes he designed used a laminated, multi-layer technique that imparted strength and aided gas retention. He is also credited with the introduction of a quick-release lever for take-off; the trail-rope - a method of low-altitude stabilisation, with modifications for use over both land and water - to ballooning and he specified a design for a rudimentary climb-and-descent indicator that was tested by him in flight.

We shall see from the examples of his exploits that follow - including piloting for scientific flights in 1828, 1838 and 1852 - his vast experience, freely and widely reported upon during his lifetime, undoubtedly made the scientific claims of those who followed (James Glaisher with Henry Tracey Coxwell, in the 1860s for example) a great deal easier to achieve. All of which gives rise to the questions: who was Charles Green; how did he arrive at his particular technique for ballooning and what was his unique contribution to the world of aeronautics?

Until his foray into the world of aeronautics in 1821, he led an unremarkable life and in consequence, information about Charles Green and his family is sparse and what is available needs careful examination, as it contains some anomalies.

Written works consulted during research for this book derive many quotes about Green from the text of the *Oxford Dictionary of Biography (ODB)*, which was compiled by G.C. Boase in the late 1890s. The most-widely quoted data source relating to Charles Green's family origins, is derived from quotes from the *Dictionary of National Biography (DNB)* or its up-dated version: *Oxford Dictionary of National Biography (ODNB)*, both of whose entries for Charles Green, aeronaut take material from an earlier entry in *Modern English Biography (MEB)* by Frederic Boase.³ Attempts by this writer to verify and/or if possible, add to the data, have identified anomalies such as:

MEB states: 'Charles Green (son of Thomas Green, fruiterer, died 1850). Born at 92 Goswell *Road*, London on 31 January 1785; fruiterer with his father.'

DNB states: 'Charles Green, aeronaut - son of Thomas Green, fruiterer of Willow Walk, Goswell *Street*, London, who died in May 1850, aged 88 - was born at 92 Goswell Road, London on 31 January 1785 and on leaving school was taken into his father's business.'

ODNB states in addition the above *DNB* item: 'He may have been the Charles Green, son of Thomas Green and his wife Anne, baptised in the local church, St Luke's Old Street, on 1 February 1786.'

Although Goswell Road still exists in the Islington/Clerkenwell/Shoreditch area of London with which Charles and his family are associated, the original number 92 is long gone.

Originally, *MEB*, *DNB* and *ODNB* all stated his father's trade as 'fruiterer' and this is widely quoted by writers when referencing Charles Green. The 2004 version of Green's biographical entry in *ODNB*, includes the above reference to the baptism register of St Luke's church in Old Street. Close examination of that register for February 1786, however, shows the full wording to be: 'Charles, S [son] of Thomas Green, *Hatmaker*, and Ann*e*. Born 31 January [1785], baptised 1 February 1786.' Parental names and birth date match, but the anomaly of his father's trade becomes obvious and is relevant because Charles was said to have gone into his father's business - making hats is a bit different to selling fruit and veg! Hat-making, for instance, would be greatly helped by better premises-lighting - which was said to be the original intention of Charles' experiments with coal gas. It might be argued that this St Luke's church may not be the right church, but there is supporting evidence. The 1861 census details Charles Green, living at 51 Tufnell Park Road, (then in the borough of Islington West) and records him as age 76 and a 'retired aeronaut'; his place of birth is given as St Luke's. Further confirmation of his father's profession can be found on the marriage certificate for Charles' third wedding in 1865, where Thomas Green signed as a witness and the word 'Hatter' is written alongside his name. It is gratifying to note that the editors of *ODNB*, having investigated evidence provided by this writer, accepted that Charles' father's occupation was *hatmaker* and published an amendment in 2020.

Charles is said, in *DNB* and *ODNB*, to have married Martha Morrell in or before 1807, but the original data source is not identified. Further research, however, yields evidence, in the form of a marriage certificate, that Charles Green actually married

Martha Pope on 8 February 1807, at St Leonard's church in Shoreditch, a mile east of Goswell Road. That certificate is witnessed by Thomas Green.

The revised 2020 *ODNB* entry also states Charles' first wife Martha died in 1834; that he married his second wife, Ann Glover (born Mansfield, Nottinghamshire), on 30 June 1835 and she, too, passed away in 1862. A death certificate has not come to light, but certainly something unusual occurred in 1834, since Charles made no ascents that year. The 1861 census shows Charles' wife is recorded as Ann, age 65, born in Mansfield, Nottinghamshire and classed as blind. Ann also appears in the 1841 census as 'wife of Charles, aeronaut' and on the 1851 census as born in Mansfield, Notts. Confirmation of Charles' link with Mansfield is as follows.

In 1849, while making a flight from Derby, Charles landed 5 miles from Mansfield where: 'In a short time he set off for Mansfield where Mrs Green, whose relations live there, was awaiting him.' Charles also told the reporter: 'I found Mrs Green in Mansfield as expected, with her family and friends.'[4]

It was Charles' third marriage that, at first, was thought to give rise to another error. The *ODNB* 2020 revision states that Charles married Jane Culling on 22 May 1865 but, in the *Islington Gazette*[5] report of the inquest into Charles' death in 1870 his widow Jane Green, giving evidence to the coroner, said she married Charles and that 'her maiden name was Shaw.' In fact both names relate to the same person. St Mary's church banns-register for May 1865 clearly shows Jane's name as 'Jane Culling Shaw, spinster.' On the certificate for her marriage to Charles Green, on 22 May 1865, the name is clearly written as 'Jane Culling.' Witnesses signed as: Thomas Green, hatter and Isaac Culling, farmer. Evidence confirms that Charles was married three times; first to Martha, then Ann and finally Jane. Well, as we shall deduce from his story, Charles seems to have had an eye for a pretty girl.

Charles' only child was George Green; born on 29 December 1807 and christened at St Luke's church (like his father) in Old Street, London on 5 June 1808. Records show his father and mother as Charles and Martha Green and that George died in 1864 at the age of 57 - thus pre-deceasing his father. In the 1861 census, George junior is listed, with his wife Elizabeth, as resident at 49 'Belgrave Villa', the house next door to his father in Tufnell Park Road. Somewhat confusingly, Charles' son is occasionally referred to as 'George junior,' but that is in order to distinguish him from one of Charles' brothers, who was also named George and who became an aeronaut in his own right. Contemporary newspapers also name Charles' son variously as 'Charles Green junior' or even 'Charles George Green.' This name issue - both forenames and surnames - certainly causes confusion when attempting to interpret newspaper reports involving the Green family's aeronautical exploits - Green, after all, is a common surname and the forenames encountered are found widely among the national population. Furthermore, this aeronautical pursuit appears to have had an attraction for the whole Green family. It is claimed that no less than ten persons of that surname made balloon ascents in the early nineteenth century, including his wife Ann, his son George - who claimed to have made over 360 aerial journeys and Charles' three brothers: George (senior; over 100 ascents); William Henry, also known as Henry (270 ascents) and James, together with a nephew William; a niece; Charles' father, Thomas and a couple of his brothers' wives. All of which has caused many writers (but hopefully not this one) to attribute flights to Charles that were actually made by one or other of his relatives - and vice versa!

From a few paintings and drawings, it is possible to see what Charles Green looked like - or at least how he was seen by the artists - but the most widely quoted description of him is that written by L.T.C. Rolt.[6]

'a bluff, massively built man with a heavy rubicund face, Green looked more like a prosperous yeoman farmer than a London shopkeeper or an aeronaut. He could have sat as a model for the original John Bull.'

It is unlikely that Rolt could deduce these physical attributes from the only paintings of Green (by Hilaire Ledru: 1835 and John Hollins: 1836/37), but may have formed his opinion from the few mezzotint, lithographic or engraved images, one in particular (1839) showing Green wearing bulky clothing. It is difficult to judge his height from any of these images. However, while evidence from reports of his flights certainly indicate he was physically strong, Charles, in his own calculations for a flight on 29 July 1828, stated his own weight as 148 pounds (lbs). Furthermore, for a flight with George Rush in 1838, he allowed for them both as 145lbs each. Now, that is either a small-ish man in stature or a lean one - not someone you would regard as bluff or massively built. For comparison: the aeronaut Henry Coxwell weighed-in at 148lbs for a flight in 1848 and the ill-fated parachutist Robert Cocking weighed 170lbs at the time of his death. Maybe Charles gained weight in later life; he certainly lived well during his voyages, since many are the times he received great hospitality in the form of hearty breakfasts and dinners. He also liked a 'tipple' while in the air and acquired an enduring taste for champagne - indeed practically dying with a glass of 'champers' in his hand!

It was not until 19 July 1821, at the age of 36, that Charles Green first came to public prominence, when he took a huge personal gamble to make his first man-carrying, free-balloon ascent. That occasion was a most auspicious event, being at the request of the Government to participate in the official outdoor festivities celebrating the coronation of King George IV in London. Furthermore, Green chose this occasion to make the first use of coal gas to inflate the balloon that would carry him aloft. If one is to gamble, then there is nothing like going for broke! Hitherto, balloonists - for example: Montgolfiere, De Rozier, Charles, Lunardi, Blanchard, Garnerin, Zembeccari, Sadler *et al* - used either heated air or hydrogen for this purpose. From this date, having (a) not killed himself and (b) having - it is assumed - been well-paid for his services, it seems Charles Green decided there was a viable living to be made and so he became a professional aeronaut for the rest of his working life. The risks were both real and great - he certainly used up his 'nine lives' - but the rewards, financially and in terms of status and reputation were overwhelming.

Green's decision to use coal gas in a balloon is attributed to his experiments, as a young man, with small-scale apparatus to make coal gas, by which to illuminate the family business premises. Coal gas is a by-product of the destructive distillation of soft coal during the process of making coke. Its basic composition is largely carburetted hydrogen gas and methane gas with additional small quantities of other hydrocarbons, carbon monoxide, carbon dioxide and nitrogen. He found that coal gas produced during the initial stage of the distillation process gave off the brightest light when ignited but gas produced towards the end of the distillation cycle gave off a barely visible flame. Green believed this phenomenon indicated that the later-stage gas contained a higher proportion of hydrogen.

It is considered that he would be aware of the value of hydrogen to aeronauts, not least because he lived in close proximity to the City Road, where several aeronauts of his youth made ascents in the locality. The Eagle Tavern Garden in City Road (the 'Eagle' and 'City Road' in the nursery rhyme *Pop Goes the Weasel*) was a venue for James Sadler in 1810 and 1811, for example and it continued to be a popular ballooning venue during Green's heyday.

This activity was already known as aerostation, which is also associated with the term aerostatics; the latter being defined as the science of buoyancy in air by means of displacement. Aerostation is the activity of that part of aerial navigation dealing with gas-borne or lighter-than-air machines, which themselves are known as aerostats and the people who carried out the ascents were known as aeronauts. To the layman though, all these technical terms simply meant ballooning.

In newspaper reports later in his flying career, Charles Green is quoted as saying he conducted his own tests upon the buoyant powers of coal gas. He said he made small balloons about 3 feet in diameter; filling them with his own-generated coal gas and changing the contents of the balloons with gas drawn off at various stages of the distillation process. This proved to him that the later-stages of the process generated the highest hydrogen content and that, while by no means of great purity, it was more than adequate to lift a useful weight. During these trials, Charles discovered that the lifting power of a balloon of 3 feet in diameter, when filled with coal gas (approximate volume = 14 cubic-feet), was 11 ounces.

Comparing his discovery (about coal gas) with the lifting power of hydrogen as made by earlier aeronauts, he found that his three-feet-diameter balloon - if filled with hydrogen - would lift not more than 15 ounces. He extrapolated these simple data to relate to weights that would be involved in lifting payloads of people and equipment into the air and used these tests to convince himself of the viability of his full-size, coal gas-filled, man-carrying balloon proposal. This was his passport to the invitation to join the Coronation festivities and to future fame.

THE FLYING ADVENTURES OF CHARLES GREEN

Information published by Charles Green while at Coventry in 1824 prior to his sixteenth ascent, for example, indicates that in practise a 14,000 cubic-feet balloon, fully inflated with coal gas, would actually lift a payload of 1,100lbs. Charles also took the opportunity to express his opinion of the superiority of coal gas over hydrogen.

'In carburetted hydrogen gas [coal gas] the principal advantages are, the certainty of inflating the machine in any given time, according to the pressure applied, the greatly diminished expense and trouble, and it's not in the slightest degree injuring the texture of the silk. Whereas, the pure hydrogen, obtained from the decomposition of water, will completely destroy it in a few inflations. In consequence of the carburetted gas entering the balloon at a lower temperature than the surrounding atmosphere, its bulk and levity [lifting power] are continually increasing, from an increase of temperature. The pure hydrogen, owing to the limited dimensions of the apparatus employed in its production, enters the balloon at a much higher temperature than the atmosphere. Its bulk and levity are, therefore, perpetually decreasing and a considerable quantity of water is deposited in the balloon which, frequently containing oxide of iron and acid, dissolves the varnish and injures the silk. To inflate a balloon 33 feet in diameter, the capacity of the vessel employed to generate pure hydrogen must be at least 500 cubic-feet, not more than one-third of which being occupied by materials. When the decomposition [of the gas-generating materials: iron and acid] commences, it follows that about 340 cubic-feet, or 25lbs of atmospheric air, must enter the balloon, unless there be a very great waste of gas as the hydrogen ascends in the vessels and the atmospheric air is not driven over until the decomposition becomes very rapid. By comparison, carburetted gas enters the balloon unmixed with atmospheric air. It may also be mentioned that hydrogen in its preparation is pernicious to every person, place and thing, with which it comes in contact. The apparatus is extremely bulky, occupies great space and is very liable to burst. All these disadvantages, difficulties and dangers are well known to every experienced aeronaut. On the other hand, the only argument that can be made against carburetted gas is, that its levity is not equal to that of pure hydrogen but even this can be altogether obviated by a small addition to the capacity [size] of the balloon.'

His decision to use coal gas thus represents a most significant change to the science of aerostation and illustrates Green's foresight in utilising a gas manufactured cheaply; in bulk; to a reasonable standard of consistency and eventually, to become universally available at home and abroad.

The Dutch academic and inventor of coal gasification and illuminating gas, Jan Pieter Minckelers (1748-1824) in 1784 and the Italian physicist, Tiberius Cavallo (1749-1809) in 1785, both postulated using coal gas for aerostation.

'It appears, therefore, that pit-coal is the substance which may be most advantageously used for the production of inflammable air [hydrogen] in aerostation and though the specific weight of this gas is greater than that of [gas from] metals when extracted by means of acids [i.e. hydrogen], yet the cheapness of the [pit-coal] materials makes ample amends. In order to enable the aerostatic machine to lift up a given weight, its size must be a little larger when it is to be filled with the gas of coal, than when [the gas] produced by metals and acids is to be made use of. On the Continent, various small balloons have been filled with the inflammable air of pit-coal and have floated exceedingly well.'[7]

Yet it was not pursued further at that time, because the means of manufacturing either coal gas or hydrogen in the requisite quantities at balloon launch sites required the erection of complex, non-permanent apparatus and thus, if all that fuss was going to be worthwhile, one might naturally elect to make the most obviously effective product, i.e. 'pure' hydrogen. Charles Green, however, was the first to put the use of coal gas for ballooning into practice and the arrival of commercially-generated coal gas at premises known as Gas Works - where gas could be generated, stored in gas-holders ('gasometers') and distributed publicly through an associated pipe infrastructure - provided the opportunity for this ballooning breakthrough.

Both outdoor and indoor artificial lighting by coal gas was demonstrated successfully on a small scale by the Scottish inventor William Murdoch, at several venues between 1794 and 1803. Another inventor, Josiah Pemberton, worked on designs to improve the luminosity of gas lights and on the design of a practical apparatus for making and storing coal gas. This work all came to a practical, public reality when gas lighting was installed in Pall Mall, London in 1807, proving to be very popular and sparking much interest in the country at large - and indeed abroad, too. A bill was finally passed in Parliament in 1812 allowing a private company to raise finance to provide public gas services and infrastructure. This led to the founding of the world's first gas company, the London & Westminster Gas Light & Coke Company, which began laying gas-carrying pipes under the streets of central London to enable public street lighting and to serve households and business premises. By 1815, 30 miles of gas main piping had been laid and by 1817, two companies operated four gas works in London. By 1820, 300 miles of piping existed in the metropolis and twenty companies were established in cities outside London. Among the key economic advantages of gas for such purposes was that artificially-lit factories could operate for longer hours; it was estimated to cost up to seventy-five per cent less than lighting by oil lamps or candles. On the social front, brighter and more stable illumination by gas light allowed people to read more easily and for longer periods of time, thus encouraging literacy, learning and social mobility. Furthermore, street lighting created a safer environment - both from a personal and anti-crime viewpoint - in which to move around.

THE FLYING ADVENTURES OF CHARLES GREEN

By 1821, as far as ballooning was concerned, compared to 'pure' hydrogen, coal gas was relatively easy to obtain, without the need for elaborate on-site manufacture and a balloon could be filled with this gas more rapidly. The financial implications were also significant, since the cost to fill a balloon with coal gas was lower than for hydrogen. Charles Green calculated that he could fill his balloon six times over, compared to the cost of generating hydrogen at the point of departure and coal gas had a less-caustic action upon the fabric of the envelope. A further advantage - one that took Green a while to appreciate - was that coal gas has a higher specific heat than ambient air, while hydrogen has a specific heat lower than ambient air. In practical terms, this means that coal gas is less susceptible to changes in temperature so that, for example, if a balloon is subjected to any number of changes while being exposed to sun and cloud, the coal gas balloon will react less to those changes and maintain its buoyancy more consistently over a longer period, i.e., it would fly further. On the down-side, coal gas has a lower hydrogen content and weighs about seven times more than 'pure' hydrogen, therefore to lift a useful payload will require a larger-capacity coal gas-filled balloon. However, when an aeronaut could 'fill up' at a gas works, he could negotiate for the contents to be drawn from better quality gas i.e., with a higher hydrogen content, usually achieved during the latter stage of production.

By 1826, Green operated a balloon of 16,000 cubic-feet capacity. This quantity of gas would have cost him around £10 (approximately equal to [≈] £815 in 2023).[8] By comparison, the husband-and-wife aeronautical duo, George and Margaret Graham were among those persisting with hydrogen-filled balloons, of which accurate dimensions are not known. In August 1825 they visited Norwich and their published costs provide an enlightening opportunity to compare financial differences between Charles Green's approach and that of one of his rivals. Both parties were at a similar point in their careers as professional aeronauts, in that Green's trip from the Eagle Tavern in April 1825 was his twenty-eighth, while that of Graham from Norwich was his thirtieth. Out of their total expenditure of £110 (≈ £8,451 in 2023) to put on their event, the cost to the Graham's for the materials alone (acid, iron, water, tank and barrels etc) to make their hydrogen came to £87 (≈ £6,684 in 2023). It should be borne in mind that, despite the laboratory qualities of hydrogen, its purity when manufactured in bulk, on-site and outdoors, was not of the best, thus impairing its lifting ability.

Thus it was to prove, with Green and his successors, that the increasing availability of coal gas allowed such adventurers to 'enlighten and amuse the public' the length and breadth of the country for almost a century. With a reputation as a genial, talkative fellow on the ground and a taciturn, 'tartar' in the air, Charles Green displayed great courage, resilience and tenacity and his personal claim to have made over 500 balloon ascents between 1821 and 1854 is widely quoted. Some put the figure at 525 or even higher but, as can be seen in Appendix 1, after a year or two, unverifiable items punctuate Charles' own flight-numbering sequence. Research of the 518 flights claimed, results in only 336 flights being substantiated by contemporary press reports and advertisements while, unfortunately, no original database or flight log survives to establish the real truth. One is left dependent, therefore, upon contemporary press information in order to paint the canvas of this great man's flying career which, even with the lower figure, remains truly monumental.

Having taken a look at the business of ballooning (aerostation) and at Charles' family background, it is time now to follow him into his flying adventures.

Chapter 2

Crowning Glory

LONDON, Coronation. 19 July 1821. Flight #1

The Times (London) of Wednesday, 18 July 1821 announced that, as part of 'the amusements' in honour of the coronation, a balloon would ascend from one of the royal parks at noon on 19 July. Charles Green had by this time, conducted a number of private experiments and concluded that a balloon filled with coal gas was capable of lifting him into the air and having made a balloon of what he felt was an appropriate size for the job - despite 'several men of science' trying to dissuade him from doing so - he determined to make a public exhibition to prove his theory.

Green advertised his intention to make his first public ascent in a full-sized balloon on Wednesday, 18 July from the Belvidere Gardens (sometimes written as Belvedere) behind the Belvidere Tavern on the corner of 1 Penton Road, Clerkenwell, London. This first incarnation of the Tavern was the location of a large garden for 'promenading,' with a tea room, 'bun-house' and areas for racquets, bowls, quoits and skittles in a venue that might be regarded as an equivalent of St James's or Regent's Parks for the City Road quarter.

It was five or six years since Londoners had witnessed a balloon ascent and desperate to increase its range of public amusements, the Government was anxious to include what most people regarded as 'a wonder of the age.' Charles Green was therefore approached to postpone his Pentonville event in order to accommodate a much more prestigious royal assignment. King George IV had gained a reputation for profligacy and was not highly regarded by the population. Furthermore, he was mired in controversy relating to his marriage. Public opinion, however, tended to favour his wife, Princess Caroline of Brunswick, so the more distractions from the feud, the better and with official expenditure on the whole pageant rumoured to be in the order of £230,000 (≈ £20,759,000 in 2023), Charles Green's inducement, whatever it may have been, was a drop in this vast ocean of extravagance.

Coronation day dawned with a clear, blue sky that found Charles Green preparing his apparatus in an enclosure erected in The Green Park, alongside the small water reservoir known as the Queen's Basin. The balloon's oiled-silk fabric was enclosed within a net gathered together at the neck by a wooden hoop from which a richly decorated car was suspended. During manufacture, the seams of the segments of the envelope - also known as gores - were sewn together by a double line of stitching, and the whole envelope varnished with what was known as drying oil - hence the term 'oiled silk,' which still retained the fabric's flexible quality. Various concoctions of varnish had been tried over the years but as a general guide, linseed oil was used as the base product.

While this oiled coating rendered the balloon fabric water-tight and gas-proof, the fabric remained pliable. It is known that French aeronauts, such as Jacques Charles; the Robert brothers, Anne-Jean and Nicholas-Louis and Andre-Jacques Garnerin, used a rubber solution in a similar way. This rubber coating, applied to the inner surface also formed an effective seal against both the potential escape of gas (hydrogen in Jacques' time) and its corrosive action upon the fabric. The rubber coating option is also believed to have been adopted by some English aeronauts who used hydrogen gas.

The rope netting of Charles Green's balloon, adorned with the King's and other heraldic arms, bore the inscription in large gold letters: 'George IV Royal Coronation Balloon' around its lower hemisphere and the total cost of the balloon and appendages was reported in the press to be £280 (≈ £25,271 in 2023). Mounted on the car was a Royal Standard flag at one end and a Union Jack at the other. Sadly, no contemporary press account has been found that gives a clear indication of the colour(s) of the balloon envelope.

At 8.00 am, inflation of this magnificent balloon began by drawing off gas through a temporary pipe run from the London & Westminster Gas Light Company's main that was installed along Piccadilly. When filled it was said to have a diameter of 31 feet. Green's maiden aerial voyage was timed to start when the sound of a cannon's boom marked the point in the ceremony at which the crown was placed upon King George's head. That was the signal for Green to release the ties and rise into the unknown.

It was a hot day. A noisy crowd pressed in on all sides so that, just before 1.00 pm, by the time he took up his position in the car to await the sound of the signal cannon, Charles had become somewhat fatigued. Many years later Charles recalled thinking he might hear better and find a bit of refreshing air above the heads of the crowd, so he asked his friends restraining the balloon to slacken off their lines and let it rise a little, intending to hold it poised above the din until the gun sounded. What happened, though, was that the balloon's power exceeded that of the ground handlers and it continued to rise. Fortunately, at that very instant, Green heard the roar of the cannon and he was away. As he climbed slowly and steadily, Charles calmly uncorked a bottle of brandy, poured himself a full glass and drank to the health of the King.

Even at a distance, the rising balloon could be seen clearly by guests leaving Westminster Abbey, who were walking along a specially constructed and richly adorned, covered walkway between the Abbey and the House of Lords.

Reportage in newspapers, books and magazines, of the progress of the flight seems to be fogged by anomalies and careful analysis of written accounts is needed in order to produce a coherent story of that landmark event. A description of his debut flight, written by Charles, was published in *The Literary Chronicle & Weekly Review*. [1]

'I felt not the least motion; it appeared as if the car in which I sat was stationary and that the earth was receding from me. The balloon took a north-east direction at first; and on my looking down upon the vast assemblage of persons in Westminster, the delight I felt is out of my power to describe. The view presented one entire mass of more than a million of human beings. Having ascended as high as I could without throwing out ballast, I determined, with the weather so fine, to keep in sight as long as possible. I threw out two bags of sand of 10lbs weight each and immediately the balloon rose with astonishing rapidity almost perpendicularly, according to my wish. When the balloon arrived at its utmost altitude, which in my opinion (due to the oscillation, I could not be certain of [the reading of] the quicksilver [mercury] in the barometer) was about 11,000 feet from the earth. I found that I had entered a current of air, conveying me directly eastward, towards The Nore [where the river Thames meets the North Sea]. The cold was extreme. I put on a cloak and on looking at my glass [thermometer], I found it was two degrees below the freezing point. Fearful of being carried out to sea, I opened the valve. The gas issued in considerable quantity and I found, by the increase of the size of objects below me, that I was descending very rapidly. The largest fields, which a few minutes before, appeared to be not more than 6 inches square, increased in size greatly and I very soon saw the sea and a number of vessels most distinctly. At this time, the balloon had a rotary motion and turned about four times in a minute.'

Thus, after first heading east towards the sea, then north, veering to north-west, over land, he decided to land and opened the valve to release some gas. He came down at 1.40 pm in a field belonging to a Mr Lamkins, 4 miles from Barnet in the parish of South Mimms, having travelled a circuitous distance of about 50 miles. While the Coronation flight was a huge success, the landing was fraught with danger. Upon the car striking the ground, Green was thrown out and dragged along the ground for a quarter of a mile while clinging to the netting hoop, but he survived without serious injury. It seems pretty much like any pilot's first few sorties - if you survived the first few, the knowledge gained improved one's survival prospects. It took a while to get the hang of making a soft landing in a balloon and Green, as we shall see, was no exception.

Expressions of altitude mentioned in this text are related to the result of a mathematical formula applied to barometric pressure and temperature readings. Charles would note a barometer reading prior to take-off, then read it at intervals throughout the flight. It is not known whether he did the complex maths personally or if, having had sets of readings worked upon by a mathematician for him, he may have decided to use an approximation for subsequent flights. From an examination of data published for many of his flights, an approximation appears to be: a fall of one inch of pressure equates to about 1,100 - 1,200 feet increase in altitude in relation to the original take-off point.

LONDON, Belvidere Gardens. 1 August 1821. #2

Having successfully completed his first flight into the unknown, Charles Green duly presented himself and his balloon at the Belvidere Tea Gardens on 1 August 1821 to have another go. An advertisement appeared on the front page of *The Times* on Saturday 28 July billing it as an ascent in company with his friend Mr Handy - who lived not far from him in Goswell Street. Inflation of the balloon would begin at 11.00 am and tickets to witness the event could be bought from Mr Green at 49 Goswell Street; Mr Handy, at 131 Goswell Street and another of the Green family - possibly one of his brothers - at 50 Penton Street; Mr Basham in Oxford Market and finally, from the Belvidere Tavern itself. No price was stated in the advertisement but press reports stated that the inflation could be witnessed for the sum of five shillings (≈ £23 in 2023).

Belvidere Gardens filled with a huge crowd of those willing to pay for that privilege, while the surrounding streets were crammed to capacity with others who were quite content to watch the ascent for free. Streets and roads leading to the Gardens were grid-locked by private and public carriages of all shapes and sizes. Open carts were even brought to town by their enterprising owners and parked up at various places where any passable view of the ascent could be found. Temporary seating in these carts offering a view over the garden walls, was priced between sixpence and two shillings (≈ £2 to £9 in 2023) according to the clarity of the view - and there were hundreds of takers!

1.00 pm was the scheduled lift-off time but that proved to be optimistic. By 2.00 pm, filling was almost complete and Charles launched a small pilot balloon to judge the state and direction of the wind. It was soon out of sight, heading north-north-east. As the clock ticked on towards 3.00 pm, Charles released a pair of carrier pigeons, each with a message paper attached. The birds belonged to Mr Green and in those halcyon days before the advent of the mobile phone, it was his way of informing his wife Martha that he was about to take-off and - perhaps - that he would be home in time for supper. Just after 3.00 pm, he sent up another pilot balloon and saw the wind had shifted a little more to the east. Now, it was time to attach the car but, before doing this he had the now inflated balloon repositioned in the Garden, so that he would comfortably clear some trees at lift-off. Then, with an air of confidence and high spirits, Charles stepped aboard - alone. His friend, Mr Handy, no doubt having had time to contemplate what he had agreed to do, suffered a bout of nerves and changed his mind earlier that morning. Green was on his own and about to prove that his first ascent was no fluke.

Approaching 3.30 pm, the restraining cords were released and with Green standing, waving a flag, the balloon rose gently and majestically into the air amidst a cacophony of cheers and applause from the thousands of watchers. Taking a yet more easterly direction as it rose, the balloon's speed of ascent slowed until, at about 700 feet altitude, Green could be seen emptying some ballast sand over the side, whereupon it began to rise more rapidly, heading almost east and was lost to view as it entered a bank of cloud.

Having experienced the cold and dampness of the cloud and higher altitude, Charles began to valve off some gas and begin his descent. Once clear of the clouds, he chose to land in a field about 2 miles from Ilford, Essex having travelled 14 miles in 30 minutes. The landing was without incident to either Charles or the balloon and he was indeed back in town that evening in time to join his wife and friends for supper.

PORTSEA, 25 August 1821. #3

Charles proved the Coronation ascent was not a fluke when he made a complete success of his second event. Charles Green was going places - and not just in the air. It is not known at what point he decided that he would attempt to make his living as a professional aeronaut but he was certainly a fee-earning professional now. Capitalising on the spectacle of ballooning and his own popularity, Charles travelled to Portsea, to prepare for his third ascent in the town on Saturday, 25 August 1821.

The venue was a field outside the Portsmouth naval dockyard fortifications in what was known as the Flat-houses area of Portsea. Gas was provided by the adjacent Portsea Island Gas Light Company's works.

A huge crowd watched the inflation and the ascent which took place at 3.15 pm to the accompaniment of a band playing the National Anthem. Owing to considerable cloud cover, watching the ascent was a short-lived affair because, in less than two minutes, the balloon entered those clouds and heading eastwards, was lost to sight. Green threw out some ballast but found the conditions uncomfortable and decided there was nothing to be gained by prolonging the flight. The chill of the clouds also caused the gas to contract and seeing he would struggle to gain altitude, he vented some gas to begin a controlled descent. Clearing the clouds, he found himself hovering over Langstone harbour where, letting out his mooring rope, unsuccessfully hailed a fishing boat for assistance. Drifting on, he reached land and came down at the water's edge near Langstone. Trapped beneath the collapsing balloon he was dragged along for a few hundred yards until a group of men from a nearby mill arrived to help him out of the car and pack up the balloon. Local brewer, Mr Lipscomb, then offered to convey Green and the balloon to Havant, where he caught a coach that returned him safely to the King's Arms, Portsea by 6.00 pm.

PORTSEA, 6 September 1821. #4

In view of the poor weather encountered for the earlier ascent from Portsea, Charles was encouraged by the organising committee from his first trip, to attempt another ascent. This event was advertised for 6 September 1821 from a venue at the Duke of York's Bastion, near Unicorn Gate in Portsea, a few hundred yards from the site of the earlier ascent.

That morning dawned cloudy but conditions looked more promising than before and the size of the crowd, estimated at 20,000 people, was much larger, too. He began the filling operation at 11.00 am under the supervision of Mr John Onthett, engineer in charge of the gas works, a task that was completed very rapidly by 12.30 pm. During his last landing Charles suffered some sort of injury which, though not incapacitating him, was troublesome.

'I suffered much inconvenience from my late accident, but was greatly assisted by several scientific gentlemen present and especially by Mr Kingston, superintendent of the steam engine in the dockyard; as well as by the gentlemen of the committee, whose services were importantly useful.'

Charles secured his equipment and instruments in the car and at 1.30 pm, took his place on board, which was the signal for a cannon to be fired, itself a signal for the committee to assemble alongside. In a most convivial gesture, wine was dispensed and Charles raised his glass and drank the health of those present and expressed his warmest thanks for their invitation and help. Amidst the usual deafening cheers and applause, Charles released the final restraining rope and the balloon rose slowly and majestically into the sky.

At this point, Charles began to take the first of regular readings from his instruments and this procedure will be dealt with a little later.

Not wishing to gain height rapidly and thus enter the cloud layer, Charles poured 10lbs of sand ballast over the side and rose gently to about 3,000 feet. He had intended to drop a small parachute to which was attached a container with a cat inside, the property of local man Mr Charles Wilcox. However, since the balloon was now drifting over water, pussy-cat had to wait for his sky-dive! Discharging more ballast, the balloon rose to 4,500 feet heading north-east but still within sight of those on the ground. After ten minutes in the air and now over land again, Charles dropped the parachute and watched it float slowly towards the ground, which he thought it reached after a fall of about eight or nine minutes. No report of the fate of the sky-diving cat has been found!

Now the balloon rose more rapidly to 10,000 feet, where it stabilised and he turned his attention to the instruments and began a series of readings. He had on board a column barometer, a thermometer and a Daniell's dew-point hygrometer which, having occupied his attention for about half-an-hour at 2.20 pm he decided to descend. By a combination of valving-off gas and releasing sand ballast now and again, he was able to control the balloon in a gradual descent. By 2.30 pm it was nearing the ground when a heavy rain shower added weight to the envelope, which combined with the cooling gas, accelerated the rate of descent. This could have proved dangerous until counter-balanced by Charles throwing out a large quantity of ballast, so that the descent rate was checked in the final moments of flight. The balloon came down in a meadow belonging to Mr J. Hollest of Mytchett Lake, Frimley in Surrey, bouncing around quite violently on landing, before being secured with help from men working nearby. Charles' track had taken him from Portsea; between Wymering and Cosham; over Purbrook Park; a quarter-mile west of Petersfield; between Empshott and Greatham; over Kingsley; one mile west of Farnham; a quarter-mile west of Farnborough, then to the landing site at Frimley. He had flown 45 miles in 45 minutes (average speed over the ground: 60mph).

Safely down, Charles was entertained at Mr Hollest's mansion where he 'partook of a good dinner,' before taking a post-chaise to the White Hart Inn, Guildford at 7.00 pm. Next morning, he was able to catch the London to Portsmouth coach to return to a rapturous welcome by the committee in Portsea. Green later reported:

> 'I was received with a hearty welcome by the gentlemen of the committee, to whose liberality and distinguished benevolence I shall ever feel grateful. I cannot forbear giving publicity to the fact that after paying me the sum stipulated, [£ not stated] they voluntarily surrendered an overplus of the money for the use and benefit of my only child [George].'

Charles expressed thanks to Messrs Barlow for the supply of gas and to Colonel Dickson and other officers for their assistance. Taken all round, this was an indication of the high regard in which he was being held and a sign of what he would have to get used to, now that he had celebrity status. A heart-warming sequel to this story can be found in a short piece in the *Hampshire Telegraph* of 29 June 1829, announcing the maturity of George's gratuity and its presentation.

'Mr George Green, son of Charles Green, the veteran aeronaut who made an aerial voyage from Portsea in September 1821, has visited this town [Portsea] for the purpose of receiving the money placed in the Saving Bank by the committee until he reached the age of 21, which sum, with interest, amounting to £68-17s-4d [≈ £6,227 in 2023] was given to him on Monday [22 June 1829].'

Regarding those scientific observations, they were scrutinised and published by the Royal Institution, with the following comment by its reviewer, Mr Daniell, in relation to Green's hygrometer data:

'He [Green] unfortunately omitted to take the point of deposition before he commenced his ascent, but the omission is of less consequence as I happened to observe at the time, at no very great distance from the spot. At an elevation of 9,890 feet, he [Green] found the dew-point at 64 degrees Fahrenheit [F], exactly the same as I ascertained it to be at the surface of the earth. At 11,060 feet it had fallen to 32 degrees, making a difference of 32 degrees in little more than 1,100 feet. Here then, we have presumptive evidence of an immense bed of rising vapour.'

Charles carried out another experiment during this trip; taking on board two large glass bottles, each filled with distilled water. At his greatest altitude, he tipped out the water and, with an assumption that they now contained air from that altitude, both bottles were re-sealed. Back on the ground, Charles gave the bottles of air to the Royal Institution whose members, Mr Solly and Mr Faraday examined their contents in the RI Laboratory. Both bottles were weighed and opened under distilled water at 60 degrees Fahrenheit (F). The ingestion of water in each was weighed and an average came out at 648.6 grains (1grain = 1/7,000 of 1lb) compared to the weight of a full bottle of water being 1,913 grains. The scientists concluded that the diminution of density of the atmosphere, at the altitude that Mr Green reached, to be one-third. They further concluded that this measurement was very close to the barometric data recorded. Analysis of the bottled air itself had also, in their opinion, confirmed the findings of the French chemist Joseph Louis Gay-Lussac (1778-1850), who postulated from his own experiments that there was no difference in the composition of atmospheric air captured at a great altitude and that taken at the earth's surface. Gay-Lussac carried out his high-altitude experiments both alone and in 1804, in company with a compatriot scientist, Jean-Baptiste Biot (1774-1862). It is Gay-Lussac's Law, on the relationship between the pressure of a gas and its absolute temperature, that Charles Green and all balloonists encountered in practical terms during their flying careers.

'The pressure of a given mass of gas varies directly with the absolute temperature of that gas, when the volume is constant.'

Joseph Louis Gay-Lussac and Charles Green - those two giants of the air - were destined to meet and fly together in Paris in December 1836.

The Royal Institution was well satisfied with all this data, with their reviewer concluding:

'It is to be hoped that Mr Green will be enabled to persevere in his exertions, as a continuation of such observations cannot fail to be of the utmost use to science. It would be desirable also that he should be a little more particular in noticing the different indications of the atmosphere, that is to say, the course of the wind on the surface of the earth and the direction of the different currents - the height of the clouds and the temperature when crossing them and whether there is more than one stratum at different heights. Now that he is aware of the tendency of the different experiments there are, no doubt, many particulars which will readily suggest themselves to him and he will not, of course, neglect to make observations before his departure and after his return, if circumstances permit.'

It is considered only right to emphasise that this scientific aspect of Charles Green's flying began as early as 1821 - and continued throughout his flying career. Furthermore, he provided the aerial platform for other men of science and meteorology to make observations in the sky. This aspect of Green's flying has been so sorely over-looked in preference to the more highly publicised and glamorised - yet no more-valuable - similarly-motivated flights undertaken by meteorologist James Glaisher with aeronaut Henry Coxwell during the 1860s.

Chapter 3

Ditching, Dutchmen and Dastardly Deeds

BRIGHTON, 2 October 1821. #5

Writing in his diary at home in Lewes, Dr Gideon Mantell noted on 2 October 1821:

> 'A remarkably fine day. Mr Green ascended in a balloon from the gasworks near Brighton. Mrs Mantell was walking with me and we perceived the balloon from the top of Keere Street. It fell into the sea off Cuckmere and the aeronaut was almost drowned.'[1]

Indeed, Charles came very close to losing his life during this, his fifth, ascent. He had taken many risks and had sustained a personal battering on nearly all his descents thus far, but this latest would come very close to being curtains for him.

The scene moves to the Brighton Gas Light & Coke Company works at Black Rock, Brighton. It was founded in 1818 and the Royal Pavilion and its grounds were among the first places in the town to be lit by gas.

Having filled his *Coronation* balloon, Charles lifted off to the now customary tumultuous applause and the balloon, heated somewhat in the morning sunlight, rose slowly to 800 feet. The sun was less evident now and the cooling gas caused the balloon to descend slightly. This was something Green could counteract by throwing out ballast sand, but he was confident he could hold the balloon close above the spectators in order for them to marvel upon the sheer spectacle of this - for Brighton - unprecedented exhibition. After hovering as long as possible, he threw out two bags of sand and the balloon rose; taking a south-east by south direction along the landward side of the shore. As the balloon rose higher the wind swung it more to the south and at an altitude of about 11,000 feet, Green found himself heading out to sea. Realising he could be heading into trouble, he searched the horizon for ships that might come to his aid, but spotting only two vessels anywhere near, a rapid descent was vital. He opened the valve and with a rush of gas venting-off, the balloon descended with great speed. Charles judged the rate of descent poorly and was unable to 'round out' before the force of the wind carried the balloon into huge waves.

THE FLYING ADVENTURES OF CHARLES GREEN

Having lost a great deal of its gas, the balloon envelope turned downwind and was forced into an umbrella shape inside its net. The wind drove it rapidly through the heavy seas. The car, with its aeronaut occupant hanging on grimly, struck the water on its side, destroying its ornaments and Green's instruments and immediately filled with water. Charles had had the foresight to take with him a life-preserver jacket, donning it hastily as the balloon fell towards the sea. He found it cumbersome and it tangled up in cordage that was whipping around in the basket, severely hampering his movements.

He hit the water some distance offshore from Cuckmere Haven:

> 'Here I was, in a perilous situation, the life-preserver useless and the car turning over repeatedly so that I was alternately under water. In this distress I continued for many minutes when, almost exhausted, it occurred to me the need to separate the cords entangling the life-preserver. With much difficulty, I did this with a knife and was then raised above the water. I was so much exhausted, I felt I could not hold on much longer.'

Charles saw a small boat pulling towards him and hailed it with what strength he had left. It was a boat from *Unity*, one of a fleet of Brighton-to-Dieppe sailing packet-vessels. Its master was Captain Clear.

'[I] was on passage from Dieppe to Brighton when, at 2.40 pm, I discovered a balloon descending very rapidly and five minutes later it dropped into the water about two miles to windward. I ordered a boat to be lowered in the charge of the mate [believed to be Francis Cheesman]. The sea was running high and the balloon was dragged through heavy surf for two miles while the boat pulled towards it. I thought the man in the basket would perish before the boat reached him, but had the satisfaction of seeing him pulled into the boat at about 3.00 pm.'

Captain Clear manoeuvred his vessel to bring the balloon and rescuers alongside. Towering 20 feet above the water, the balloon envelope was still drifting before the wind and Captain Clear could not hold it. The rescue boat, still fast to the basket, was being dragged along with the balloon so, in order to subdue the beast, risking his spars, Captain Clear rammed the balloon and forced his bowsprit through the netting.

Charles was pulled on to the deck and the rescue boat recovered. Captain Clear administered a reviving tot of brandy to the bedraggled aeronaut, then had him taken below, where he was stripped of his sodden clothing, wrapped in blankets and put to bed. The master then addressed the balloon, which was impaled on his bowsprit. It remained there until all the gas escaped, whereupon it slithered back into the sea and sank beneath the vessel's keel. The mangled envelope was hoisted aboard by block and tackle, during which progress, suffering from the effect of wind and tide the silk gave way, tearing in all directions and being left as a sodden, tattered heap on the deck.

Rendered insensible for several hours, Charles recovered enough to ask Captain Clear about the fate of his balloon; to be informed that it was literally torn to ribbons and that all his instruments and apparatus were lost or destroyed. Looking at the heap on deck, he considered the balloon irreparable.

Having to wait for a favourable tide, it was 1.00 am next morning (Wednesday) before the *Unity* could tie up in Newhaven and Charles stepped on dry land at last. He took a coach back to Brighton, reaching the Gas Works at 10.00 am that morning.

Had it not been for the fortuitous presence of *Unity* and Captain Clear, it seems highly likely that Charles Green would have drowned and the world of aeronautics would have been all the poorer for it.

CHELTENHAM, 30 July 1822. #6

Charles had escaped with his life; his balloon was in tatters and the winter of 1821 was fast approaching. He seems to have mastered the process of preparation and ascension quite well, but it was the landing phase in which he consistently encountered problems. There was no 'dual-control' here; he had never flown with other aeronauts to gain experience and with no-one to show him how to judge height, while balancing rate-of-descent with buoyancy and local weather conditions, his actions were a process of trial and error. He was, however, hooked on his new profession and determined to continue with his hazardous adventures. It appears to have taken him until July 1822 before he was ready to enter the public arena once more. It has to be said at this point that it is not known for certain how much fabric was recovered from the original *Coronation* balloon that went into the sea. In this flight from Cheltenham, for the first time we find the colour of his balloon clearly described in press reports as blue, red and yellow. Unfortunately, the colour of the balloon he used at the coronation was not stated in any of the contemporary accounts of that event, so confirmation that he had lost his 'original' was difficult to prove.

However, for the clearest indication about the fate of the original *Coronation* balloon, if we are patient until 1836, examination of newspaper reports in February of that year shed light on the matter. It was during a civil court case that a statement made by Charles Green, a witness for the defence, was reported as follows.

'In the year 1821, [when] the *Coronation* balloon [was] destroyed, [they] had used the waterproof fabric and given it to their friends to use as cloaks.'[2]

'The silk of the *Coronation* balloon had been torn up and made cloaks of and when worn was found to be waterproof.[3]

THE FLYING ADVENTURES OF CHARLES GREEN

This is evidence that the original *Coronation* balloon was indeed destroyed after it ditched in the sea. The deduction can be made that Charles constructed a new balloon over the winter of 1821/22, which was first used at Cheltenham. This court case will appear again later.

The choice of Cheltenham as his next venue also seems to be linked to the demise of his first balloon. The original car was destroyed during the ditching off Brighton and the new car - 'a costly and most elegant structure' - was a gift from Colonel Riddell of Wellington Mansion, Cheltenham. Perhaps Charles felt some obligation to appear in Cheltenham as a result of this gift. Whatever the reason, a committee invited Charles to make an ascent and even scheduled a celebratory public dinner for the following day.

During the morning of Tuesday 30 July, launch preparations took place in a yard behind the London Hotel, with gas filling operations commencing at 1.00 pm, supervised by the manager of the Cheltenham Gas Light & Coke Co., Mr Thomas Spinney. A huge crowd of 'nobility, gentry and fashionables' assembled in the town, with visitors arriving from as far afield as Bath; Bristol; Gloucester; Tewkesbury and Worcester.

By 3.00 pm, Charles Green's new silk balloon, 50 feet tall, was full of gas and the lustrous blue, red and yellow segments, shimmered in the afternoon sunshine. This trip would be another first for Charles, since he was to be accompanied by Samuel Young Griffith, proprietor of the *Cheltenham Chronicle* newspaper. At 3.30 pm, the two men climbed aboard the car in high spirits. The cords by which the car was attached to the hoop of the balloon were secured and the intrepid aeronauts shouted their farewells to the crowd.

Then a strange thing happened. As the breeze caught the towering balloon, it swung to windward across the yard while still being restrained by the ground handlers. Now it could be seen that one of the ropes, by which the netting over the envelope was attached to the hoop, dangled loosely and appeared to have been deliberately severed. The cry went up for Mr Green to stop the ascent and repair the rope, but he was having none of this. With a bellow, he ordered all restraining ropes to be let go and up they went. With cheers ringing in their ears, the balloon remained in sight of the crowd for twenty minutes, heading east.

It transpired later, that the slashed line was sabotage linked to heavy gambling, wagered locally and in London, on the distance that the balloon would travel. Charles told his companion that he was: 'of the opinion that the cord was cut by black-legs from London, with something as sharp as a razor and done with such dexterity to avoid being seen.' Someone betting on a short distance had clearly tried to 'nobble' the ascent. As a result of this and other, as yet unseen, knife damage, the netting was weakened and stress came on the car-suspension ropes on one side. The two travellers' lives were in grave danger.

In the meantime, Green and Griffith were climbing and heading east, passing over Northleach and the home of Lord Sherbourne. Thirty minutes into the flight and a mile and a half from the village of Salperton, Charles decided that the strain on the balloon net and its possible effect on the stability of the car, was too great a risk, so he set about a landing. Gas was vented off and the balloon descended steadily. Near the ground, he tossed out a grappling iron that, with the help of some people on the ground, gained purchase on a wall but did not hold. The speed of the balloon tore it free. Still venting gas, the balloon lost buoyancy but the whole mass was dragged across four fields, ploughing through hedge after hedge, before the car became trapped in the branches of a tree as the balloon rose over a spinney. It was here, at Notgrove, that more ropes parted suspiciously easily and the car was flung to the ground from about 30 feet. Charles Green lay unconscious while Samuel Griffith fared a little better, although badly bruised and shaken.

The pair were rescued by Mr Day of the King's Head Inn, Northleach, who, together with his son, had ridden out to watch the descent. When Charles regained consciousness, he and Samuel were carefully placed on the Day's horses and taken to the home of Mr J. Stone at Turkdean, 2 miles from Northleach. Here they were given a very warm welcome and put straight to bed. Mr Lamley, a surgeon from Northleach who had also ridden over, expecting to greet the aeronauts on landing, turned up and 'promptly let blood' from the invalids. Mr Murley; Mr Beavan; Mr Brown and Lord Sherbourne, of the committee hurried to Turkdean to express their sympathy and offer help. Early on Wednesday the following bulletin was issued to the populace of Cheltenham and to members of the press.

'Turk Dean 31 July 1823 at 1.00 am

We have examined Mr Green and the gentleman who ascended with him, in consequence of their accident from the descent of the balloon and find them very seriously injured. Mr Green has a severe contusion on the left side of the chest, but unattended with a fracture of the ribs. The other gentleman has received a severe injury of the spine, but unattended with paralysis of the limbs.

Signed
Charles Lamley, Surgeon, Northleach.
S.H. Murley, Surgeon, Cheltenham.'

The balloon, reported to have cost £500 (≈ £49,000 in 2023) now released from the weight and encumbrance of the car leapt into the air. It was seen, apparently intact drifting over Woodstock and must have picked up an air current that pushed it northwards, because it was eventually captured at 6.00 pm, collapsed in Mr Wright's wheat field at Ecton, a village east of Northampton, having travelled a distance of about 54 miles. Miraculously, it was said to be 'very little injured,' which is more than can be said for its former occupants. A public subscription opened in Cheltenham to raise funds to recompense Charles Green for his injury and to help pay for a new balloon but, while that now seemed unlikely, it looks as if the fund would be needed for repairs.

Mrs Green and their son, George, accompanied Charles to Cheltenham and, not unsurprisingly, was very distressed by the accident and in particular by a story put about by a farmer who arrived in town declaring Mr Green to be dead! Fortunately, that was completely false and Mr Murley was able to set Mrs Green's mind at rest within the hour by telling her that both men were much improved.

It was a murderous episode and one that Charles would not forget in a hurry. Samuel Griffith of course got the scoop of his life and was able to bring the whole sorry tale to the attention of readers of the next issue of the *Cheltenham Chronicle*.

Six months later, having made good progress in his recovery Charles Green found there was another day of reckoning in this sad episode. On 20 December, the management committee of the Cheltenham Gas Light & Coke Co., directed Thomas Spinney, its chief engineer, to 'apply to Mr Green for the amount due for the gas used for the ascent of the balloon.' To his credit, he had had a great deal on his mind and the bill was settled with good grace. Indeed, Charles seems to have remained on very friendly terms with Mr Spinney, since he was one of the passengers accompanying Charles in the *Royal Nassau* balloon for its first flight outside London; staged at Montpellier Gardens, Cheltenham on 3 July 1837.

MERMAID TAVERN, Hackney. 3 June 1823. #7

The Mermaid Tavern - the most famous inn in Hackney, London - had existed since 1636 and by 1823, grew to encompass an Assembly Room and extensive pleasure gardens which, among its many delights, was the venue for a number of balloon ascents in the years before Charles Green arrived on the scene; the most notable being that of James Sadler and Captain Paget in 1811. In Green's time, the Mermaid Tavern was located on the west side of Mare Street but was demolished in 1845 and re-built on the opposite side of the road. That establishment closed in 1944 and is, in 2023, a shop.

Only a couple of his first seven flights were without landing difficulties and mishaps and indeed the injuries sustained by both himself and his balloon on his sixth flight put him out of action from July 1822 to June 1823. Even though he mastered his landings eventually, it was a while before the public learned to treat coal gas with a measure of respect - particularly in the quantities being vented off from a balloon upon landing! Such perils were demonstrated at Romford on 3 June 1823, at the end of Green's first trip after his layoff.

The weather was awful. A strong wind delayed the start of inflation, which in turn had a detrimental effect on the number of people coming to watch - and pay - to see that process. First it was announced that filling would begin at 11.00 am but, when the violence of the wind did not diminish, it was delayed again. Filling finally began at noon, but with the balloon being snatched and pummelled by the wind, it was a slow process. The weather improved around 2.00 pm; clouds parted and the sun emerged to brighten things up. The wind dropped and now many more spectators were attracted to the enclosure – 'and this had great effect in filling the pocket of the aeronaut.'

By 3.00 pm, the time scheduled for the ascent, the balloon was less than half-full but the crowd, fortunately, accepted this was due to the weather and did not voice its impatience. By 4.30 pm, Charles Green declared he was satisfied with the amount of gas in the balloon and ordered the car to be brought to the viewing enclosure for attachment to the balloon.

This job was not done well. When placed beneath the suspended, filled balloon someone dropped it on the coils of control ropes, one of which was the valve release cord. This mis-handling caused the valve to open and out went a substantial amount of precious gas before the ropes were sorted out and it could be closed again. The result was that the filling process had to be re-started. 5.00 pm came and went; then 6.00 pm chimed out from the nearby church. The spectators became very restless – even the band playing resolutely, seemed to have no soothing effect. By this time bets were being wagered noisily on the odds of Charles making an ascent at all that day. The potentially ugly situation was finally calmed down by none other than Henry Hunt MP [Member of Parliament] (1773-1835) being brought on to the stage to speak up for Mr Green and to plead for patience a little longer. Charles was lucky indeed to have such a man among the spectators. Known throughout the land as 'Orator' Hunt, he was a man of imposing stature – over 6 feet tall and hefty – notorious as a radical politician; champion of parliamentary reform and scourge of mal-practice in public life. Hunt was reputed to be the best mob-orator of his day and as the *Bristol Mercury* said of him in 1826: 'No-one perhaps possesses greater tact in managing a mob – and never fails to carry the crowd along with him'. Thus, was calm restored to the scene.

Around 7.00 pm, Charles called for the handlers to pay out their ropes to see if he could clear some trees, but the balloon drifted into them, so it was back to putting more gas into the envelope again – with yet more delay!

By 7.30 pm, Charles was satisfied all was ready for take-off. At 7.45 pm, he gave the order to release all the restraining ropes and up he went – alone – to strains of *God Save The King* from the brass band below and hearty cheers from the crowd. Bowing and waving a flag as the balloon rose, he cleared the trees and nearby Hackney church tower and dropped some ballast. This allowed the balloon to rise steadily to 10,000 feet and take a course, first to the east then veering north-east. Still just in sight of the spectators at 8.00 pm it seemed to be heading for Epping Forest, but most people had decided to go home by then.

THE FLYING ADVENTURES OF CHARLES GREEN

The balloon's track took it over Hackney Wick; over Hackney marsh lead mills; Leytonstone; Barking Side; part of Epping Forest and west of Romford. This time, Charles made a good descent, by balancing discharge of gas with dropping ballast and landing quite gently in a field belonging to Mr Staines, at Noak Hill, 4 miles north of Romford.

Mr Staines, however, was far from amused by his unexpected aerial visitor. As Charles himself put it:

> 'I should have gone further had I not pledged myself to return to Hackney the same night; but I was prevented from effecting, by being detained by Mr Staines. He forcibly seized my balloon because of some trifling injury had been done to his clover by persons who ran into the field to witness my descent and who were curious to inspect the aeronautical machine.'

The *Lincoln, Rutland & Stamford Mercury* reported another far more alarming event:

> 'Mr Green ascended with his balloon at 7.45 pm from the gardens of the Mermaid Tavern, Hackney, London and landed safely at 8.20 pm 4 miles north of Romford, Essex. A circumstance occurred which nearly proved fatal to the lives of two people and shows how pernicious is the coal gas. Mr Green was sitting in the car and the balloon was discharging its contents very fast through the valve which was wide open. Two men came up to render assistance and one took hold of the valve and breathed deeply of the gas being exhausted. He inhaled so much of the noxious gas that he fell, insensible, to the ground. The condition of the man was not observed by Mr Green and another man came forward to render assistance to the aeronaut and met with the same misfortune and fell to the ground apparently dead. By this time the balloon was nearly empty and the men were seen and carried away to some distance where they were resuscitated with difficulty.'

Despite all this bother, Charles arrived back at The Mermaid in Hackney at 2.00 am next morning.

A few interesting facts are thrown up amidst the reporting of this event. There is the first clear indication that some of Charles' income for this event was derived from the entrance money taken from spectators paying an admission price to enter the enclosure set up around the inflation process. These enclosures were just that; a 'no-go' area where the perimeter was built of hessian sacking or other opaque fabric, to such a height as to prevent casual, non-paying people from seeing the spectacle for free. Seating for the paying spectator was usually provided, together with entertainment, usually in the form of a band. He also seemed to be grasping how to balance the balloon during the descent phase, so that a gentler, controlled landing could be made.

OXFORD. 13 June 1823. #8

Isaac Earlysman Sparrow was a young man who lived and worked in Bishopsgate, London as an ironmonger, nail manufacturer and brass-founder. It is not known how he came into contact with Charles Green, but Sparrow offered Charles the prodigious sum of £50 (≈ £4,900 in 2023) to 'take him aloft for the privilege of being allowed to encounter the perils of the voyage.' Charles Green accepted the fee and so the two travelled to Oxford, the venue for Charles' eighth flight on 13 June 1823. Some accounts state this to be his fifth flight but that is incorrect. Furthermore, upon his return to London after the flight, Sparrow produced a number of metal tokens celebrating his experience. Some tokens are undated; some have dates incorporated into the design, while others appear to have had a date stamped on them later. The date of Friday, 13 June 1823 is confirmed by newspaper reports, not least by *The Times* (London) of 16 June quoting a despatch from Oxford dated Saturday, 14 June stating that the aeronauts 'returned to Oxford by midnight on Friday [13th]'. As we shall see, this dual ascent was also not without incident.

A crowd, estimated at 5,000, assembled to witness the event at the Oxford Gas Works. This is believed to represent the 'paying punters' which, if correct, at two shillings each (a ticket price known to be charged the following year) would give Charles about £500 'on the gate' (≈ £48,900 in 2023) before expenses; a tidy sum indeed for his work - and the risk.

Once again inflation was delayed, this time for two hours, because two poles, between which the balloon was suspended in order to keep it upright while the gas gradually filled and enlarged it, partially collapsed. All was complete, though, by 2.30 pm and Charles Green and Isaac Sparrow climbed into the car and the restraining ropes were released. At first, the balloon rose very slowly, but when Charles threw out some ballast, the ascent was more rapid. At this point the balloon drifted and its netting snagged the corner of one of the gas-furnace chimneys. There was a loud thump and the car was almost upset. A collective cry of horror burst forth from the spectators. Fortunately, the intrepid aeronauts were not tipped out; the net freed itself and up they went, heading south-west, with Isaac frantically waving his flag to signal all was well. Still climbing rapidly, they picked up an easterly current until at 3,000 feet a variety of air currents tossed them around a little. Isaac Sparrow said it took him a while to accustom himself to cope with his fear of great height, but did so and was then able to enjoy the vista below and the clouds above.

THE FLYING ADVENTURES OF CHARLES GREEN

Despite the barometer taking a knock during take-off, it did not prevent Charles being able to calculate their altitude. As usual he noted the barometer reading prior to lift-off and on this occasion, it stood at 29.7 inches. The lowest reading obtained during the flight was 21.3 inches, indicating that they had reached an altitude of about 10,000 feet. Thermometer readings fluctuated between 33 degrees F and 70 degrees F. When the barometer stopped working at the start of their descent, it made it difficult to judge whether the balloon was going up or down - or even standing still - so Charles had the bright idea of hanging one of their flags out from the side of the car and then watching to see if it moved to the effect of the airflow and in what direction. If it flapped upwards, they were going down and *vice versa* - simples! To make matters worse, after being in the air for ninety minutes, the cap plugging the neck of the balloon fell off and gas began to leak out; calling for more improvisation to stop the escape. This was tricky, because it required Charles to stand tall, in the flow of noxious gas and tie both men's several silk handkerchiefs, knotted together, round the fabric in an attempt to close the neck of the balloon. While not completely effective, the flow of gas was greatly reduced. Now all they had to do was get back to Mother Earth. They were coming down on Nettlebed Heath, 4 miles north-west of Henley-on-Thames - and it was going to be rough.

With a thousand feet to go, Charles cast the remains of the ballast over the side; ordered Sparrow to toss the seat cushions out; told him to grab hold of the hoop above his head - and hang on tight. Charles did likewise just as the car hit the ground with an almighty thump and rebounded 50 feet into the air. The balloon lifted a little, moved forward and the car crashed again to the ground. Losing his grip on the hoop, Isaac Sparrow pitched overboard and fell sprawling on the ground. What happens when the balloon is suddenly lightened in this way? Well, of course, it goes UP - with Charles still hanging on! It bumped and bounded along for another 150 yards before Sparrow sprang to life and grabbed some of the trailing ropes. Pulling for all he was worth, he tried to slow the balloon but was prevented from getting himself into a more dangerous situation when its progress was brought to an abrupt halt by the fabric, netting and car becoming ensnared in the tops of some tall trees. Charles was rescued from his precarious perch by labourers who ran up from Lady Stapleton's estate - upon whose land they had fallen. The men secured the balloon from further movement and Charles was able to shin down a rope to the ground. Once more, the car was smashed, but at least the two aeronauts were intact.

Lady Stapleton was informed of this unexpected arrival just 300 yards from her mansion and immediately invited the two men to take refreshments and rest, while her workmen separated the balloon from the trees and the process of dismantling and packing it up could begin. A coach conveyed the balloon and aeronauts back to Oxford, 22 miles away, which Charles and Isaac reached at midnight on Friday night; it had indeed been a real 'Friday the thirteenth' event and Isaac Sparrow had certainly fulfilled his wish 'to be allowed to encounter the perils of the voyage'.

He was, however, so impressed by his experience that he re-named his Bishopsgate warehouse: 'Balloon House' and incorporated a balloon image in advertisements for his products.

READING. 1 August 1823. #9

With the need to effect repairs to his balloon and replace the car, it was two months before Charles Green took to the skies again. The venue for this next aerial exhibition was in the gardens of The Forbury in the centre of Reading, on 1 August 1823. Charles was accompanied on this trip by Mr Henry Simonds (1785-1874) of Broad Street, Reading, second son of William Blacknell Simonds, founder of Simonds Brewery. The family also had banking interests in the locality and Henry, who was both deaf and dumb, was a director in the family business. Charles considered Henry's disability was no bar to his taking part in this aerial adventure and after the event, complimenting his companion on his coolness and nerve, he said: 'the risk of being unable to communicate with [Henry] during the descent was a possibility, but his undeviating attention to orders he was given at the outset, together with his extreme steadiness and presence of mind to remain calm and stay in place when the balloon dragged along the ground, were above all praise and such conduct contributed much to my own safety.'

Long before midday, huge crowds gathered, filling every street around The Forbury and on any vantage point outside the town that would give a view of the spectacle to come. A large space was set aside for the platform on which the balloon would be inflated. This area was barriered off by wagons and fencing to allow only one entry gate to the 'inner sanctum,' where a vast number of paying spectators could witness the inflation, take-off and see the intrepid aeronauts at close range. Nobility and gentry from 20 miles around came to see this event and it looked as if, from the sheer quantity of carriages of all descriptions lining the streets, the majority of the population within that distance had turned out, too. Contemporary press reports describe the balloon quite clearly.

'In the centre of the enclosure, the balloon, which was extremely magnificent, being 107 feet in circumference and [was made from] 700 yards of oiled silk in alternate stripes of blue, red and yellow and was calculated to contain 136,280 gallons of gas [≈ 21,000 cubic-feet]. It was covered with a net-work, from which ropes proceeded and to which the car was attached.'

Entertained by the Reading military band, thousands watched the inflation process, which was almost complete by 3.00 pm. A small pilot balloon was sent aloft to check the wind and was last seen passing over Play Hatch chalk-pit, heading in a north-east;

then, at 4.00 pm a second pilot balloon was launched and took a similar direction. Yet another small balloon was sent up at 4.30 pm and about fifteen minutes later, a shouted announcement from the enclosure warned the thousands of spectators that the aeronauts were about to lift off.

The band struck up with a lively rendition of the National Anthem and at 4.53 pm, accompanied by tumultuous applause, the balloon rose majestically into the sky. As it rose, Charles stood in the car, bowing to his audience, while a beaming Henry Simonds waved his flag vigorously. In favourable weather and on a brisk south-west wind, the balloon gained height quickly, heading north-east, passing over Wargrave while dipping in and out of the clouds. It remained in sight of the crowd for almost half an hour before it was finally lost to view.

Now above the clouds, with his barometer reading 24.2 inches, Charles calculated they had reached an altitude of 6,250 feet while the thermometer fluctuated between 42 degrees F and 62 degrees F. It was at this height, after picking up a current of air from the north-west and the balloon moving along quite rapidly, that Charles decided it was time to look for a landing site and opened the valve to begin the descent. Having dropped below the clouds, he could discern no favourable site, so he heaved 20lbs of sand ballast over the side to stop the descent and stabilised their height at 2,000 feet while the balloon continued on its way. At about 5.30 pm, Charles saw a likely landing area that seemed free of woods, growing crops and houses and opened the valve to go down again.

A controlled descent brought the car down with a gentle bump, but the wind drove the balloon over the ground at quite a pace. Some labourers grabbed at the trailing ropes but these were snatched from their hands and the balloon escaped. The grapnel hook caught in a tree, but tore off a branch and the balloon bumped on across the fields until another person snatched a rope and quickly secured it to a strong gate-post, bringing the balloon to a halt. Peace returned to the scene; the rest of the gas was vented off and the process of dismantling and folding-up the balloon began. They landed at 5.45 pm in a field belonging to Mr Franklin in the parish of North Mimms in Hertfordshire, north of London. It was about 40 miles in a direct line from Reading, although Charles reckoned that, with course deviations, they had actually travelled 50 miles over the ground. Several gentlemen arrived on the scene on horseback to offer help, including the same Mr Lamkins, upon whose land Charles had descended on his very first aerial journey. During the course of the flight, Mr Simonds jotted down notes of his experience.

'The ascent produced a sensation not unlike that caused by the action of a swing. I kept my eyes on Reading as long as it was visible and tried to distinguish other places as we passed over them, but the distance rendered them too small to be recognised with any certainty. The London Road and river Thames looked very small, but the view of fields, woods and towns was grand and pleasing beyond expression, until all disappeared as we were enveloped by the clouds. Masses of clouds like snow were on one side blue and green and red on the other. I thought the green clouds contained rain and the red colour to be produced by sunshine. We remained at a steady height for twenty minutes while Mr Green calculated the height by consulting the barometer and our bearing by the compass. I had no sensation of giddiness while climbing or descending, but a slight tendency when the balloon rotated.

When Mr Green told me he would shortly descend, I thought we were about 20 miles from Reading and I put my writing apparatus in my pocket. Mr Green opened the valve by pulling the rope affixed to it and jumped upon the edge of the car. I followed this movement according to the instructions I had previously been given. It was a rapid descent, with little time for preparation. The balloon touched the earth in the middle of a field and rebounded about 45 feet, then took the ground again close to an oak tree, in which it was a little entangled. It then fell on one side, dragging us over a hedge and through a field, with our sides to the ground and our faces toward each other. We were then drawn over another hedge into a cart road about 5 feet deep. The car was driven against the opposite hedge on the road side and the balloon against an oak tree and our progress was stopped until persons arrived to our assistance.

During the descent, I experienced a strong air current pressing upwards. During the flight I felt different currents of air, some genially warm, others cold and at one time, I was quite chilled.'

The two aeronauts were none the worse for their bumpy landing and declining several offers of rest and refreshment, a messenger was sent on their behalf to Hatfield to procure a post-chaise. Charles and Henry Simonds arrived back in Reading at 3.00 pm the next afternoon: Saturday 2 August, almost a day after they had begun their flight.

Chapter 4

Flying Tours

LEEDS. 5 September 1823. #10

Having lined up a number of consecutive engagements, Charles Green ventured north for the first time. His exhibition in Leeds took place in the yard of the (third) White Cloth Hall, in The Calls area, on 5 September 1823 – but it would not end well.

A calm day and an absence of wind helped the gas-filling process, which was completed in the remarkably quick time of just over an hour. The scheduled time of lift-off was 3.00 pm but, with so many people still flocking in for another half-hour, Charles delayed his departure accordingly - it was all good for his pocket! Sending up one final pilot balloon was the signal for departure and stepping aboard the car, to the accompaniment of cheers and applause, the balloon carried Charles almost straight up into a cloudless sky. He stood on the side of the car holding on to the hoop, waving enthusiastically to the vast crowds gathered in the yard, on surrounding buildings, on church towers, on hillsides and in all the open spaces of the city. After a few minutes he sat down in the car and continued to wave a flag at those below. Some watchers, with the benefit of a telescope, saw him let out a rope to dangle below the car, then pour a few bags of sand ballast over the side. The balloon remained in good view of the ground for almost 40 minutes, glistening in the sunlight, before it was lost behind some cloud, heading towards Pontefract.

Charles began his descent in the vicinity of Haxey, a village 9 miles north of Gainsborough in north Lincolnshire and about 40 miles from Leeds. It was now, as he dropped ever lower, that he began to experience very strong, almost gale-force winds. Close to the ground he threw out his grapnel, hoping for it to bite into a grass field below - but it would not hold and the balloon dragged it for some distance. The car struck a stout fence with such violence that Charles was momentarily stunned. The grapnel snagged the same fence but the speed of the balloon was too great and caused the rope to snap suddenly, pitching Charles over the side to fall on the ground. This time he was knocked out and severely bruised.

Even though there was, by now, very little gas left in it, the loss of Charles' weight and nothing to hold the balloon in check, sent it springing back into the air and in less than twenty minutes it had vanished from sight. All hope of trying to catch the beast was gone - it was now too high to reach - and was heading towards the coast.

Charles, in considerable pain, could do nothing, so he set about organising transport to return him to Leeds, which he reached at 1.45 am the next morning. Despite his loss and injury, he was upbeat about the trip, telling his committee that he had had a delightful voyage; he had climbed to about 10,000 feet, at which point the thermometer registered a cool 28 degrees F.

Charles then made it known that he was offering a reward of £10 (≈ £980 in 2023) to anyone who recovered his balloon (on which he placed a value of £400, or ≈ £39,100 in 2023) and returned it to him intact. There was every chance that the balloon might be lost in the German Ocean (the North Sea) and it was not long before this was confirmed as true. A few days after the ascent, a message reached Charles Green from Holland. On Saturday, 6 September, a silk balloon with the English coat of arms upon it and with its car still attached - but with all the instruments lost - was recovered from the sea by fishermen, near Wijk-aan-Zee, north of Ijmuiden. They carried the much-torn balloon back to the Texel where the remains were placed in the charge of Mr Tiede Christians who eventually got in touch with Mr Green. It is rumoured that the Dutchman demanded £18 (≈ £1,700 in 2023) to return it to England, but there is no confirmation of the sum paid. There is, however, evidence in the *Leeds Intelligencer* of 1 April 1824, that it was returned and repaired for further use - which speaks volumes for the strength of the design.

'Our readers will be glad to learn that Mr Green had fixed the day of his ascent from Halifax for Wednesday next [14 April]. We understand that, although his balloon was considerably injured on its arrival from Holland (where it descended after its voyage from this town [Leeds] in September last), it has undergone such repairs as to render it again fit for the purpose of aerostation, besides having received additional embellishments [un-specified].'

HALIFAX. 19 April 1824. #11

Poor weather upset Charles Green's plans for his ascent from Halifax, scheduled for Wednesday, 14 April 1824 and he was obliged to hang around for quite some time until it improved. This, his eleventh ascent, would be his first since his balloon had escaped to Holland. In discussion with the organising committee, Charles agreed that the weather looked promising for Easter Monday, 19 April and he agreed to make an ascent from the central court-yard of the Piece Hall on that day. Dating from 1779, the Piece Hall, is one of the most magnificent buildings of that era in Yorkshire; used for the trading of cloth and becoming a symbol of great wealth and civic pride.

A strong wind still blew on the day of the ascent and the gas-filling operation was slowed by the balloon being buffeted. Filling was completed just before 4.00 pm, when the car was attached and Charles lifted off at 4.35 pm for his solo flight.

THE FLYING ADVENTURES OF CHARLES GREEN

Rising slowly, the balloon took a northerly course. Concerned that this might take him towards very hilly ground, Charles let out some gas and descended until he detected a different air current, which took him to the north-east. His track was to the left of Bradford; Otley; Ripley and Kirkby Malzeard and passed directly over the villages of Masham and Bedale. Seeing that he was now well out of sight of Leeds, he sought a landing place and at 6.10 pm, despite the blustery wind, came down quite gently into a meadow near Hornby Castle, home of the Duke of Leeds, 4 miles north of Bedale. He reckoned, in all, that he had travelled 63 miles from Leeds. Assistance in the form of estate workers quickly arrived on the scene and the balloon was rapidly secured and dismantled. It was taken to Squire Mitchell's house in the village of Hackforth, where a messenger was sent to Bedale to rustle up a chaise. Meanwhile, Charles was very hospitably entertained by Colonel Percy Henry Pulleine of nearby Crakehall Hall, who put him up for the night. Next day, he gathered together all his equipment, loaded it on the chaise and set out from Bedale for Leeds, arriving at 12.00 noon to the acclamation of his committee and the townspeople.

Green's exhibition in Halifax, for example, gained no coverage in *The Times* of London, although, fortunately, the *Leeds Intelligencer* printed a detailed account of the event. However, there survives a diary account written by local lass Anne Lister (1791-1840), who at this time lived with her aunt in Shibden Hall, a centuries-old manor house located about a mile from the centre of Halifax. Anne was well educated; took a keen interest in the world affairs and is known to have been an avid diarist and traveller. Her diaries (which ran into millions of words, written in a system of code she developed herself) record that she joined the crowds thronging to Halifax on 19 April to see Mr Green take to the sky. He took off at 4.30 pm and remained in sight of the spectators for about twenty minutes. Anne believed that Mr Green had taken some £400 in receipts (≈ £36,000 in 2023) at the entrance to the enclosure, for which the admission prices were one-shilling and two-shillings-and-sixpence, depending on the quality of the view required. Anne wrote that she returned home by 5.15 pm but, from the Talbot Inn to the top of Old Bank, her carriage had to meander and push its way against a veritable tide of thousands of people wending their way back to the city from high vantage points all around. Anne Lister's colourful, sexually-liberated life-style as a lesbian is the inspiration for a critically-acclaimed TV drama series *Gentleman Jack*, which was aired by the BBC in 2019.

Another, contrasting, view of events that day was penned by the 'Bard of Airedale,' the poet John Nicholson, in a rambling, 140-line ode entitled: *On the Ascent of Mr Green's Balloon, from Halifax, April 19, 1824.*

Behold th' assembled myriads near,
The shouts, the drums, the trumpets hear,
When expectation's on the wing
To see of aeronauts the king,

Rise in his ornamented car,
On wings of gas to soar afar!
Etc, etc.

Charles went up on his own and descended without mishap - saying later that he 'never had a more pleasant excursion.'

LEAMINGTON. 18 May 1824. #14

'The public are respectfully informed that Mr Green the Aeronaut, will make an ascent from Leamington Spa on Tuesday, the 15th day of May at three o'clock in the afternoon. The balloon will be exhibited to the public at Elliston's Assembly Room in Leamington, till the day of the ascent.'

Thus ran an advertisement in the *Coventry Herald* announcing Charles' first in a series of flights from towns across the Midlands. In his account of the event in the *Warwick Advertiser* this flight is number fourteen but, so far, no venues for flight numbers thirteen and fifteen have come to light.

Charles Green drew a crowd estimated at 15-20,000 people to the grounds of the Bowling Green Inn on New Street, with carriages; people on horseback and watchers thronging the surrounding streets, in and on houses and vantage points for miles around. Many took up position in front of Elliston's Library and the Royal Hotel which commanded particularly good views. Pickpockets, too, were drawn like moths to a flame on just such occasions as this and many were the tales of pockets being lightened while the attention of the victim was focussed skywards. Even Charles' wife Martha was targeted while busy collecting admission money; losing £9 (≈ £800 in 2023) when thieves cut away her coat pocket amidst the hustle and bustle at the enclosure gate!

Under the supervision of Mr T. Roberts, superintendent of the Leamington Gas Works in Ranelagh Terrace, the inflation process began at 11.00 am. Despite a rumour that Charles would be accompanied by 'a military gentleman' he made the ascent alone. This being the case, by 4.00 pm the blue, red and yellow-striped balloon was about three-quarters full and Charles deemed this quite adequate for his solo trip. He made his customary buoyancy tests by allowing the balloon to rise a little under restraint from ropes and moved the balloon each time to present it in front of a different section of the crowd.

At 4.15 pm, at his signal, the ropes were released and with Charles waving a flag and bowing to all those below, the balloon rose majestically into the sky amid loud applause, enthusiastic cheering and strains of *God Save The King* from the band. Spectators had just six minutes to watch its progress before it was enveloped by a huge cloud and lost to sight from Leamington. From barometer readings, Charles calculated this to be about 4,000 feet thick and the most-dense layer he had ever flown through.

A brisk wind blew from the west and as it pushed the balloon eastwards, it was spotted for some time, well to the south of Coventry. Charles then found a current that took the balloon in a south-easterly direction and having passed through the thick cloud layer he burst into bright sunlight which gratefully warmed him up and sent the thermometer soaring from 58 degrees F to 86 degrees F. However, fifteen minutes into the flight, he reached his peak altitude of about 14,200 feet, where the cold was intense and with the thermometer falling towards freezing, he decided it was time to call it a day and go down. His track took him to the left of Southam and a few miles to the right of Daventry and further on, coming down at about 100 feet per minute, he rounded-out to a good landing at 4.50 pm in the parish of Milton Malsor, 4 miles south-west of Northampton. It was on land owned by Francis Montgomery, Rector of Holcot and nine labourers toiling amongst the bean crop were so alarmed by his sudden, silent approach, that only by bellowing at them and promising reward for their trouble, was Charles able to persuade them to come to his aid. Indeed, during the time the balloon was dragging along the ground, a bulldog took a great dislike to the car and attacked it with some ferocity, leaping at it barking, growling and hanging on to the car covering with bared teeth. It was removed before having a go at Charles; order was restored and the balloon quickly dismantled and packed up. Charles was entertained by the Reverend Montgomery at his nearby mansion; given a bed for the night and returned to Leamington Spa in a chaise and four at 9.00 am the next morning.

COVENTRY. 25 June 1824. #16

Bad weather was again responsible for a delay from Monday, 21 June 1824 to Friday, 25 June 1824, for Charles Green's balloon ascent during the annual fair in Coventry. He arrived in the city on Monday, 14 June in order to set up the balloon - filled with atmospheric air - in St Mary's Hall, where it would remain on view from 9.00 am to 8.00 pm until Saturday, 19 June. Admission to the exhibition hall was one shilling for ladies and gentlemen and sixpence for servants and children.

The location of what the advertisement billed as Mr Green's sixteenth flight, was to be in a 'commodious enclosure' in a field owned by Mr Edward Gulson, situated between the east side of Hill Street and the original Gas Works in Gas Street. An area enclosed to prying - i.e. non-paying - eyes, by an arrangement of sheets of cloth on tall supports, contained seats and marquees for those who wished to be in close proximity to the whole spectacle of filling and ascent and not one, but two bands of music would play for their further entertainment. For this privilege, the entrance price was three shillings (≈ £14 in 2023 terms) and the enclosure would be opened at

11.00 am, with the aeronaut going up at 3.00 pm. Mr Gulson held a private reception and light luncheon for his friends - described eloquently by the local newspaper as a *Déjeune a la Fourchette* - in one of the marquees.

Friday dawned with weather little better than the previous Monday but, despite rain falling, the prospect of an ascent being confirmed drew great numbers from the city, although there seemed to be fewer people arriving from outside the city than on Monday. Shops even closed early, so that the city centre became almost deserted as the time for the ascent drew closer and an estimated 25-30,000 people assembled in the field and the surrounding area.

It stopped raining around 11.00 am. Filling began at 1.00 pm, under the watchful eye of Mr Hands from the Gas Works, marked by the firing of a signal gun and the release of a pilot balloon to check the wind strength and direction. Filling was completed by 3.15 pm and again marked by the signal gun and the launch of another pilot balloon, which tracked off to the south. These brought Mr Green to load ballast, grapnel and his instruments before taking his seat in the car. Now he tested the buoyancy two or three times and expressed his satisfaction and readiness to launch.

At this point in proceedings, Mr Gulson beckoned to Mr Green and ran over to the car, where a short, but earnest, conversation took place between the two men. It transpired that a young gentleman expressed a wish to fly with Charles that day and Mr Gulson was negotiating a seat and its fee. According to the *Coventry Herald*, Gulson is said to have offered Charles £25 and this sum was agreed there and then. However, according to the *Leicester Chronicle* account a week later, the sum agreed was 50 guineas ($\approx$ £4,700 in 2023).

The lucky fellow turned out to be Henry Brookes, a solicitor from Coventry. Beckoned forward by Mr Gulson, Brookes took his seat in the car; ever one for decisive action, Mr Green tossed bags of sand over the side equivalent to the young man's weight; tested the buoyancy twice more, called for the ropes to be released and up they went at 5.37 pm.

Green had adjusted the ballast to give about a '20lb positive lift,' which kept the rate of ascent slow and allowing the balloon to keep below the grey cloud base. Avoiding the spire of St Michael's church by a hundred yards, the balloon drifted south at around 600 feet, remaining in view of the vast crowd for thirty minutes, while passing Ryton-on-Dunsmore and Stretton-on-Dunsmore then over the London Road, 3 miles from Dunchurch. Here, more ballast was dispensed and it rose through a cloud layer to about 4,500 feet - Charles was unsure of the altitude because his barometer was damaged just prior to take-off.

In order not to stray too far from Coventry before nightfall, Charles decided to descend slowly through the cloud once more. At about 1,000 feet, he became concerned that there were many buildings below, so he steadied the rate of descent until the balloon drifted over an area clear of obstructions. Then he opened the valve again, tossed out the grapnel and rope and made a gentle, safe descent, at 6.35

pm, in a grass field belonging to Mr Taylor at Grandborough, near the village of Willoughby, having travelled 15 miles in just under an hour.

While the gas was being vented off, almost 1,000 people flocked to the scene from Dunchurch and the balloon was soon packed up. Among the crowd was the Reverend Dr Hue of Braunston who cordially invited the travellers to take refreshment at his nearby home, but Charles declined on the grounds of wanting to return to Coventry as soon as possible. A chaise and four was found so that Charles Green and Henry Brookes could return to the Castle Inn by 9.30 pm.

It is from the various press reports of this exhibition that more detail of the balloon and its appendages can be gleaned. Charles described it as follows.

'When fully inflated the balloon would take 14,000 cubic-feet of gas, the weight of which is 550lbs. The weight of the balloon structure, its netting, the car with two passengers, ballast, grapnel, ropes etc., is 530lbs. A total of 1,080lbs.

The car is 5 feet long, 2 feet in width and 2 feet, 4 inches deep, in a boat-like shape made of wicker, covered with leather, upon which is painted subjects from mythology. On one side is Aeolus, the god of winds. On the other side is Juno, queen of the Heavens, seated in a golden chariot drawn by peacocks. At one end of the car is the figure of Fame, with her trumpet and at the other end is Aurora, rising in the east. The car is lined with pink satin and the ropes by which it is suspended from the balloon are ornamented at the top with festoons of blue silk. Rosettes are placed at regular intervals down each rope as far as the edge of the car, round which are painted the twelve signs of the Zodiac.'

With two persons plus instruments on board there would be little spare space between them and with three persons (as happened a little later), the one in the middle would need to hang on to the hoop to maintain some degree of safety. Most of all, though, one would need a jolly good head for heights!

NORTHAMPTON. 8 July 1824. #17

On Saturday, 3 July 1824, Charles Green set up his balloon, car and appendages in the County Hall as a taster - at the usual prices - for the local population for his forthcoming flight scheduled for Thursday, 8 July.

Thursday morning found Charles arranging for the balloon to be set up for gas-filling in an open space next to the new Northampton Gas Works. Filling began at 6.00 am and took up most of the day. At 5.10 pm Charles stepped aboard the car and after quaffing a glass of porter with members of the organising committee, he took off alone a few minutes later. It was a fine, warm evening with just a few light clouds and a fresh breeze from the south-west. Remaining in sight for twenty-five minutes, the balloon occasionally passed behind some small clouds before being lost to view, heading now more easterly towards Kettering; Thrapston; St Ives (Huntingdonshire), in the general direction of Cambridge. This ascent was advertised on posters and handbills as his seventeenth flight. Rather confusingly, the same handbill stated that the balloon 'was first used in his ascent from the Green Park, at His Majesty's Coronation and subsequently in fourteen other ascents, with complete success,' thus - if the handbills are to be believed - suggesting this was his sixteenth flight!

In the town, the number of spectators was immense and those admitted within the space enclosed by a canvas screen were estimated at 2,000. Martha Green accompanied her husband to Northampton, but she was occupied on *terra firma*, collecting admission money at the gate of the arena.

Green intended to land near Haddenham, 5 miles from Ely and opened the gas valve to begin his descent as the village hove into view. However, as he went lower, a great deal of water could be seen below, in the area known as Grunty Fen, and he threw out some ballast to avoid a 'splash-down'. Having then passed over Ely and Soham itself, he was able to alight safely 2 miles from the village but the landing was not without difficulty and a little danger from a quite unexpected quarter.

At first the grapnel hook would not hold in the light fenland soil but as the rope trailed along the ground Green espied a labourer close by working on top of a haystack. Calling out to this fellow to lend a hand, so startled was the man by the stealthy arrival of this apparition that he threatened to run his pitchfork through both Green and his balloon if he dared approach closer! Throwing out the grapnel once more, it fastened onto a gate and held, thus allowing the balloon to sink safely to the ground, where he was this time assisted by more friendly natives making hay - no doubt while the sun still shone! A thousand or more people streamed to the landing site to witness this wondrous event and were gamely controlled by young Mr Henry Fox of St John's College, Cambridge, without whose help, the balloon and its equipment was in danger of being un-intentionally overwhelmed and possibly damaged.

Far from being upset by his brush with the aggressive labourer, Green's verdict on the journey was:

> 'The day being perfectly serene added very materially to the grandeur and magnificence of the scene. My extreme height was two-and-one-half miles [13,000 feet] and the distance covered was 50 miles in the 2½ hours since my ascent began [average speed 20mph].'

Deflation complete, the balloon was placed in a cart and the party retired to The Crown Inn, Soham for refreshment. Suitably rested for a couple of hours Green, together with his balloon and accoutrements, hired a post chaise to Northampton. He arrived at the George Inn at 1.00 am next morning, Friday, to be greeted by the ringing of church bells and most cordial civic congratulations from the mayor.

THE FLYING ADVENTURES OF CHARLES GREEN

LEICESTER. 26 July 1824. #18

On the day of what his advert billed as ascent number eighteen, the *Leicester Chronicle* averred:

> 'Never, in the recollection of the oldest inhabitant living, has any circumstance taken place in Leicester which occasioned more interest, or brought a greater influx of company into the town.'

Carriages, gigs, horses, carts - anything that could carry people - was pressed into service to bring visitors into town. The location of the ascent was on a piece of ground, owned by Mr Bradley, adjoining the Leicester Gas Light & Coke Company (founded 1821). The gas works was about half a mile north of the town centre and near the Leicester canal, which brought in coal for the works. A unique feature of Leicester Gas Works in those days was that it had its own brewery on-site, for the purpose of allowing its shift-workers to have two beer-breaks per shift. Now that's what you call a proper employee benefit!

The gates to the enclosure opened at noon and as the seats and standing room filled up, a brass band played some favourite airs. Outside the enclosure, spectators filled every open space and it was estimated that 20,000 people were gathered on Abbey Meadow.

The inflation process was supervised by Mr B. Robinson and Mr H.M. Robinson managers of the gas works. Evidently it was filled pretty well to capacity as, coupled with a brisk north-east wind, it took all the strength of forty strapping workmen, heaving on the guide ropes to keep the beast on the ground. By 4.30 pm, the filling was complete and the car attached. Charles stepped on to the edge of the car; grabbed hold of the hoop and hollered for the ropes to be cast loose. Up she went, with Charles holding fast with one hand, while making flamboyant bows to the crowd below. Heading westwards and rising steadily, he stepped down into the car, sat down and waved his flags energetically.

Charles Green recalled later that he had taken a barometer reading of 29.8 inches on the ground. After lift-off he encountered an air current from the north that helped push him upwards above a cloud layer over Nuneaton and to the left of Coventry. He then flew in glorious sunshine; basking in its heat with the thermometer fluctuating from 40 degrees F to 80 degrees F. It was here, too, that he saw a beautiful phenomenon that he had witnessed during several previous voyages, namely the formation of an 'Iris,' composed of all the prismatic colours appearing on the upper surface of the clouds and through which the shadow of his balloon appeared to dance. Charles was witnessing 'cloud iridescence' or 'irisation,' an optical phenomenon displayed on a stratum of cloud, arising from diffraction caused by (particularly) small water droplets or small ice crystals individually scattering the sunlight.

His barometer fell to 18.5 inches, indicating he had reached an altitude of 12,000 feet above his take-off point. He had been sailing along for almost two hours, when he deemed it time to return to *terra firma* once more. Valving off some gas he dropped below the clouds to find himself almost over Warwick and Leamington. As he went lower, the balloon picked up a current that again took it westwards over Stratford-on-Avon and to the left of Alcester. At around 1,000 feet in the air, the balloon suddenly began to rotate rapidly and was pushed violently upwards by a sort of whirlwind, a sensation that Mr Green had not experienced before. Quickly regaining control of the descent, he brought the balloon down in safety and without any great impact, in a field belonging to Mr William Webb. The passage of the balloon was halted when its netting became entangled with a pear tree and there it stayed until help arrived to pack it all up. He had landed in the parish of Haselor, a couple of miles from Alcester, having made a track of about 53 miles from Leicester.

Mr Webb and his family greeted him with great hospitality and provided a bed for the night. Next morning a chaise and four conveyed Charles back to the Bell Hotel in Leicester, where he arrived at 2.00 pm. The reason for his late return was because he had stopped off in Warwick to unload the balloon and car ready for his ascent from that town. It was reported in the *Leicester Chronicle* that Charles had, after settling all his expenses, cleared £150 for this event (≈ £13,500 in 2023 terms - not bad for a week's work).

WARWICK #1. 5 August 1824. #19

Were Charles Green's gentlemanly nature and good judgement unfairly compromised when a sweet, self-assured young lady was suddenly thrust into his car as he was about to take to the sky in Warwick? What was going on?

Thursday, 5 August 1824 found Charles preparing for an ascent from the Factory Yard adjoining the Gas Works, in the Saltisford area of the borough. The weather that morning looked unfavourable, with a low grey overcast scudding along on a strong south-westerly breeze. Ever the optimist, Charles continued his preparations and was rewarded around midday when the clouds began to break up and glimpses of the sun looked more promising. An immense number of people had gathered in the streets and in the enclosure. Around 1.00 pm though, the sun disappeared; clouds rolled in on a freshening breeze and it stayed like this until the time came for take-off.

Such was the availability of good viewing from outside the special enclosure, it was evident that on this occasion, comparatively few people dug into their pockets and bought tickets to the inner sanctum, even with the attraction of a close-up view of the huge balloon; seats and music to ease the wait. Instead, thousands were content to stand on St Mary's Common and the surrounding higher ground or take up spaces in the many houses that had a commanding view of the proceedings.

THE FLYING ADVENTURES OF CHARLES GREEN

This hit Charles' takings, but at least he was provided with the launch space and supply of gas free of charge.

At 1.30 pm the boom of a gun marked the commencement of the inflation of the blue, crimson and gold striped balloon suspended upright between two poles. Gas Works engineer Mr Bradley was in charge of the filling arrangements. Coal gas was supplied from the Works by a branch pipe, laid from the main pipe running beneath the Saltisford and through Mr Pratt's business premises to the balloon. Some 16,000 cubic-feet of gas was dispensed to fill the balloon, whose lift capability was tested as 648lbs. The weight of the balloon, its car, netting, grapnels, instruments and other oddments was 280lbs. We learn here that Charles Green weighed in at 148lbs (so, he was a pretty lean fellow in those days) and his child companion for the trip scaled 95lbs. Ballast packed on board weighed 125lbs; all in all, giving an equilibrium point.

Another gun fired at 4.20 pm signalling the completion of filling and a pilot balloon was launched to check the wind direction and strength. It shot off rapidly to the north-east and disappeared into the cloud layer. Just before 5.00 pm all was ready for Charles to step into the car, when something entirely unexpected took the spectators by surprise. Mr Bradley, the gas engineer, walked hand-in-hand with a young girl to the car and lifted her over the side. She sat down and with that, Charles - who must have known about this in advance - let go the final ropes and the balloon rose into the air to tumultuous applause.

The young girl was Miss Harriet Bryant, age 14. She lived in Warwick with Mr Bradley the gas engineer, who had interests in a number of gas works across the Midlands. She had watched Charles Green ascend from Northampton and expressed a great desire to fly with him when he came to Warwick. While touring the Midlands, Charles said he had reason to consult Mr Bradley for his expertise on several occasions at various gas works with which Mr Bradley was involved. It seems that Mr Bradley now called in his favours and pressed Charles to allow Harriet to go up in the balloon. The deal came down to Bradley giving his final permission right at the point of departure, it being subject to Charles Green's own decision that it was safe to launch. When Charles announced that he was going, Mr Bradley went across to his ward, seated among the honoured guests, said: 'Now, Harriet;' up she jumped and calm as you please, beaming from ear to ear, walked to take her seat in the car. While making her way through the crowd, young Harriet displayed her firmness of mind by refusing no less than four offers of £50 from gentlemen who tried - unsuccessfully - to persuade her to sell her seat to them. How could Charles refuse her if he was going up himself?

Upon their return to earth, Charles said the girl had shown no fear and had done everything she was told to, including untying the small bags of sand ballast when required. When it rained heavily, soaking her clothes and leaving her feet covered in water, Harriet was uncomfortable but did not complain. She also helped to wrap up and stow the instruments in canvas to protect them from the deluge and during the landing.

About forty-five minutes after take-off the balloon was lost to view as it passed through banks of cloud, heading east. Veering to the north-east at height, Rugby was left 4 miles to the right of track and Coventry about 8 miles to the left. As the lime-kilns of Lawford were flown over, with those at Brinklow seen some distance away to the left, the balloon ran into a rain storm. Due to the cooler atmosphere and the weight of rain on the netting and in the car, it lost altitude rapidly and in order to stabilise the craft, Charles had to pour overboard nearly 50lbs of ballast. He slowed the descent and they flew over Lutterworth at 2,000 feet. Spotting open fields 2 miles further on, Charles chose to land there and opened the valve again. There was no great impact but the wind drove the balloon on over several fields, tearing out the grapnels, on the end of 100-foot ropes, from the ground so violently that some of their prongs were actually straightened. The balloon was brought up short by a thick hedge and Charles heaved on the valve line, holding it open to get rid of the gas. Another bound across a road and it finally flopped to rest. A few labourers ran up to steady the car and allow the two travellers to alight. A vast crowd soon gathered around the balloon. It was nearly the last view for a pair of over-curious fellows, though. They ventured to inspect the valve opening very closely and were gassed insensitive for their curiosity. Dragged away by the crowd, they eventually revived - but only after the balloon was packed up and long gone.

They had landed safely, between Gilmorton and Lutterworth after an hour in the air, during which time the balloon reached an altitude of 9,000 feet. Having packed up the balloon and its accoutrements on to a chaise that was too small to carry them all, it was sent off to Lutterworth while the bedraggled Charles and Harriet walked a couple of miles into town. Here though, they received a most hospitable reception from Mr Smith, a local linen draper and his wife. Harriet was greatly fussed over and given a change of clothes while hers dried out. Entertained to refreshments and now rested and dried out, the travellers returned in a larger chaise and four to Warwick, stopping off for a change of horses at the King's Head in Coventry and arriving in Warwick at 9.00 pm that same evening. Harriet Bryant had had the ride of her life and no doubt would remember it - and regale everyone who would listen - for the rest of her life.

SHREWSBURY. 23 August 1824. #20

Shrewsbury Gas Light Company was founded in 1820 and its original gas works was built on St Michael's Street, close to a canal to facilitate the transport of coal to the premises. Shrewsbury Gas Works eventually incorporated three gas holders but, at the time of Charles Green's latest exhibition, one of these had not yet been built. Sunk 15 feet into the ground, however, was the 40 feet diameter, circular cistern base for the new holder and it made an excellent platform for Charles' balloon to be filled from the adjacent gas holder. Placed inside the cistern, the balloon was held by numerous sandbag weights hanging from the envelope netting. Most conveniently, a pipe ran through an existing underground duct, later utilised to connect all the gas holders, into the neck of the balloon. Gas was fed through this temporary pipe from the working gas holder, while ropes and pulleys from two upright posts held the balloon steady as it filled.

Filling began early on Monday, 23 August but, as the balloon grew in size and gently swayed side to side in the cistern, its increasing buoyancy began to overpower the weights and it threatened to break free. Several workmen were drafted in to drop into the cistern and hang onto the lower netting, to keep the balloon in place until filling was complete. They were down there for several hours because that operation was not completed until 4.00 pm. Now the car had to be passed down into the cistern and attached beneath the balloon, which of course could be eased upwards to allow that to happen. Next, his instruments were placed inside and the ropes and grapnels hung from the outside of the car and so fine was the equilibrium that now with hardly a breath of wind, only the strength of one man was required to hold the balloon in place. Charles milked these last few moments, by walking around the yard to the adulation of the paying crowd - and even the sun came out to bathe the whole scene in light and warmth. On the ground he read the barometer at 30.2 inches and the thermometer at 72 degrees F.

At 4.40 pm, Charles climbed into the car alone; called for the single rope to be released and the balloon cleared all the buildings; climbing vertically into a clear blue sky. With so little wind, it remained in view for nearly an hour at great height, drifting slowly eastwards towards Wellington. After a while, the balloon's track swung to south-east by south, taking him to the left of the Wrekin Hills. The sun made Charles quite hot but as he rose to his greatest height, the thermometer fell to 44 degrees F and the barometer, at 20.5 inches, translating into a gain in altitude of 11,000 feet.

After two hours, passing over Much Wenlock, Charles began an uneventful descent and landed safely 5 miles from the town, in a clover field on Symblecot Farm, Weston, in the parish of Monkhopton at 6.00 pm. He restrained the balloon with the help of a dozen labourers running over from the next field. Having discharged all the gas, he packed everything up and was entertained by a gentleman named Moore who lived nearby. As there was no inn close by, Charles waited with Mr Moore until one of his men, who was sent to Much Wenlock to obtain a chaise, could return. This took quite some time and it was 11.30 pm, before Charles made it into Wenlock. Too late to set out for Shrewsbury, he was quickly persuaded to stay the night by a party of thirty local gentlemen who, hearing of his impending arrival, had laid on a band to play music and ordered up a good supper for him. Royally entertained, he regaled his hosts with tales of this and other adventures in a thoroughly convivial evening.

By 9.00 am the next morning, Charles was up and on the road to Shrewsbury where he was met at 10.30 am by his committee and a huge crowd that showered him with congratulations - and no doubt he revelled in it and relished every cheer.

PORTSEA. 25 October 1824. #24

As a result of his mishap at Brighton in 1821, Charles did not fancy a repetition of his dunking in the sea and paid particular attention to the wind direction when arranging exhibitions on the South Coast. It was with great reluctance, therefore, that he admitted defeat due to a strong north wind blowing on the day of his planned ascent from Portsea on Saturday, 16 October 1824. By 3.30 pm, the balloon was filled and ready to go, but the wind showed no sign of veering to a more southerly quarter and so the committee insisted that he and his intended companion, should not fly, as the risk to life and limb was far too great. Being reluctant to disappoint his adoring fans, the committee relented only as far as to permit him to let the balloon rise, tethered securely to his longest rope and with a large party of strong men hanging onto it. The wind persisted in that quarter for many days and Charles was obliged to delay his trip until Monday, 25 October.

The venue for this event was the same as for Charles' earlier visit: the Duke of York's Bastion close by Portsea Gas Works, where the public would be allowed to enter this military area by an entrance opposite the hospital. Many had already bought tickets for the original date so, in order not to entice bad publicity by charging full-price again, Charles placed new advertisements making it clear that those who had paid before would be re-admitted for just sixpence each. It was also made clear that, if the wind did not play ball again, then Mr Green would stay until the wind was in a safe direction.

Inflation began at 11.00 am on the 25th and a signal gun was fired. Take-off was scheduled for 2.00 pm, but it was an hour later before a gun was fired to indicate that operation was complete. Charles took along Lieutenant Gandy of the Royal Engineers, stationed at Portsea and the balloon rose into the air at 3.10 pm. The wind had settled in the south-west and though steadily climbing to a maximum altitude of 6,500 feet, it remained in sight of Portsea; Portsmouth and Gosport for a quarter-of-an-hour, before being lost to view.

After a voyage of 35 minutes Charles brought the balloon down at Heyshott, 2 miles from Midhurst. It touched earth initially near the brow of a hill but the grapnel hook prongs became entangled with its rope and would not bite into the ground. The wind drove the balloon further towards Heyshott, until its progress was checked by the netting becoming entangled with a poplar tree. The balloon's impetus broke off a large chunk of branches and then it was free again to bump along, striking trees, buildings and a chimney on its merry way - each hit damping its speed a little.

THE FLYING ADVENTURES OF CHARLES GREEN

The balloon and its travellers finally came to a halt when the netting again snagged an apple tree in the garden of Mr Perry. A young man ran out of the house to render assistance and for his trouble, was struck by the grapnel and his clothing ripped but, fortunately, was not greatly hurt. With the balloon now tied securely to the apple tree, the pair were able to climb down from the car, having themselves escaped injury. The landing could have been less difficult if only the inhabitants – never having seen a balloon before – were not so alarmed by its sudden appearance that they cowered indoors! In a most generous gesture, Lieutenant Gandy gave the young man a gold sovereign to repair his clothes and as reward for his help.

The balloon was packed up; loaded on to a chaise and the pair headed for the Swan Inn at Chichester, where the balloon was left in the care of the landlord, pending Charles' return to Chichester for his next engagement on 9 November. Green and Gandy then carried on to Portsea where they arrived, much to the relief of his committee and friends, at about 9.15 pm.

Chapter 5

Sophia, The Girl Who Fell to Earth

1824 was Charles' busiest year so far. It saw both him and his blue, crimson and gold-striped balloon, on the road for many months, touring to twelve different venues from Halifax in the north, via Shrewsbury in the west midlands to Chichester on the south coast. It was all done by horse-drawn transport, too. He had reaped high financial rewards and greatly enhanced his celebrity status, but it was a gruelling tour, too, involving Mrs Green and their son George, so he is almost certain to have looked forward to a long winter's rest.

EAGLE TAVERN, London. 4 April 1825. #28

Charles used his winter rest to plan his forthcoming season and made a major decision to construct a new, larger balloon than the one he had been using since he lost his original *Coronation* balloon. His second balloon - which he also called *Coronation* - the blue, crimson and gold aerostat, had had an extremely rough life; had been ripped, soaked, dried out and patched up time and again, but it had served him very well indeed since 1821. Passenger trips featured at his venues more frequently these days and he really needed a balloon that could support a bigger payload more reliably than his current one. His car, too, would need to be enlarged to accommodate the changes he had in mind. All this came to fruition at his first exhibition in April 1825 at the Eagle Tavern which, on the basis that he claimed his last trip in 1824 was his twenty-fifth, then this one should surely be his twenty-sixth. However, newspapers referred to it as 'Mr Green's twenty-eighth balloon ascent,' so he must have given them that information. Of course, it is quite possible that he had made a couple of non-public test flights in the new balloon which may account for the number discrepancy.

Here at the latest venue, it was a new crimson and gold striped balloon, still styled '*Coronation*' but somewhat larger than the two earlier ones, with an envelope comprising 1,100 yards of oiled silk and a capacity well in excess of 16,000 cubic-feet of gas. During interviews with the press, Charles made great play of the fact the balloon 'was manufactured using an ingenious new method of binding the seams of the stripes.' Furthermore, Charles said his son George, now age 17, had spent three months actively involved in the construction process. It is believed the 'ingenuity' was a vague reference to the use of a revolutionary glue product, invented by Charles, by which the fabric joints were cemented instead of being sewn together. A speedier construction process and a technique he would apply very effectively to his later balloons, such as the *Royal Vauxhall*.

There was a new, larger car, too. Oblong in shape; it was made from light wickerwork, with a comfortably upholstered seat at each end; a canopy above; lined with straw-coloured silk and decorated on the outside with paintings of mythical aerial characters. The hoop to which the car was attached to the balloon netting, was richly covered in crimson silk edged with a gold fringe and the six cords by which the car itself was attached to the hoop, had artificial flowers wound around each cord. It was indeed a colourful sight.

The Eagle Tavern, in Shepherdess Walk, was noted for its vast pleasure gardens and Charles would ascend from the bowling green during the afternoon. The Eagle - and indeed other taverns in London, such as the Golden Eagle on the Mile End Road; the Star & Garter at Richmond and the Mermaid in Hackney - was a venue often frequented by aeronauts over the years but the Eagle is best remembered in modern times for its mention in the nursery rhyme *Pop goes the Weasel*. The present building dates from about 1900.

Admission to the Eagle Tavern bowling green area was one shilling, but those wishing to have a grandstand seat close to the balloon were charged an additional one shilling. Here they could watch the filling in comfort, while being entertained by a band of musicians. The day was fine and sunny and from early morning the gardens began to fill with people until, by 2.00 pm it was heaving, while the streets and houses in the surrounding area were all crowded with spectators. Pickpockets were again in evidence but they were given a hard time by the vigilance of constables of the Bow Street Patrol.

A small pilot balloon was sent up at 10.00 am and the wind judged to be from north by north-west in a steady breeze. At 11.00 am the empty balloon was hoisted by ropes to be suspended between two stout poles. Under the supervision of Mr Ayres from the Independent Gas Company, temporary pipes had been laid from the nearest main gas pipe in the street and used to illuminate the Eagle gardens on its Gala Nights. This 3-inch diameter piping was used on this occasion to run coal gas to fill the aerostat, with delivery pressure being specially increased back at the local gasometer. The balloon valve was checked out at noon and the splendid new canopied-car was brought out at 1.00 pm.

Filling continued during the afternoon and by 4.00 pm all was nearly ready. Many applications had been made to Charles to accompany him - including his son George junior and Lieutenant Gandy of the Royal Engineers from Portsea - but all were turned down as he had decided to take up his brother George for his first aerial trip. After the buoyancy was tested, the gas supply was turned off; the pipe removed and the neck-valve sealed. A signal gun warned the crowd that filling was complete and the launch of a pilot balloon told of imminent departure. The wind had veered to north-west but was still in a good quarter. Now the car was securely attached and ropes, telescopes, compass, barometer, thermometer and grapnel irons loaded aboard. It was time to go.

At exactly 5.00 pm on a signal from Charles the balloon was allowed to rise on a rope to 20 feet, while he checked all was still well, then he unhitched the final rope and they were off. Naturally, the band played *God Save The King* and the crowd cheered itself hoarse.

After shaking out a bag of ballast, the balloon rose, caught the breeze and took a southerly track, heading towards Croydon and remaining in sight of large tracts of the capital for about half an hour. Rising steadily to 4,000 feet, the balloon crossed the river Thames between Waterloo and Blackfriars bridges, giving the travellers good views of St Paul's and The Monument. At one point, a pigeon was released to test the claim that it would find it difficult to fly at such height. It flew off, zig-zagging downwards with ease until they lost sight of it, so they concluded the claim was untrue.

On the ground, the barometer read 30.2 inches and at their highest altitude it showed 21.5 inches, which translated to about 9,000 feet while the thermometer fluctuated between 69 degrees F and 75 degrees F. Although their view was sometimes obscured by clouds, the balloon did not pass through any and so the voyage was made in quite comfortable, sunny conditions.

After an hour and three-quarters in the air over open countryside, Charles deemed it time to go down. He noted that, at 4,000 feet, the first sound he detected from the ground was the barking of a dog. The balloon came quite gently down to earth into a ploughed field which, if they remained there, would make packing up the balloon a messy job. They agreed that George would vacate the car and Charles would lift off and drift the balloon to a grass field about a quarter mile away. That field was found to be on the land of Lady Glynn, in the parish of Ewell, near Epsom in Surrey. The usual crowd of willing helpers arrived and the balloon and accoutrements were soon packed up. A chaise and four was also rustled up and the intrepid travellers returned to the Eagle Tavern by 11.00 pm.

Amongst the great and the good assembled at the Eagle to watch Charles Green, leaning on the arm of a friend was a small, pale, delicate-looking young woman named Sophia Stocks. This young woman would have attracted little attention in normal circumstances, but she was no ordinary person and was the subject of nods, long looks and whispered asides among the crowd in the Eagle gardens. Aware that people recognised her, Sophia bore her notoriety well, for it must have taken considerable will power for her to have visited the Eagle when one considers what she went through the last time she was there. That occasion was on 25 May 1824, when Sophia Stocks went aloft with Thomas Harris, a novice aeronaut who made his first - and last - flight in his own balloon that day from the very same Eagle Garden.

Harris was involved with the manufacture of his balloon and the design incorporated a novel dual-action main gas vent. It was from either a malfunction or mis-handling of this valve, that resulted in a catastrophic loss of gas when he and Sophia were thousands of feet in the air and they both plunged to the ground aboard the car. Thomas Harris was killed on impact but, miraculously Sophia survived, although badly injured. Sophia was slowly recovering her health but her narrow escape had by no means dampened her spirit of adventure. She wanted to fly again and approached Charles Green - she was seen shaking hands with Charles and George upon their return to the Eagle that evening - to allow her to do so with him on a future voyage. It will transpire that Charles agreed to do so and they made several, successful, flights together later in the year.

It was shortly after this meeting that Charles Green travelled to Stamford to arrange an exhibition there in a few months. The *Stamford Mercury* of Friday, 29 April provides an interesting insight to Charles' professionalism.

'Mr Green, the aeronaut, has been this week engaged in making experiments as to the purity and strength of the Stamford gas, with a view to correctness in his calculations when filling the balloon for his ascent at the time of our races. He pronounces the gas to be excellent.'

NEWCASTLE #1. 11 May 1825. #29

It was now time for Charles to journey north again. Although it is surmised that Charles took his wife and son along, there is no firm evidence for this. Advertisements and subsequent newspaper reports, however, confirm that Charles' brothers George and William Henry (also referred to as Henry) not only accompanied him, but also undertook a separate flying programme of their own. We are thus witnessing another subtle phase in the flying career of Charles Green; one that suggests he was developing his aeronautical activity into a family business. In this new season, Charles had begun to involve brother George in aerial matters; son George was involved in balloon manufacture and wife Martha supported the ground management side of things.

Charles made three ascents from Newcastle at this time and it is on a further ascent from the city, that his brother George took his first step as an aeronaut in his own right. There are indications that two balloons are involved now and the venue locations and dates for Charles' and George's separate events lend weight to that fact. It will be recalled that at the end of 1824, Charles still used a blue, crimson and gold balloon, believed to be his 'old faithful' steed that survived many mishaps from his early days as an aeronaut. However, for his first 1825 event at the Eagle Tavern, he used a new crimson and gold balloon. Now, in adverts for the first and second of the Newcastle flights, the balloon used is described as being crimson and white in colour but the advert for the third Newcastle ascent did not mention the colour of the balloon. However, in an advert for George Green's own ascent at Stockton on 16 June - and his first flight in command of a balloon - his balloon is described as being crimson and gold. Having examined all the press adverts and reports for Charles' own itinerary during the next two months - first to Leeds, then joining George at Stockton; then down to Stamford, Leicester and Worcester - it is not until he advertises the Worcester event that the colour of his balloon is stated as blue, crimson and gold. The conclusion drawn, therefore, is that Charles introduced George to flying while testing the new crimson and gold balloon at the Eagle; he then gave his brother George more dual instruction in it at Newcastle before handing it over to his brother George who, with William, went on to fly at Stockton; Newcastle (#4) and Durham while he, Charles, got on with his own programme in the Midlands. The use of the words 'crimson and white' crops up in a later advertisement and also in an article about the first flight from York (#40). This term 'crimson and white' may be explained as an alternative way of describing Charles' own balloon - for example when the sun glistens on the crimson and gold, perhaps the gold appears to be white and maybe the blue does not show up so well - rather than suggesting a different balloon.

The first of Charles' three ascents at Newcastle (his brothers George and William made the fourth one) was scheduled for Wednesday, 11 May 1825 from the Nun's Field, by permission of its owner, Major Anderson. It was billed as Charles' twenty-ninth flight. Tickets to the general field were priced at two shillings each and for those who wished to enter the grandstand arena to see the inflation up close and be entertained by a band, this cost an extra shilling. For a few days prior to the actual event, the balloon, car and appendages were exhibited to the public in the Long Room of the Turk's Head Inn in Bigg Market in the city.

On the day of the ascent, the weather was cloudy but remarkably calm. The balloon was removed from the Turk's Head and taken the short distance to Nun's Field, where it was filled through a pipe from the gas works, under the supervision of Mr Mather. At 3.50 pm the balloon, with Charles and George aboard, rose easily and vertically into the air but was swallowed in the cloud-base after just three minutes. Charles vented some gas to stop the ascent and the balloon dropped into view again. After some minutes hovering beneath the cloud to the accompaniment of loud cheering from below, a quantity of sand ballast was released (falling in Albion Place) and the balloon disappeared once again in the cloud. It was damp and chilly passing through the 3,000 feet cloud layer, but they rose steadily into the warmth of bright sunlight in a serene blue sky. Cruising gently along over a sea of cloud, they basked in warmth as the thermometer rose from 57 degrees F to a balmy 85 degrees F. That same warmth expanded the gas and helped the balloon climb to 13,000 feet.

Having spent an enjoyable hour in the air, just before 5.00 pm the travellers descended cautiously through the cloud and seeing they were over open countryside, dropped into a field belonging to farmer Mr Scott at Peck's Houses. This was on the estate of Henry Bell Esquire of Newbegin House, located a few miles north of the city on the Ponteland Road. With help soon arriving the balloon was packed up and placed in one of Mr Scott's barns until transport could be arranged. In the meantime, Mrs Bell invited Charles and George to take refreshment with her, which they were delighted to partake. It seems to have been an ideal, problem-free training flight for George, too.

NEWCASTLE #2. 23 May 1825. #30

It was commented upon in the newspapers that the crowd for Charles' first ascent at Newcastle was not as large as could be remembered for other ballooning events in the city a number of years previously. This may have resulted in lower receipts than anticipated and so, Charles and George arranged to stay in the city a little longer and make a second ascent on Whit Monday, 23 May 1825, from the venue in Nun's Field. It was hoped that, being a general holiday, their flight was likely to attract many more people. Fortunately, despite another cloudy day with the odd light shower, this turned out to be the case and according to press reports, £430 was taken for admission to the field on the day. In the air, though, all did not go quite so well.

Filling the balloon was trouble-free and several people were allowed to sit in the car - for a consideration, of course - and be taken up for tethered trips, which proved very popular. A few minutes before 4.00 pm a signal gun was fired to indicate the Green brothers were about to set off. Taking a south-west course, the balloon was hardly airborne for a minute before it was seen coming down again. Finding the cloud layer base was again quite low, Charles wanted to keep the balloon in sight of the crowd for as long as possible. He therefore opened the valve to release some gas in order to hold the balloon beneath the cloud, which was fine - until he found the valve would not close again. Gas was now venting at quite a rate and there was no option but to land as quickly as possible.

In trying to slow down the increasing rate of descent, 300lbs of sand ballast, together with seat cushions and the precious barometer, were all thrown overboard. After a hefty bounce in a corn field and a hop into another field, they came to a safe full stop near the White Lead Factory at Low Elswick. A large, unruly crowd descended upon the balloon and thinking its occupants had short-changed them with such a short flight, the mob set about stripping the car of its ornaments and anything else they could lay their hands on. The two aeronauts were constantly barracked and harassed while they were still venting off the gas and dismantling the balloon. In the mob-melee, one man had his leg broken and his ankle dislocated; another suffered a broken arm, while others received various cuts and bruises. Two young men inhaled such a quantity of gas that they were nearly asphyxiated and had to be dragged away to recover. Even Charles inhaled so much gas that he became quite ill and leaving George in charge, he was taken to a nearby house and put to bed to recover - which he did within a few hours with no lasting effects.

The premature crash-landing was due to a piece of deal wood, to which the valve hinge was screwed, splitting along the screw-line. This split occurred when, at a height of about 1,300 feet, the valve rope was pulled and because the whole hinge failed, the valve would not close and gas escaped rapidly. In-flight attempts to force the valve shut also caused a tear in the fabric near the top of the balloon.

In order to placate the local population and show their own goodwill, Charles and George made swift arrangements to make another ascent from the same venue on Monday, 30 May.

NEWCASTLE #3. 30 May 1825. #31

In a comprehensively worded newspaper advert it was explained why the last ascent was cut short; the Green brothers also made it clear that, while tickets to the grandstand area would be priced at one shilling or two shillings and sixpence each, admission to a substantial area of the field would be priced 'at the very low charge of sixpence each.' Furthermore, they announced that:

> 'one half of the net proceeds, arising from the admission, will be appropriated to that excellent Institution, the Newcastle Lying-In Hospital and the Committee will deal with the application of such of the receipts as are set apart for the Hospital.'

At 4.00 pm, in lovely sunshine, Charles and George began their third ascent from the Nun's Field. It went particularly well and the balloon remained in sight of the vast crowd for nearly an hour. Initially the track was due west but, as it gained height, the course swung southwards, carrying it over Chester-le-Street; Durham and Stockton, all of which had a good view of its flight. So clear was the sky, that the balloon was even seen by people as far apart as Sunderland and Northallerton. At one stage, while still climbing, the balloon passed through what Charles called 'frozen cloud' and after a longer-than-usual voyage of three hours, an almost perfect landing was executed a little to the east of the Tontine Inn near Potto, in Cleveland, having travelled a distance of 48 miles from Newcastle.

A chaise and four was obtained from the Tontine and the brothers travelled to Stockton, where, arriving at 9.00 pm, to great applause, they left the balloon ready for its next exhibition, which was to be held in that town. They stayed in Stockton overnight and returned to Newcastle the next morning.

It was not until late July that the Hospital Treasurer received the sum of £17-13s-7d, which was half of the net receipts (after expenses) as promised. This delay caused some more ill-will in certain quarters of Newcastle society but was, in fact, quite unfair to Charles and George. It took the publication of a robustly-worded anonymous letter in the *Durham County Advertiser* of 30 July 1825, to set the record straight on behalf of the aeronauts - described by the letter-writer as 'victims of calumny and misrepresentation.'

Unaware of this acrimony, Charles set off for Leeds, where he was to make his thirty-second ascent from the grounds of the Coloured Cloth Hall with a special passenger.

LEEDS. 9 June 1825. #32

Sophia Stocks travelled independently to Leeds to await the arrival of Charles Green, for the ascent scheduled for Thursday, 9 June at noon. Ticket prices for the enclosure were two shillings and a further one shilling would allow access to the grandstand itself. The weather dawned fine and a good crowd gathered both in the enclosure and in the streets all around. By 11.00 am however, the sky had clouded over and rain threatened. Preparations continued and soon the sky cleared again, remaining fair up to the time of departure. Sophia was obviously a star attraction and she played the crowd.

'During this time, Miss Stocks, accompanied by two or three other young belles, walked about the Yard. She is a young lady of a small, neat figure and rather inexpressive countenance, which betrayed not the slightest symptom of alarm, even for a moment. She frequently smiled and entered the car as composedly as she could have seated herself on a sofa. She was dressed in green, with a white silk bonnet and carried with her a parasol.'

Sophia was lifted into the car and all was ready. At 12.15 pm the balloon rose steadily into the sky, heading north-east and in five minutes, upon entering a large cloud, it was lost to view.

Passing through this cloud, the travellers encountered a heavy fall of fine snow, the weight of which caused the balloon to descend. Dropping some ballast allowed it to rise again through another layer of cloud and emerging from that one they could see yet another dark cloud layer above. From this layer fell a heavy hail storm, but it washed away the snow on the balloon envelope, thus allowing it to climb easily through that layer and burst out into warm sunlight at an altitude of about 9,000 feet. To counteract the expansion, Charles vented off some gas and set up a gentle descent through the clouds. Emerging from the lowest cloud layer, Charles found it was raining hard and the wind quite boisterous but, with the effectiveness of his improved grapnel design, he made a tricky but safe landing at 12.55 pm. The landing site was in Mr Fearby's field near the village of Askham Richard, 6 miles from York and 18 miles from Leeds.

Charles and Sophia were hospitably entertained at the house of Mr Russel, before setting out for Tadcaster, 5 miles away, to obtain a chaise to carry themselves and the balloon back to Leeds by 8.00 pm.

Charles Green wound up things in Leeds, then went off to meet his brother George in Stockton, where the latter had been setting up everything for his first ascent actually in command of a balloon. Sophia Stocks did not accompany Charles to Stockton and appears to have made her way down to Stamford, to await the arrival of Charles in that town.

At Stockton, the balloon is clearly described in George's advertisements as coloured crimson and gold. The ascent – the first ever seen in the town – was planned for Thursday, 16 June 1825, from a field owned by Mr Botcherby, located behind the premises of Skinner & Thompson, wine merchants in the High Street. No doubt Charles checked out George's actions and procedures and gave him some tips, but the voyage made was without incident and at 4.15 pm a safe descent was made between Acklam and Marton. Lady Turner and Mr and Mrs Hustler followed the track of balloon in their carriages and the landing was made about a mile from Mr Hustler's home at Acklam Hall. As usual, plenty of people gathered at the site to help pack up the balloon and the travellers were very hospitably entertained by Thomas Hustler at his nearby home. Here they awaited the arrival of Messrs Jennet and Milburne, two members of the event management committee. Mr Jennett had given a homing pigeon to Charles before the ascent and this was released upon touch-down. It duly returned to its loft about half an hour later, carrying the message: 'Safely landed in the parish of Marton, in a pasture field. We have just escaped a sea voyage. Send a post chaise and four.' (Who needs smart-phones when there is a smart-pigeon handy?). They duly obliged, collecting the Green brothers and returning them to Stockton – but not before all four of them: 'partook of a very elegant dinner and excellent wine at the table of Mr Hustler.' One needed a strong physique and a hearty appetite to be an aeronaut.

Now George was off on his own itinerary (Durham; Newcastle and Kendal) while Charles set off for Stamford on his.

STAMFORD. 2 July 1825. #35

Having considered Charles' application to put on an event at the gas works, the committee of the Stamford Gas Company appointed the Saturday after the Town Races as the most suitable date.

Saturday, 2 July 1825 at Stamford was a glorious mid-summer day with not a cloud in the sky. Charles Green and his balloon were objects of enthralled attention

THE FLYING ADVENTURES OF CHARLES GREEN

from quite the largest crowd ever assembled in that small town for this, billed as his thirty-fifth flight. He could reasonably call his flight with George: #34. An estimated 25 - 30,000 people, many from as far away as 50 miles, assembled to witness this first balloon ascent from the town. Inns were filled to overflowing, few private houses were without guests and a carnival atmosphere pervaded the whole proceedings. Much interest - and revenue - was generated already by a static exhibition of the balloon and appendages and a working model gas-balloon, in the Assembly Rooms for three days.

After a few years as a professional aeronaut Green had developed an astute commercial approach to his exhibitions. The *Lincoln, Rutland & Stamford Mercury*, that oldest and most respected of provincial newspapers, carried advance notice of the event and in view of its vast catchment area, made a practice of reporting on all Green's (and other's) ballooning activity in the region and beyond.

Focus of attention was on the gas works enclosure. Admission on the day was two shillings (≈ £8 in 2023) for the general enclosure and three shillings for the grandstand area, where seats on platforms and in waggons were provided. Displayed in the Assembly Rooms for three days prior to the launch, partially inflated with atmospheric air, the balloon was put on show to the public. An additional attraction took the form of a model, gas-filled, balloon of 9 feet circumference, made from gold-beaters skin, which was made to ascend and descend within the confines of the Assembly Rooms. Tickets to enter the Rooms were on sale: 'at one shilling for Ladies and Gentlemen and sixpence to Children and Servants.' Here is a subtle insight to the prevailing social order of the day; one which continued in evidence in the wording of advertisements and prices quoted for aeronautical events well into the twentieth century. It will be observed on several occasions that these prices represent a considerable sum to the ordinary person in those days. Some may argue that air show prices in modern times have, relatively speaking, have become equally exorbitant! Nevertheless, £100 was taken during the three days and a further £200 at the gate on the day of the ascent but, for the majority in all the advantage points in the town and beyond, it was a free show.

It was reported that Mr Green and his companion for the trip, the mysterious and attractive Sophia Stocks, 'would be left with a handsome remuneration for their hazard.' In financial terms, Green was occupied in Stamford for at least four days, during which time his income was £300. His coal gas would have cost him about £13 and of course he would have had other expenses such as the hire of the hall, seating, band, accommodation, travelling etc., but he would have cleared well over £200 (≈ £15,400 in 2023).

On the question of remuneration, some indication of the vast sums of money such men could command can be gained from reports that Vincente Lunardi, for example, earned £2,000 (≈ £244,000 in 2023) after making the first flight in Britain in 1784. Entrance fee to his take-off ground was no less than one guinea (£1.05 ≈ £120 in 2023). In 1810, the celebrated aeronaut James Sadler offered to carry a passenger aloft for the sum of 100 guineas (£105 ≈ £6,900 in 2023) - and a certain Lieutenant Paget took up his offer.

In the gas works yard off Wharf Road, between - appropriately enough - Gas Street and Albert Road, by 3.30 pm inflation of the balloon with coal gas was complete. Charles Green, accompanied by the doughty Miss Stocks, stepped aboard the ornate car, cast off and balloon and passengers rose into a cloudless sky amid tumultuous applause. They responded by waving brightly coloured flags. With a gentle wind from the west the balloon rose quietly and steadily, remaining in sight of the watchers below for an hour. For a graphic description of their journey the *Stamford Mercury* quoted him thus.

'My course was east by south at first. Being fully inflated, some gas was displaced from the balloon as we rose higher and thus the lifting power was decreased. This was compensated for by throwing out a quantity of ballast and eventually an altitude of 7,500 feet was reached and maintained as the balloon passed first over Burghley House, then the villages of Ufford and Glinton. During the journey, the temperature fluctuated between 65 degrees F and 73 degrees F.

A most splendid view of Peterborough cathedral was afforded us some 5 miles away to our right hand and in a short while, we passed over the south side of Thorney. I decided that, as the surrounding countryside was favourable for a safe descent and numerous people could be seen running towards us, we should descend at this place. No time was lost, therefore, in making a controlled descent. With little forward motion, the carriage came to earth in a field of standing corn. As I did not wish to damage the crop, I decided to allow Miss Stocks to alight with the flags and recording instruments, before proceeding to another, clearer, field in order to deflate and dismantle the balloon. Those good people who had assisted my descent by holding on to the trail ropes were urged to release their grip, whereupon I re-ascended. Unbeknown to me, one of their number, a labourer by the name of Bolton, taken by surprise was carried aloft still clinging to a rope. He retained the presence of mind to hold his grip but fortuitously it required only a passage of about a mile before I was able to descend in to a grass field belonging to George Maxwell Esquire. As the balloon sank gently towards the ground Mr Bolton judged his moment and dropped to earth from a height of 15 feet. He was stunned only momentarily and this splendid fellow recovered quickly enough to follow me once more in order to render further assistance to secure my balloon. Miss Stocks joined me within minutes of my arrival and Mr Crane whose residence was very close by received us most hospitably. A chaise and four was generously procured for us by our host and we returned to Stamford by 9.30 pm.'

This relatively short but eventful, journey of some 15 miles in all, marked the end of Charles Green's thirty-fifth flight and Sophia Stocks seems no worse for her aerial adventure, travelling with Charles to his next venue in Leicester.

LEICESTER 27 July 1825 #36

Once again Charles announced that he would be accompanied by Miss Sophia Stocks and all the advertising material spoke of her escape from the jaws of death on her trip with Thomas Harris. The venue on this occasion was an enclosure and grandstand, in which the inflation and ascent would take place, surrounded by a very large meadow. The enclosure was of course priced at the usual rates, but the whole of the meadow was open and free to the public. It was therefore likely that a huge number of people would not be paying for their view of proceedings. According to the *Leicester Chronicle* reporter:

> 'The day was uncommonly fine, the sun shone with a powerful, yet not oppressive lustre. The Cerulean canopy of heaven was almost cloudless, with a few slight strata of white filmy, transparent rack; the wind a gentle, refreshing breeze from the south.'

It was a different venue to his previous Leicester event; this time in a much more open environment, in Mr Bradley's Close, adjacent to the gas works. After a few trial rises, that showed off the balloon and car to the spectators, Charles and Sophia climbed aboard and at 4.30 pm the ties were released and 'a more beautiful ascent was never seen.'

With little or no wind, the ascent was almost vertical and the balloon remained in sight of those below for a long time and it was said to be visible from Loughborough; Ashby-de-la-Zouch and Hinkley. Release of more ballast still only achieved a maximum altitude of about 6,200 feet, which was much less than on the previous occasion. After an hour of flight, Charles made a safe descent in the vicinity of Atherstone, Warwickshire, 20 miles from Leicester. The descent was watched by Mr Wilday, a banker and businessman, from his home in Atherstone and he despatched some of his servants to assist the travellers and to invite them to join him for refreshment and rest at his house. This they did most gratefully and it was past 10.00 pm when the pair returned in a chaise, with the balloon on top, to The Bell Hotel in Leicester. The Bell was headquarters of the local Gentlemen Cricketers who cordially invited Charles (but not Sophia) to join them immediately for supper, which he happily accepted. It is recorded he ate a hearty supper and rid himself of the fatigues of the day by helping to dispose of a magnum of champagne. There were great benefits to being a celebrity! However, on the financial side, it was reported that Charles was 'handsomely remunerated for his daring enterprise' by the usual entrance fee takings and although Mr Bradley did not charge him for the use of the meadow, Charles gave him a donation of £10, to be given to the Leicester Infirmary. It had also been announced prior to the event that, because the meadow was open to uncontrolled public access, a voluntary collection would be taken among the crowds in that space. Not surprisingly, the sum of £21-16s-4d collected was a bit disappointing, 'considering the immense number of persons congregated together.'

Charles Green left Leicester on Friday 29 July bound for his next exhibition in Worcester, but, since Sophia Stocks did not make any more flights with Charles, it is assumed she returned to London. It was almost a year later before Sophia's name was once more associated with ballooning, but not with Charles Green. She was billed to go up with George Graham from the White Conduit Gardens in London on 28 June 1826 but, due to insufficient buoyancy in his hydrogen-filled balloon (a frequent occurrence), Sophia was obliged to give up her seat and George's wife, Margaret Graham, went up solo instead.

Although fading from the public eye, Sophia was evidently still keen to fly, as an item in the *Leicester Chronicle* of 25 Nov 1826 indicates.

'Miss Stocks is appealing to the public for subscriptions to enable her to purchase a balloon to make aerial flights for the benefit of herself and her mother, who is dependent on her for support. Donations will be gratefully received [in this instance, by *Leicester Chronicle*] and forwarded.'

This appears to have been a plea, possibly originating in London and picked up by provincial newspapers in general, but what transpired is not known, except that there is no evidence of Sophia owning a balloon or making any more flights thereafter.

Possibly the last known reference for Sophia Stocks is a marriage record found in St Leonard's Church, Shoreditch, London in which a Sophia Stocks was married to Edwin Cole on 25 December 1839. Her birth year was stated as 1808, which would make her about the same age as the girl who flew with Charles Green.

Chapter 6

Another Balloon Lost

WORCESTER 20 August 1825 #37

Charles Green's thirty-seventh flight was scheduled for Saturday, 6 August from the bowling green of the Saracen's Head Inn, Worcester. Prior to this event, Sophia Stocks was advertised to accompany Charles, but did not do so; neither did the ascent take place on the day planned.

On the scheduled day, inflation began at an early hour, but the wind was very strong and particularly boisterous, so much so that the balloon suffered some tears in the fabric and the ascent had to be called off. About £19-worth of tickets were sold in advance and Charles had to refund that money, so his pocket took a hit because he had already spent about £100 for the gas and various travelling expenses. The *Worcester Journal* reported this loss to its readers and suggested a public collection be made to recompense Charles - but that plea fell on stony ground.

Accustomed to this sort of setback, Charles soon organised repairs to the balloon and let it be known that he would set another date for an ascent in the town in due course. The *Journal* duly announced that date as Saturday, 20 August and if an unfavourably strong wind were to blow on that day, then he would move the ascent to the gas works itself. Supervised by Mr Hill, the works engineer, the balloon was indeed inflated at the gas works, where according to Charles, the gas was of excellent quality and it took only an hour and a half to fill the balloon to capacity. Then, by man-handling on ropes, it was moved to a barge on the adjacent canal and thence along the waterway to the Saracen's Head. It suggests that, for this to happen, the wind could not have been very strong. Arriving intact at the bowling green, Charles took the opportunity to raise his takings by offering short, 'tethered' ascents until around 5.00 pm when it was time to make his free ascent.

He went up alone and none of the newspaper reports of the event mention Sophia Stocks, so perhaps she had left for London by that time.

Lift off was uneventful and the balloon, with Charles waving his flag energetically, remained in view for nearly half an hour. It took a southerly direction over Worcester, following the course of the River Severn near Tewkesbury and could be seen by watchers in Cheltenham. At 8,000 feet altitude Charles released one of two homing pigeons belonging to Mr Chapman of Worcester and the second at 11,000 feet, both birds having to be coaxed to leave the car. At 6.00 pm the balloon passed over Gloucester at 12,000 feet altitude, its slow passage being followed by a number of the city inhabitants on foot and horseback. Charles said he had a wonderful panoramic view, encompassing Worcester; Hereford; Gloucester; Tewkesbury; Cheltenham and Malvern and a fine view of the Bristol Channel, shining like polished silver. Descending lower, at 4,000 feet he encountered a new air current from the north-east which pushed him to the west of Gloucester, where he made a safe landing at Beauchamp Lodge, near Highnam at 6.05 pm. A messenger was sent in to Gloucester to acquire a chaise but this took quite a while to arrive; delaying his return to Worcester. The balloon was dismantled; everything was packed on top of the chaise and after a stop for refreshment at the Hop-Pole Hotel in Tewkesbury, Charles arrived in Worcester at 12.30 am the next morning.

Charles also reported seeing a sun-light phenomenon he had witnessed before, when flying among cloud banks. He said the shadow of his balloon projected onto a cloud, was encircled by a rainbow of the most brilliant colours. He recalled seeing this phenomenon during a flight from Cheltenham.

So far, Charles' work in Worcester was 'rather unprofitable,' so the following day he inflated the balloon again at the gas works and had it taken to the Saracen's Head bowling green, where he spent the whole day doing tethered flights for the paying public in order to recover a little profit. There were many takers for these 'flights,' which carried two or three persons each trip to a height of 500feet, for the price of five shillings each, but Charles was probably glad to see the back of Worcester.

KENDAL #1, 16 August 1825 #38

At the end of July, the *Cumberland Pacquet* newspaper announced that Kendal horse races would start on 27th; that Mr Green had arrived in the town to make an ascent shortly and that new gas lights would be lit in the town for the first time. Kendal Gas Light & Coke Company had received permission to form and on 25 July 1825, its new gas works, built alongside the Kendal to Lancaster canal; coal wharf and two gasometers, each with a capacity to store 11,000 cubic-feet of gas, came into operation. Originally scheduled for Friday, 5 August, Charles Green, assisted by his brother George, was engaged to put on a show to encourage the public to buy into this new civic amenity.

On the day, the weather did not oblige and a very strong, gusty wind played havoc with the inflation process in the gas works enclosure. The balloon was almost fully inflated when Charles called a halt and made it clear that he was not going to risk his balloon or his life by attempting to fly that day. This news was met with angry whispers and accusations in the press that the whole event was a hoax, but Charles was adamant that he had made the right decision and he was happy to arrange another day. The *Cumberland Pacquet* back-tracked on its censures and wrote: 'Mr Green intends to ascend at Kendal tomorrow (16th). His late failure appears, from the most respectable testimony, to have been solely to do with the elements and not to any intent not to gratify the crowd.' Very magnanimous.

The ascent took place on Tuesday, 16 August but the *Pacquet* gave it scant coverage, merely saying that the weather was fine and the spectacle was magnificent. The trip itself lasted 45 minutes and an altitude of 9,000 feet was reached, but the distance travelled over the ground was only a few miles from Kendal and the actual landing spot was not mentioned.

KENDAL #2, 30 August 1825 #39

The *Carlisle Patriot* was more kindly disposed towards Charles' second ascent from Kendal which took place on the planned day of Tuesday, 30 August 1825. Perhaps this was due to Charles taking up an amiable young local lady by the name of Miss Dawson as his companion for the trip.

Take-off was at 5.30 pm and with a few scattered high clouds and little wind to speak of, Charles was able to keep the balloon in sight of the town for three-quarters of an hour. He then cast out some ballast and the balloon drifted north-north-eastwards, cruising along at 5,300 feet, for another half-hour. Approaching Appleby-in-Westmorland, a current turned them more to the east and with the high fells approaching, if he was to stand a chance of any helpers reaching him quickly, Charles deemed it prudent to descend. Initially the descent-track threatened to deposit the balloon into Flakebridge Wood, so more ballast went over the side and the trees were avoided. After flying 27 miles, a safe landing was finally made at the foot of Murton Pike at 6.45 pm, when the balloon netting became entangled with an oak tree, but suffered no damage.

The two travellers were assisted by onlookers arriving on foot to pack up the balloon. They were then given refreshment by Mr Dixon of Harbour Flatt, remaining there until a post-chaise arrived from the King's Head Inn, having been sent from Appleby by its mayor, the Reverend Milner. Such was the merriment in Appleby that, upon the arrival of the chaise carrying the pair back to Kendal, that the church bells were rung in their honour and the chaise was drawn into the town by a host of people, while the horses followed on behind. George Green and Miss Dawson's brother then arrived in Appleby in a carriage and four and everyone having enthusiastically acknowledged this civic rapture, the two carriages returned that same night to Kendal.

Leaving George to go off and do a solo exhibition in Preston, Charles wended his way across the Pennines to York for his next event.

ANOTHER BALLOON LOST

YORK #1. 17 September 1825. #40

Despite being reported as 'a most beautiful ascent, to the great pleasure of a crowd of spectators,' Charles Green's first flight from York was not a financial success. He was out of pocket by £30; his outgoings for gas and contingencies being £60 and his gate receipts being only £30.

It was the week of the York Festival and for those who could afford it, many were able to attend sublime performances at the Minster, exquisite music at various concerts and the gaiety and splendour of a Fancy Ball. They were to be further enticed and entertained by an aerial ascent by the famous Charles Green, from the gas works, without Monk's Bar, on Saturday, 17 September 1825. Charles made the usual arrangements for seats and space in an exclusive enclosure inside the gas works yard; musical entertainment was provided by the band of the 7th Hussars all for the usual entrance price of three shillings per person. The problem was that the 'continually accumulating throng' was mostly outside the gas works gates and in the surrounding streets - where they were happy to have such a view for no entrance fee at all. One dense mass of people occupied the area in front of the gas works; more were on Monk's Bridge and they spread far up the Malton Road and into fields near Grove Terrace. People could even be seen on the tower of the Minster while the castellated entrance to the city and its walls also attracted a share of the throng. Thus, as the *York Herald* put it: 'We regret the interior of the gas works was but thinly attended.'

Inflation began at 1.00 pm under the supervision of gas engineer, Mr John Onthett who, it will be recalled, was the gas engineer for Charles' ascent from Portsea in 1821 and was now employed by the York gas works. By 3.00 pm the car was attached and Charles stepped aboard. With the balloon still securely tethered by a long rope, he made a few trial ascents to the delight of the small crowd inside the yard. Now ready to go, Charles drank a glass of wine to the health of the crowd, his flags were handed to him and the restraining rope cast off. At 4.10 pm the balloon emerged from the buildings into a sunlit sky and into full view of the whole city. The *York Herald* account states that 'the sun finely beamed upon the crimson and white stripes of the balloon.' Perhaps the blue and gold stripes, were made pale in the sun's glare?

Taking a north to slightly north-west track, Charles poured out some sand ballast and climbed steadily to about 5,000 feet, remaining visible for half an hour. Then a new air current veered the balloon to north-north-east and this course continued for the rest of the voyage.

Afterwards, Charles said he reached an altitude of 13,000 feet and had an uninterrupted view of the coast of Yorkshire from the Humber to the Tees. He had planned to descend near Malton but on descending a little, encountered another current that took him 4 miles to the left of Malton and then over the magnificent Castle Howard, all in the general direction of Pickering. Having flown well out of sight of York and faced with a hilly district coming up, he decided to land. Dropping his grapnel, it took a firm hold and Charles made an uneventful landing at 5.00 pm in a stubble field belonging to Mr Hayes, in the parish of Pickering, 2 miles north of the town. It was not long before he had a bevy of helpers and a chaise was soon brought to the site. He added:

> 'I received invitations from several respectable inhabitants of the neighbourhood, particularly Colonel Mitchelson, a magistrate from Pickering, which I accepted and partook of the hospitalities of his table. Having been refreshed by a good dinner and excellent champagne [Charles seems to have developed quite a taste for 'bubbly'], I set out for York and arrived at the gas works at midnight.'

The *Yorkshire Gazette* reported:

> 'The loss that Mr Green sustained by his first ascent on 17th, induced several gentlemen to wish him to repeat the exhibition at a reduced rate of admission. Tuesday, 27th was fixed upon for that purpose.'

YORK #2. 27 September 1825. #41

Setting up this time in a field outside the York gas works, in order to further boost his takings, Charles sorted out his longest ropes and carried out tethered ascents to 200 feet for thirty ladies and gentlemen. During one of these lifts, an overly-bold young fellow literally put his foot in it by stepping into a loop in the rope. It tightened up too rapidly for him to jump clear and he found himself whisked up into the air. Fortunately, he had the presence of mind to grab hold of the rope above him with his hands and this enabled him to stay safe until the balloon could be drawn back to earth and he could jump clear. Cries of alarm then turned to gales of laughter at his predicament. A cat, in a basket with a small parachute attached, was taken up several times and dropped over the side, just to add spice to the entertainment.

At 4.20 pm, having topped up the gas once more, Charles, complete with the cat as his passenger, stood in the car, quaffed a glass of wine 'to the health of all friends on *terra firma*' and cast off into the blue sky. With the sun glistening on the balloon, he headed south-east and upon reaching a good height, he let drop the parachuting cat.

Climbing gently, the balloon veered due east and after hovering in sight for some time, it was lost to view behind a cloud. Emerging into view once again, it could be seen by people in York for almost an hour. A landing was made without much difficulty on the estate of Mr G. Calvert, near Osgodby in the parish of

Hemingbrough, 2 miles east of Selby. Again, there was no shortage of willing helpers and Charles was then hospitably entertained by Mr Stringer of Barlby, who helped him to obtain a chaise for all his gear. Charles arrived back in York by 9.00 pm where the *York Herald* claimed the flight to be: 'unquestionably one of the finest ascents that has ever been witnessed in York.'

CARLISLE #2. 11 October 1825. #42

Charles' brother George had progressed from Preston to Carlisle, where he made an ascent from Carlisle Castle on Thursday, 29 September in a balloon described by the *Carlisle Patriot* as red and yellow in colour. He was injured during the landing near Beattock Bridge, Moffat, north of the border and the *Carlisle Patriot* reported:

> 'Mr [George] Green was considerably hurt by the violent manner in which the car afterwards [its second impact] came into contact with the earth. He was, however, well enough to return to town early this morning and having kept himself quiet, is in a convalescent state and will probably regain his strength in the course of a few days.'

Upon his return, George received many invitations to make a second ascent from Carlisle and agreed to do so. It is surmised, however, that his injury was troubling him somewhat - and possibly his confidence was a bit shaken, too. He decided to send word to York for his brother Charles to travel to Carlisle and make the second ascent from the town on his behalf. This accounts for the arrival of Charles in Carlisle, just before Saturday, 8 October, where the second trip from the town was advertised for Tuesday, 11 October. Temporary gas pipes were already laid from the Castle, all the way down to the bottom of Castle Street, where a connection was made to the town gas main.

Here, the vexed question of keeping track of balloons the Greens were operating, crops up again. George is reported to have gone up at Carlisle in a red and yellow balloon on 29 September. On 27 September, Charles was in York and the description given there was for a crimson and white balloon. In an article describing Charles' ascent at Carlisle on 11 October, the balloon is described as red and yellow, so he appears to be using 'George's' balloon, while presumably leaving his own (red, blue and yellow) behind either in York or, perhaps in Richmond, where he was due to make an ascent later that month. Busy fellow!

The weather - always a vital factor - was rainy, driven on by a boisterous wind on Saturday, 8th until the morning of the event on Tuesday, 11th. Despite these adverse conditions, Charles organised the inflation while keeping a wary eye on the weather. Sheltered by the castle walls, spectators in the inner sanctum of the Castle were entertained by a band playing popular airs. Inflation to about eighty per cent of the balloon's capacity was completed by noon, by which time the weather had greatly improved, though the wind was still blowing nearly a gale from the south-west. The specific gravity of the gas used was found to be greater than that which Charles had used in York and after a few trial lifts, with many stout-hearted men tailing on to the mooring ropes, he declared there was insufficient spare buoyancy to take a passenger on this trip. Apologetically, he turned down an offer of £40 from one would-be passenger and cancelled his intention to offer some tethered flights. By 2.00 pm, the time announced for departure, the crowds, though considerable in number both inside and outside the Castle, were much smaller than for George's earlier flight. That strong wind still made the balloon buck and roll against its restraints and the car was tossed about like a small boat. But, as the afternoon wore on the wind subsided quite suddenly. It was time to go.

It was 3.35 pm when the balloon cleared the battlements with ease and glinting in the sunlight, rose slowly, heading north-east. Charles had, that very morning, received a new barometer from London and taking it up with him for the first time, he calculated his highest point as 8,250 feet. George's barometer was broken when the car hit the Cloth Hall roof at the start of the Preston flight. After three-quarters of an hour in the air, he began his descent and with the wind no longer presenting a difficulty, Charles made a safe - but interesting - landing in a pasture on the Earl of Carlisle's estate, farmed by William Winter esquire, of Billestan in the parish of Haltwhistle.

The landing had already seen some merriment. In view of the breeze being likely to be favourable, Major Mounsey proprietor of The Shaws Hotel in Gilsland and master of the local pack of hounds, decided that the hounds should be led out that morning in the hope that the hunters might have the good luck to be able to ride to see the intrepid aeronaut make his landing and thus be on hand to render assistance. Just as the last hare was killed, Charles was heading earthwards right towards the spot where the huntsmen were gathered. It was agreed that this hare would be presented to Mr Green, whereupon he materialised in front of them and the hare was tossed into the car just before it touched down. Never a man to be lost for words, Charles smiled broadly at the hunters and shouted: 'Gentlemen, I thank you, but it is not very common for me to receive the present of a hare before I actually land.'

The descent path began near Gapshields, a mile or so from Gilsland Spa Villa and was seen by many folk who rushed, cheering and waving ecstatically, to the pasture to lend a hand. Having expelled all the gas and packed up the balloon Charles was wined and dined by Major Mounsey at his Spa Villa home, along with the great and the good of the district. A chaise and four was found to convey Charles and his equipment back to Carlisle, where he arrived at 1.00 am next morning - but not without incident. It is not known if Charles was driving the chaise or not, but in the pitch-blackness of the road between Gilsland and Brampton, the chaise was 'overset' and progress was delayed. Fortunately, neither Charles nor his equipment were damaged.

ANOTHER BALLOON LOST

RICHMOND. 18 October 1825. #43

After a very short sleep at the King's Head Hotel in Carlisle, Charles caught a stagecoach and re-crossed the Pennines yet again, bound for Richmond in Yorkshire, where he was scheduled to make an ascent from the castle on 18 October. This was expected to be an arduous task as the capacity of the gasometer in Richmond was only 3,000 cubic feet and the balloon would require nearly 16,000 cubic feet - so the filling operation was going to take a few days.

On Tuesday, 18 October, a vast concourse of spectators gathered in and around Richmond castle to witness the final part of the inflation and the ascent of Charles' faithful blue, red and yellow balloon. Once again, the weather was playing its tricks and there was a gale blowing from the west. Casting off at 1.30 pm, Charles needed all his skill to cope with this tricky launch and the balloon was driven rapidly in the direction of Cleveland. Having covered a distance of 20 miles in only 14 minutes (average speed: 86mph), Charles decided that he had better land, or at this rate he would be driven out to the Yorkshire coast.

Four miles west of Yarm, Charles brought the balloon down as steadily as he could in the tempestuous wind, trailing all his grapnels in an effort to stop the craft from bouncing endlessly - and dangerously - along the ground. His efforts were in vain. The car struck the ground at 2.00 pm at Trafford Hill, near Middleton and Charles managed to clamber out but, in the absence of any helpers whatsoever, there was no way he could hold on to, let alone restrain the manic gyrations of the balloon.

Wrenched from his grasp, the balloon and car pounded its way across the fields and the car began to disintegrate. An eyewitness to the landing had the following to say to the *Hull Advertiser*:

> 'Accompanied by a friend, [I] was on a journey on the turnpike road from Stockton to Yarm in a gig, when we nearly met with a singular accident. Mr Green's balloon was coming driving along the road, with half a car and a pair of grapnels dangling on a rope. It just passed over our heads. We both expected the gig would have been hooked by the grapnels and that we should have been taken in tow into the North Sea. After passing us, it rose into a dark cloud and was lost sight of. Shortly afterwards, we caught a glimpse of it again, at a great height, going rapidly to the eastward. It went into a second range of clouds and disappeared altogether. It has gone out to sea, it is supposed. Mr Green came into Yarm with one of his hands bleeding, his coat covered with mud and without his hat. After taking some slight refreshment, he set off in a post-chaise to Richmond. Except for the scratched hand, he was not personally hurt.'

Speaking later to people in Yarm and Richmond, Charles seemed resigned to the disappearance of his balloon and the fact that it was irretrievably lost somewhere in the North Sea.

BLACKBURN. 24 October 1825. #44

'Notwithstanding his mishap, Mr Green again ascended at Blackburn on Monday last, with the balloon that was in Carlisle.' Thus ran the article in the *Carlisle Patriot* of Saturday 29 October 1825. It was now Charles' turn to ask George for some help. Bouncing back from his physical and financial loss of his old faithful balloon, he asked George to transport the red and gold balloon over from Carlisle to Blackburn, where Charles was billed to make an ascent on Monday, 24 October 1825.

The venue for this event was described as follows: 'The machine was inflated in the new square, by means of branch pipes from the gas works,' but it is not known to which square this refers.

Being October, a season of gales, it comes as no surprise to find the weather facing Charles was again marred by a strong north-west wind. At 3.00 pm a small pilot balloon was released to check the wind strength and direction and Charles made a few tethered test lifts to check the buoyancy. All was pronounced in order and at 3.10 pm, being sufficiently confident of his ability to handle the conditions Charles, accompanied by Mr C. Radcliffe of Blackburn, took the balloon up into the teeth of the gale, before which it bounded along to the south-east. Crossing the Pennines, even with two people on board, the greatest elevation reached was 9,200 feet as it tracked between Rochdale and Huddersfield, towards Rotherham. A safe landing was made at Braithwell, 6 miles east of Rotherham, at 4.05 pm after travelling about 65 miles (average speed: 71mph). Due to the rural locality and overall distance involved, it was 6.00 pm in the evening of the next day before the aeronauts returned to Blackburn, in a chaise and four with the balloon and equipment packed securely on its roof.

This ascent was the last trip made by Charles for this year and he, George and the rest of the family retreated to London to review their work, start making a new balloon to replace the one lost at Richmond and to plan the next year's itinerary.

Chapter 7

The Eagle & The Horse

**EAGLE TAVERN #2, City Road,
LONDON. 30 March 1826. #49**

If there is any doubt that ballooning for the Green's was a family business, then surely this next flight will dispel that doubt. The event was to be a family affair since Charles chose to take up his son George and his youngest brother William Henry - usually known as Henry. Charles had planned to take up his brother George, to give him more training but, since the lift and car capacity was limited and the youngsters pleaded to go, George the elder stepped aside to allow them both to go up. Press reports once again referred to the involvement of Charles' son George having experience in the manufacture of balloons.

Inflation began at 7.30 am under the watchful eye of Mr Hinds and was completed by 4.00 pm when the balloon was filled to capacity of around 20,000 cubic-feet of gas. The 'normal' lightweight wicker basket was not really adequate for a crew of three people and so it was replaced by a heavier but more-roomy car that was equally richly decorated.

Pilot balloons launched showed the wind was steady from the north but was increasing in strength. At 5.10 pm the trio entered the car and it took all the immense effort of fourteen strong handlers to hold the balloon down, until Charles bellowed the command: 'Away!' and they left the ground. At about 20 feet up, it needed some ballast to be dropped in order to persuade the balloon to climb more positively and then ever rapidly towards the south. It caught a new current that took it more to the east and within a few minutes was lost to view.

After a time, the wind swung it back to the south and the travellers crossed the Thames below London Bridge, marvelling at the beauty of the river and all the ships along its length. They passed over the villages of Limehouse, Deptford, Stepney and Greenwich and then, still climbing, entered thick cloud which was both dense and cold, at one point enduring a heavy snow shower. At this point the thermometer showed 2degrees of frost.

After 40 minutes in the air and finding it chilly, they dropped back through the clouds and made an easy landing in a field 5 miles from Sevenoaks.

EAGLE TAVERN, City Road, London. 16 May 1826. #51

Charles was back at the Eagle Tavern on City Road for his ascent on Whit-Tuesday, 16 May. The gardens were divided into two areas; the general entrance was priced at one shilling and entrance to the inner enclosure was an additional one shilling. Monday saw the balloon partially filled and viewable in the inner enclosure for the price of sixpence. Also, the popular tethered 'flights' were again on offer for five shillings each and Charles had clearly decided this was a great way to boost his takings. He would have laughed off an item in the newspaper *British Press*, which commented on 17 May: 'Green's ascent attracted a great number of spectators to view a thing which is now as common as it is uselessly perilous.' In contrast, an anonymous contributor to the *Literary Chronicle* - under the title of 'Rambles of Asmodeus' - wrote:

> 'You know I am fond of holiday sports and on Tuesday I sauntered to the City Road, where I found a new species of amusement. It was Mr Green, giving persons of elevated ideas a ride in his balloon at five shillings a head. Mr Green resorted to a very ingenious artifice. When the balloon had risen some three or four hundred yards [*sic*], he gave his passengers the wrong end of the telescope to look through and made them believe they were half a dozen miles high. This was an innocent fraud, Mr Green, which gave much gratification at a little risk and you are not censured for it by me.'

Just after 6.30 pm Charles, his son George and Mr Barham of Oxford Market (London) entered the car and he gave the signal to release the ropes. With hardly a breath of wind, the balloon rose steadily before drifting southwards. The flight which, even with three people aboard, reached 7,000 feet, was uneventful except when they encountered quite a heavy snowfall while passing through some cloud. A safe landing was made on the estate of Percy Hart Dyke Esquire, of East Hall, St Mary's Cray in Kent, at whose mansion the three aeronauts were very hospitably entertained and suitably refreshed, returned to the Eagle Tavern by midnight.

Despite the undoubted prominence of Charles Green, on this occasion much press publicity was given to a terrible accident that occurred indirectly as a result of the balloon event. In a street named Tenter Row, to the rear of the Eagle, were what were described as 'cottages of the meanest description.' On the rooftop of a row of these cottages, some occupants had built platforms on which people could watch the balloon proceedings at a fraction of the cost of entry to the garden itself. One platform was a heavy scaffold erected by a Mr Bartlet, said to be a dealer in cat's meat and it was crowded with people. Shortly before Mr Green's ascent this scaffold collapsed, sending many people crashing to the ground, where at least five sustained severe injuries but, fortunately without fatality.

HERTFORD. 31 May 1826. #52

Foul weather caused Charles to postpone his ascent from Hertford from Tuesday, 30th until late in the afternoon of Wednesday, 31 May. A general election was in the offing, too, and the reason for the lateness of his departure was so that it would not compete with an election rally and parade through the town by Thomas Slingsby Duncombe, who was trying to become the MP for the local constituency. In fact, 'Honest Tom,' as he was known, an advocate of the Chartist cause, was successful and entered Parliament on 15 June.

By 6.00 pm on the 31st, the weather was still poor but flyable and a huge crowd braved the elements to assemble around the gas works yard. It is interesting to learn that the gas manufactured at this works was 'generated on Mr Broadmeadow's patent principle.' This is a reference to the work of Simeon Broadmeadow, a civil engineer from Abergavenny who, in 1825, patented his invention for exhausting, condensing or propelling air through gas - in this case - during the coal gas production cycle. His method was said to purify the gas by expelling, with fanned air jets, many of its carbon impurities. As far as Charles Green was concerned, he was of the opinion it improved the specific gravity and 'levity' of the gas to such an extent that less gas volume was required in the balloon to achieve his buoyancy requirements.

Accompanied by his brother George, the balloon rose from its moorings in grand style and headed south-west towards Essendon and Barnet. It took just four minutes to disappear into the clouds. Climbing steadily, the balloon emerged from thick cloud into bright sunlight and welcome warmth, reaching 8,000 feet altitude at its highest point. Charles and George cruised along for about an hour then released gas to descend through the cloud. When they emerged beneath it there was a convenient pasture below, into which the balloon made a gentle landing just after 7.00 pm. The landing spot was near Gannick Corner, half-a-mile from Potter's Bar, in the parish of South Mimms, the third time Charles had made a landing in that parish.

BOSTON, LINCS. 8 June 1826. #53 (advertised as #52)

Boston town gas works had been operating for only seven months and this was a good way for the owners to promote the benefits of their wonderful town improvement. Once again, the partially inflated balloon together with its 'car and appendages' was on view to the paying public the day prior to the event. Tickets to witness the process of inflation and launching of the craft could be had for the sum of two shillings and sixpence. Ladies and gentlemen were assured that secure (!) seats were to be erected for those honouring Mr Green with their presence in the gas works enclosure, where they would also be entertained by a band of music. Six hundred of the local gentry were induced to part with this not inconsiderable entrance fee and availed themselves of the spectacle at close quarters. Meanwhile, a crowd, estimated at 20 - 30,000 people, filled the streets to overflowing to catch a glimpse of this wonder of the age. For this ascent Charles chose to be unaccompanied, although no reason was given for his decision.

It is not often that a first-hand account, other than that provided by a journalist, can be found of such an event in the early nineteenth century. Writing was not a prolific skill in those days and diaries were even rarer. On this occasion, however, such a rare combination existed in the form of the diaries of John Peck, gentleman farmer and patron of all things modern, of Parson Drove, Lincolnshire. Written in a beautiful copperplate style, John Peck kept a meticulous diary every year from 1814 until his death in 1851. The following extract is one of several references to ballooning taken from his diaries, now in the custody of Wisbech Museum.

Of Green's visit to Boston, John Peck wrote:

> '8 June 1826. Started at 6 [am]. Breakfasted at Kirton. On with Mrs Peck and a party to Boston to see Mr Green ascend with his Balloon, which was indeed a truly Grand sight. I offered him £5 to go up with him but he would take no-one. Never saw Boston so full of Company. Returned and tea with Mr Palethorpe. Home to Parson Drove by 11 o'clock [pm].'

Although the sum of £5 was a prodigious inducement in those days (≈ £400 in 2023) it was far below the fee Charles could command - but he was never a man to let greed over-ride his better judgement.

On first leaving the ground the balloon took a south-westerly course which in a short while changed to due west. This carried Green between the villages of Swineshead and Heckington, in a direct line for Grantham and Belton Park, the home of Sir John Thorold. Boston by that time had become in Green's words: 'resembling a mass of rubbish covering about an acre of land.' Knowing that its inhabitants must have lost sight of him, Green commenced a descent while still to the east of Grantham.

Having passed the town, on reaching 4,000 feet he encountered a south-easterly air current which now swung him northwards, towards Newark. However, as the countryside was still favourable for a landing, he continued to descend, coming to rest at 5.05 pm, in the grounds of the home of Thomas Earle Welby Esquire, in the parish of Allington near Bottesford, just within the Lincolnshire boundary.

Green had, on this occasion, travelled 30 miles in just over two hours. His barometer readings showed a drop in pressure from 30 inches on take-off, to a low of 20.2 inches, indicating having gained 12,000 feet at his greatest elevation.

By the time he had dismantled the balloon and car, several gentlemen arrived on horseback from Grantham to acquaint themselves with this aerial celebrity. One of them kindly lent Green his mount, while another horse belonging to Mr J.B. Tunnard of the Blue Lion Inn, Grantham, had the balloon packed upon it and conveyed to the George Inn, where Green himself was greeted warmly by a large gathering of local gentlemen. Mr Welby sent an invitation to the aeronaut which he accepted and 'partook of a sumptuous dinner' that same evening. Charles Green, duly replete and basking in the adulation of the gentry of Grantham, transferred his trusty balloon once more to a chaise and four; left Grantham at 10 pm and arrived at the Peacock Inn, Boston at 3.00 am next morning, where no doubt he enjoyed a much-deserved sleep.

KING'S LYNN. 21 June 1826. #54

The spectacle of ballooning fed by a local gas supply presented ideal opportunities for town councils to draw attention to their civic efforts. It was this context that brought Charles Green to King's Lynn for the first time on 21 June 1826, for the opening of the town gas works and his fifty-fourth aerial journey. All roads to the town were jammed with people on foot, horseback and in carriages of every description. Accompanied on this auspicious occasion by his brother George, Charles Green's reputation by now guaranteed a large audience anywhere in the land.

It was 5.35 pm when the aeronauts rose majestically into the air beneath their magnificent balloon in the presence of a crowd estimated at 15,000 people. Drifting southwards, gaining altitude, they were carried towards Downham Market. They flew in and out of clouds, some of which deposited snow on the balloon and car before passing back into the warmth of sunlight.

After a flight lasting an hour, the Green brothers descended without mishap on the estate of Robert Martin Esquire, in the parish of Southery, 6 miles from Downham. The travellers and balloon were conveyed by horse and cart to that town where, upon their arrival, church bells pealed out in their honour. Congratulated by a group of local gentlemen, led by the grandly named Christopher Thomas Agrippa Hunter Esquire, by whom they were most hospitably entertained at the Castle Inn, Charles and George returned to King's Lynn in a chaise and four where, preceded by a band of music, they arrived tired but elated at 9.30 pm.

Farmer John Peck did not visit King's Lynn but expressed a keen interest in the event described above, as his diary entry records.

'21 June 1826, Roll and harrowing, 11 acres sown. A cold day. Mr Green ascended from Lynn with his balloon and alighted near to Southery. I went up Parson Drove church with a telescope expecting the wind to drive him this way but turning more to the north, was disappointed.'

Now brother George, equipped with the smaller red/yellow balloon used at King's Lynn, set off on a separate tour of the midlands and northern England. He went to

Derby; Nottingham; Leicester; Bolton and Carlisle, while Charles headed back to London, where he was to commission his newest balloon, another crimson and gold beauty of 20,000 cubic-feet capacity, whose manufacture was supervised by George junior. Furthermore, Charles was about to undertake a new venture, too; entering a business relationship with Frederick Gye and Richard Hughes, the owners and operators of London's premier entertainment venue, the Royal Gardens, Vauxhall. In his thirst for adventure, self-fulfilment and perhaps a dash of the emerging showman, Charles was going to take another big leap into the unknown - and fly at night.

VAUXHALL GARDENS, LONDON #1. 21 July 1826. #55

One of many public indoor and outdoor entertainment venues scattered across the city - including Marylebone Gardens and Ranelagh Gardens, for example - the Royal Gardens, Vauxhall, by 1826, could claim to be the longest-established and most diverse of such commercial pleasure gardens in London. Located in the borough of Lambeth, close by the modern Vauxhall railway station, the existing business was bought by Frederick Gye and Richard Hughes in 1825 and it was not long before their jam-packed daily entertainment programme included balloon exhibitions. And who better to draw in the crowds than Charles Green: the most popular aeronaut in the land. Although not exclusively committed to Vauxhall, Charles maintained his connections with Gye and Hughes for over twenty years during which time his aerial exploits from the Gardens proved to be extremely lucrative for both parties and as we shall discover later, gave rise to Charles' most famous flight of all.

Meanwhile, on 21 July 1826, among a long list of performances that included concert music, popular and operatic singers, ballets, fireworks and tightrope walkers, Charles Green made the first ascent with his new balloon; his own first ascent at night and the first night ascent to be seen in this country.

Filling the balloon with coal gas, supplied by the Phoenix Gas Light & Coke Company of Bankside, began early that morning and was completed during the afternoon. In the evening Charles made the balloon available for a small number of tethered flights by the more daring among the gathering crowd, to a height of about 100 feet. Up to 9.00 pm, several pilot balloons were launched and the upper winds carried these off generally to the north-west. All was ready by 10.00 pm, for the main event and Charles, his son George and a gentleman by the name of Whittaker, took their seats in the car. As a precaution, Charles loaded two-hundredweight (224lbs) of sand ballast but, in the event, very little was used.

At 10.17 pm a pistol was fired to signal the release of the ropes and the balloon rose like a shadowy spectre into the darkness. Charles had, of course, thought this flight through carefully and armed himself with one of Sir Humphrey Davy's famous Safety Lamps. This enabled him to read his instruments - barometer, thermometer and compass - with ease and in case of unforeseen accident, he would not precipitate a gas explosion if the balloon sprang a leak! The lamp was also a means of signalling to the ground.

Charles was not anxious to achieve a great altitude - he held the balloon around 4,000 feet - nor distance, in view of the unknown territory into which he was venturing. The balloon track crossed the Thames three times and he could identify several bridges; Regent's Park, Battersea and Wandsworth districts and was both helped and impressed by the twinkling gas lights spread across the metropolis. The general direction was west by north and after clearing the built-up area, he looked for a landing site in the vicinity of Richmond. At this point, Charles placed the lamp so that its light would reflect off the shiny balloon fabric and be a beacon to anyone on the ground who might be able to assist with the landing. Unaffected by any wind the balloon, however, came down softly at about 11.30 pm, on King George's Farm in Marsh Gate, Richmond.

Prior to the ascent taking place, the proprietors of the Vauxhall Gardens had announced in the London newspapers:

> 'A Present of Ten Guineas. The proprietors wish to inform those inhabitants who reside within about 20 miles of the Metropolis and all other persons, that it is their intention to present Ten Guineas to the person or persons who may afford the greatest facilities to Mr Green in his descent this evening, in the packing up of the balloon and in forwarding the aeronaut in a post-chaise and four to the Royal Gardens. Mr Green is to decide to whom the reward shall be given. Should the wind continue to blow from the same quarter as present, he may descend in the neighbourhood of Romford and will ascend, as near as possible at a quarter after ten at night.'

It seems likely, though, that the ten-guinea gift was not paid out, since Charles reported:

> 'A horse-patrol was the only person on the spot, but on account of the dead calm which prevailed, we required no assistance. We returned to Vauxhall Gardens at 2.00 am [next morning] precisely and were heartily congratulated by the numerous assembly.'

BOSTON. 30 August 1826. #59

'Mr Charles Green most respectfully announces to the Gentry and inhabitants of Boston...that he intends making his fifty-ninth ascent with his new, beautiful and stupendous balloon *Royal Coronation* on Wednesday, 30 August 1826.'

It was also announced that he would be accompanied by an un-named lady and gentleman, well-known in Boston and its neighbourhood. Furthermore, should the day's weather prove calm, a parachute containing a live animal would be dropped from the car, to descend in safety (hopefully!) into the enclosure. Topping even this, weather permitting, Mr. Green would be offering tethered flights. This was indeed bringing aeronautics to the masses!

When the great day dawned, however, the wind was considered far too strong and this prevented both the tethered flights and the parachute drop. The un-named lady who was to have ascended with Mr Green was also 'windy' and declined the trip but eventually Mr Henry Brooke junior, editor of the *Boston Gazette*, accompanied him aloft. Their journey was uneventful and one hour and ten minutes later, at 5.15 pm, a safe landing was achieved in the village of Manby, near Louth, 25 miles to the north.

Green's commercial instincts seem to have influenced his subsequent strange actions. No doubt he wished to return to Boston in an attempt, at least, to honour his promise to give tethered 'flights.' This latter state occurred when the balloon was not completely inflated as for full flight but still had sufficient buoyancy for lift. Long ropes, securing the craft to the ground and controlled by a steam winch, allowed the balloon to rise with its passengers to a height and for such a time that would simulate the sensation of flying. The process of ascent and descent could be repeated many times before buoyancy was lost and it became necessary to top up again with gas. Perhaps his thoughts were mercenary too, since by keeping the balloon semi-inflated he would save time and expense in re-filling it completely. In turn this would enable him to take up fare-paying passengers in quick succession and thus improve his earnings before nightfall. And so it was, that the strange spectacle of a flaccid balloon could be seen being conveyed in its semi-inflated state along the country lanes into Louth, 'for the purpose of gratifying Mr. Green's friends in that neighbourhood.' From there it was transported to Burwell, 10 miles further along the main road to Boston. Here, it was reported:

> 'In consequence of the wind being excessively boisterous, it became quite unmanageable and was found necessary to deflate the balloon to avoid damage. Otherwise, it was Mr. Green's intention to have conveyed it in a state of inflation to Boston.'

STAMFORD. 11 September 1826. #60

The scene moves once again to Stamford. Thursday, 7 September 1826 was the day chosen for his sixtieth ascent but due to extremely bad weather it was postponed until the following Monday.

During Green's visit to Stamford in 1825 he had promised a trip aloft for one of the more valiant among the local gentry. When the day of the event dawned, it was declared that Mr Green would take up with him two passengers. One was to be Octavious Simpson, the son of Alderman Francis Simpson to whom Green had made his earlier promise. The other person was William Reed, son of the Town-Serjeant of Stamford.

Blessed with favourable weather, their journey terminated in the village of Whittlesey near Peterborough. Octavious Simpson made copious notes during his trip of a lifetime, thus providing posterity with an excellent passenger's-eye view of a typical balloon flight of that era. This is his account.

'It was 4.08 pm when the balloon lifted off from the gas works enclosure to the sound of cheers and clapping from assembled onlookers. As we rose, our course was easterly and I did not experience the giddiness I had expected. Instead, I found the view of churches, streets and the profusion of buildings quite delightful.

Still rising, the balloon followed the silvery course of the river Welland. At a height of about 5,000 feet, air currents gently carried us in a south-westerly direction, over the twinkling spires and turrets of Burghley Mansion.

We passed over Barnack and left Pilsgate to the right. At 6,500 feet there was a splendid view of the panorama of the Fens, with an occasional glimpse of the sea between the clouds. On we went over Milton House, the Fitzwilliam's home near Peterborough, with Wansford and Castor to the right.

After half an hour in the air the barometer fell from 29.7 inches to 23.3 inches, indicating a height of 8,000 feet. I found the panorama passing below me imposing beyond imagination.

Next a view of Thorney Abbey, with the ruins of Crowland Abbey in the distance, could be discerned, while the balloon itself approached the west end of that magnificent cathedral at Peterborough.

Mr Green began a controlled descent at this juncture so that we might gain a better view of the impressive architecture of the cathedral and to present the citizens of that city a good view of the balloon. The top of the cathedral seemed to be covered with human beings. Having descended to 2,500 feet over the city, Mr Green threw out some ballast and the balloon once more rose steadily and Peterborough was slowly left behind.

The next object to capture my interest was Whittlesea Mere. The clouds were more-dense at this point and bright sunshine danced playfully through them, reflecting upon the glassy surface of the lake. Now another straggling town, with much thatched roof architecture, hove into view. It contrasted sharply with the stone and tiles of the Stamford we left earlier. As the town drifted into view crowds of people could be discerned in the streets, waving and cheering. This was Whittlesea. The surrounding flat countryside seemed favourable for a landing, so Mr Green began a skilfully controlled release of gas, until the grappling hook on the landing rope began to find purchase and the balloon sank easily and gracefully to earth. It landed half-a-mile from Whittlesea at 5.15 pm after a journey of 18 miles.

Many willing people had ridden on horseback to the site and all helped to deflate and pack the balloon. Among the helpers were Mr Barber of Willow Hall, Whittlesea; Mr Maydell and Mr Wilson also from Whittlesea. Mr Green and I were then invited to partake of ample refreshment at the Haynes mansion in Whittlesea. A chaise and four conveyed us to Stamford which was reached at 9.30 pm where we were met by a relieved crowd of thousands.'

Curiously, no mention is made, in Simpson's account, of William Reed who, according to a later newspaper report, was a passenger on that flight. No mention is made of Reed being invited to join Simpson and Green for refreshment at the Haynes mansion nor of being conveyed in the chaise back to Stamford. In fact, the newspaper states a chaise and four conveyed 'the pair' back to Stamford. Perhaps in the end young William Reed decided not to go aloft after all? On this occasion too, some indication is given of the cost of filling a balloon with coal gas. The *Stamford Mercury* was:

> 'Happy to report the number of persons who paid to watch the inflation process in the enclosure (and who alone were the means to Mr Green of recompense for his outlay and professional skill) was larger than on former occasions. It is understood the Gas Company charged £10 for the exhaustion of the gas receiver [*sic*] and Mr Green's receipts were £88.'

Inspired by Green's visit in 1825 and coinciding with his return the following year, the owners of a new public house built in 1826, in Blackfriar's Street and within sight of the gas works, were moved to name it the Balloon Inn. Sadly, by 1959, no longer used as an inn, the name disappeared. In 1964, however, the property was renovated for domestic use and now converted to a delightful private residence, the present occupiers, having discovered the earlier name in the deeds, were moved to re-establish its connection with the past. Taking up residence in 1987, they re-named their home Balloon House.

BOSTON. 7 May 1828. #93 & 14 May. #94

Between September 1826 and May 1828 Charles Green claimed another thirty-two balloon ascents to his tally, before returning to Boston on Wednesday, 7 May 1828. The ascent was made from Mr C.K. Tunnard's paddock in Bargate, in the centre of Boston, with one passenger on board. It turned out to be a most hair-raising flight, ending in the village of Gosberton, 6 miles north of Spalding.

Charles Green's companion on this trip was John Willerton, a wool buyer from Swineshead and the pair lifted off from Bargate at 3 pm, buffeted by a blustery wind as they rose. After a while, Green evidently grew unhappy with the conditions. His experience and natural concern for the safety of his passenger in the now quite violent wind led him to decide to descend through the murk of the clouds to ascertain their whereabouts.

Nearing the ground, in the vicinity of Gosberton village, still being bowled along by the boisterous wind, the grapnel on the trail rope struck the tops of trees, breaking off some branches in its manic passage. It dragged a further half-mile, tearing at trees, hedges and buildings in its path, like a demented snake. At one point it struck such a resounding blow on Mr Crosby's granary that the noise 'frightened a labourer working inside and made him quite ill.' Eventually the grapnel held in a cornfield but the effect of this violent decrease in speed was to eject poor Mr Willerton overboard from his seat in the car. He saved himself from almost certain death only by clutching the carriage suspension ropes and dangling 150 feet above the swaying ground, until the balloon finally came to rest. 'He displayed great presence of mind,' observed the local newspaper!

With considerable difficulty, the balloon was deflated and the battered travellers were then free to sample local hospitality. Mr Everitt, mine host of the White Hart Hotel in Spalding, 6 miles away, who happened to be passing the spot, generously gave up his seat in a post-chaise for Mr Green and his companion. They were conveyed to Gosberton House, the nearby home of the Reverend John Calthrop, for 'most gratifying hospitality,' before returning to Boston by 9.00 pm.

Charles was not done with Boston yet, because he advertised his next, ninety-fourth, trip for Wednesday, 14 May. In the days prior to this event, Charles made a number of tethered 'flights' for people and - wait for it - himself while sat astride a pony! Several newspapers across the land picked up this horsey story, but it was the *Tyne Mercury* of 27 May that made it clear that:

> 'Green the balloon man has been using a pony instead of a car in an ascent at Boston. The pony was well-trained and bore Mr Green on his back without alarm. On the preceding days, the elder Mr Green twice ascended to a considerable height on horseback.'

This report indicates these were tethered 'flights' and lead us to the ascent of the 14 May. An advertisement stated that Charles would make this, his ninety-fourth, ascent but almost all of the subsequent newspaper reports read as if his son George was actually in charge of the flight and no mention is made of Charles being aboard. Emphasis is given to the fact that 'Master' Green had not yet come of age (21) and that his two companions were Mr John Willerton of Swineshead (again) and Mr Henry Brooke junior, the editor of the *Boston Guardian* newspaper.

However, a report found in, of all places, the *Cork Constitution*, suggests that, on this occasion, Charles also went up with his son and two passengers. It is, therefore, by no means clear if Charles flew this trip, or not. The landing site for this flight was near Sleaford.

It is also worth noting that, during 1827 and 1828, the family ballooning business was flourishing up and down the country. Charles' brother George spent many months touring the west Midlands and the north-west of England; going to places such as Coventry; Birmingham; Wolverhampton; Chesterfield; Wigan; Salford and Preston. His flights were not without incident and he had a number of mishaps during which he sustained minor injuries. By the end of 1828, George senior had accumulated at least sixty-five flights. Brother Henry, too, put on exhibitions around the land, including Canterbury; Exeter; Ipswich; Northampton and Stamford and while his shows were less frequent than his brothers,' he also met with several trials, tribulations and even the occasional brush with death.

EAGLE TAVERN, MILE END, LONDON. 29 July 1828. #99

Having trialled his exhibition with a pony at Boston, Charles brought this phenomenon to London. On Tuesday, 29 July 1828, Charles entered the realm of showmanship when he made a complete free flight sitting astride his Welsh pony. It was an amazing sight that deservedly brought thousands of people to the Eagle Gardens and into the streets of Islington. Charles' wife took it all in her stride and came to watch the take-off, where she was said to have been un-concerned about the potential perils of the ascent. Such was the vast crowd in the Eagle Gardens that those who paid one shilling were quite unable to see the pony when it was taken into the sheeted-off inner enclosure - entrance to which cost another shilling. This set off a minor riot and the sheeted barrier was torn down in an angry scene. Now everyone could see the equestrian star of the show!

Charles described the arrangements for the horse and himself as follows.

'The usual car was not used. In its place was a circular shallow wicker tray with sides about six inches in height, a green cloth lining and four straps to secure the animal's feet. The platform was secured to the balloon hoop by six cords. My pony, dressed with colourful ribbons, was led from its stable and took its place on the platform. His fetlock-joints were each secured by the straps and he licked my hand calmly while this was done. The saddle was connected to a hoop that passed over the pony's back and to this hoop was attached my grapnel, the valve control lines, a bag of beans and about 250lbs of ballast in eleven bags. I took my place in the saddle.

On release of the ropes, the balloon rose slowly and perpendicularly. The pony strained at the straps at the great sound of cheering but, in seconds, was calm and still again as we passed over the Thames. He ate some beans from my hand, that I easily gave him by leaning forward in the saddle.

I now hung out the grapnel and dismounted to arrange some ballast, but my weight on one side made the platform tilt and discomposed my little companion. I resumed my seat and, discharging a little ballast reached a height of about 6,000 feet, where it snowed upon us. This changed to rain when I descended a little, then it cleared up when descending even further. During this time the pony finished eating his bag of beans and seemed quite at home.

Having been in the air about half-an-hour I prepared for a landing. With hardly a breath of air, I brought the balloon down without the slightest injury to all, in a clover field in the parish of Beckenham, Kent. The moment my pony was liberated from the platform, he took advantage of the clover and began to devour it with a keen appetite, even though he had eaten more than a pint of beans while in the air. My first task was to find someone to take care of the pony. Fortuitously, a gentleman named Lister, residing at Plaistow and whom I had met on a previous occasion, made himself known and procured the use of a stable from a friend of his who lived in Beckenham.

The weights carried by the balloon on this flight were:

Balloon, appendages and equipment:	508lbs
Weight of the pony:	250lbs
My weight:	148lbs
Total:	906lbs.

The loss of gas in my descent was comparatively trifling, so I determined on retaining the remainder overnight and either myself or my son - whom I expected to arrive with the [balloon] car - to make an ascent in the morning with Mr Hemmings.'

Among the enormous number of newspapers that reported this event, the editor of the *Liverpool Mercury* made it clear to his readers that he 'thought such exhibitions were preposterous and should not be permitted.'

BECKENHAM, KENT. 30 July 1828. #100

While in modern times, a one-hundredth event is felt to be a notable milestone and celebrated as such, in Charles Green's time - apart from perhaps a birthday - not much was made of that sort of thing. This seems to apply to Charles' milestone ascent, which he had hoped to make from Beckenham accompanied by Mr Hemmings, a professor of chemistry and natural philosophy, who was his passenger on an ascent from the Swan Inn, Stratford, London on 9 July. Due to bad weather during that flight, Mr Hemmings did not complete all the experiments he wanted to do and expressed the wish to ascend again to complete his work. Since gas was not readily available in Beckenham, Charles' idea was to retain the gas in the balloon overnight, then mount another flight on 30 July.

However, when the day dawned, Charles deemed the wind to be far too strong and since it also blew from the west, would likely take the balloon out to sea. Although the wind abated during the day, the volume of gas left in the balloon after so long since its original inflation, was now insufficient to carry two people aloft, so he had to disappoint Mr Hemmings. At about 5.00 pm, Charles decided to make a solo ascent because he had promised the local villagers and did not want to disappoint them, too. However, it was just a short flight; ending on Bromley Common just 5 miles from the take-off point.

Charles' equine travelling companion - now christened 'High Flyer' - was the centre of attention in Beckenham all day and travelled separately back to his quarters in London; the first horse - except mythical ones - to fly.

Eventually, Mr Hemmings did manage a second flight. It was, however, Charles' son George who was at the helm on that occasion, which saw the pair take off from the White Conduit Gardens in Pentonville, London on 15 August 1828. That Charles - who had wanted to make another 'equine flight' but deemed the weather unsuitable - was not on board seems to be confirmed by Mr Hemmings' press release, which included: 'I express my admiration at the cool and skilful manner in which the machine was managed and directed by my conductor, Mr Green junior.' They landed at Bexley, a mile beyond Maidstone.

Mrs Martha Green was still doing her ground management role and was on duty at the White Conduit Gardens for her son's ascent, as an amusing report in the *Morning Advertiser* under the heading of Police Business recalls.

'Hatton Garden - George Bowles, the proprietor of White Conduit House, was yesterday brought up on a warrant, charged with assaulting the officers of this establishment in the execution of their duty.

Andrew Lloyd and George Waddington, two of the most active [plain-clothes] officers of this establishment, stated that Friday last, the day on which Green ascended in the balloon, they went to White Conduit House and Mrs Green refused to admit them unless they paid two shillings a head. They produced their staffs [*sic*]; informed her that they belonged to this establishment and that several bad characters were in the ground. She still, however, would not admit them, so they persisted and forced their way in. At the time the ropes which held the balloon were loosed, an immense rush took place and the officers were following two reputed thieves, when they were stopped by Mr Tollington, a check taker and Mrs Green, who abused them in the most shameful manner, declaring that she did not want officers there at all. The defendant also came up and he and another man struck the officers several times, Mrs Green shouting all the while "Turn them out!" Mr Skillen, a conductor of the Bow Street Dismounted Patrol, stated he and his two men were refused admittance. Mr Bowles, in his defence, said that Lloyd was in liquor at the time. Mr Laing said the officers were not in liquor and were doing nothing but their duty at the ground. The defendant was given bail pending an appearance at the Quarter Sessions.'

Mrs Green was evidently a formidable lady on the gate!

Chapter 8

Log-Book Puzzles

It appears that, following his trip from Ludlow in October 1828, Charles called it a day for that season and returned to London. The next time he is attributed by the British press with an ascent is on 19 May 1829, when the vice-chancellor of Cambridge university engaged him to ascend from Mr William Warwicker's enclosure, behind his house in the Barnwell district of the city, for what was advertised as his 115th flight. This latter, incidentally, is a prime example of the difficulty encountered with Charles' flight numbering scheme. The number for his Ludlow flight on 10 October was advertised as #104 and yet here, on 19 May 1829 - apparently his first trip in seven months - the *Cambridge Chronicle* states it will be his flight #115. Where have the intervening ten flights gone? Is it possible, in this case, that any notes passed to the newspaper - hand-written of course in those far-off days - were mis-read and perhaps it should have been #105 - a number that would match the sequence better? Ten flights, spread over a period of seven months is 'do-able' but, considering such flights would have to have been made during the winter and early spring, that is too much to accept - and is unsupported by his previous programmes. Maybe he made some non-public and un-publicised test flights? Who knows?

This latest flight ended after an hour and twenty-five minutes, near Wellingborough.

Between 9.00 am and 2.00 pm, on the day of the ascent, Charles' new 'star,' billed as his 'docile and highly-trained animal; Mr Green's Aeronaut Pony,' its special carriage and all the other balloon accoutrements, were displayed for public inspection for one shilling (ladies & gentlemen) or sixpence (servants & children). The final stages of inflation, attachment of the car and the launch itself, could be viewed from the enclosed area, admission to which was two shillings. It can be seen, therefore, that entry prices were still holding-up after almost eight years on the exhibition trail. According to some press reports, Charles could generally expect to receive an appearance fee of at least £50 from the local organising committee, who would raise this sum by personal donations and public subscriptions. As with his other passengers, the two young gentlemen from the university who flew on this day with him, paid a fee for the privilege, but it was un-specified on this occasion, as were the names of the gentlemen. It was merely reported as 'a liberal sum for the purpose of enjoying the excursion' - but it is likely to have been £40 or £50 each, which would add upwards of another £100 to his takings for the day. Although not carried out at this event, Charles could also increase his event income by charging up to five shillings per person for tethered 'flights.' Charles would also receive the gate takings - organised by the formidable Mrs Martha Green - which, taken all altogether, after settling his expenses, would leave him with a tidy sum as profit.

There are signs this year (1829), that Charles did less flying himself. He appears to have spent much of his time supporting the aeronautical career of his son George, by passing on his knowledge and skill to the young man, who was now aged 21 and a competent aeronaut in his own right. George junior flew at Portsea and Derby (25 September) during the year and also intended to make a trip from Chesterfield, which he claimed would be his own thirty-eighth ascent (both solo and as a passenger). Although he, too, carried fee-paying passengers there is no evidence of Charles going up with him on these latter excursions.

Charles and his son were, of course, using the same balloon for their flights and the Chesterfield ascent had to be cancelled. The reason was damage to the balloon as a result of extremely high winds experienced when the Chesterfield district was hit by a bad storm a day before the event. The wind was still very boisterous during the filling process and tossed the balloon about so badly that it was extensively torn and rendered 'un-gasworthy.' It was emptied, dismantled and packed off to London for repair.

Charles' brother George, too, was still touring the country very successfully and by the end of 1829, having flown at such venues as: The Golden Eagle, Mile End; Jamaica Tavern, Rotherhithe; Chelmsford; Colchester; Dudley; Walsall; Kidderminster and Birmingham, was rapidly approaching his eightieth ascent.

Brother Henry, on the other hand, by his constant and sometimes quite serious mishaps, together with acrimonious and widely reported disputes during his own, separate tour, now posed a real threat to Charles' excellent reputation - and to his brother George's, too. Matters came to a head in ugly, dangerous scenes after Henry's two failed ascents at Devizes in July 1829. Henry's balloon was in a shocking state of repair and fabric failures were to blame for much of his woes.

When Henry's second attempt at Devizes (said to be his fifty-seventh ascent) failed, the crowd turned into a baying mob, intent on destruction of the aeronaut and his balloon. Stones and other missiles were thrown at the balloon, tearing it severely. When it collapsed to the ground, the mob hacked it to shreds with knives - hundreds of knives were produced - and it finished up as a pile of silk rags. The netting went the same way; the valve mechanism was torn off and kicked down the street and the grapnels stolen. All this mayhem was accompanied by cheering and shouting - much of it drunken - until the cry went up: 'Now for Green!' A mass rush thundered towards the gasworks superintendent's house, where it was thought Henry, his wife and their business partner Mr Pickering had been hidden. It took an immense effort by a group of local magistrates 'to prevent the infuriated populace from taking vengeance on the aeronaut.' The unfortunate trio were indeed hidden - but in a dark corner of a room beneath the gas condenser building - and were only able to slip away, unseen, around midnight. Things turned so ugly that, had the mob caught him, Henry was in grave danger of being murdered.

All this venom came on the back of similar situations in Brighton; Bath and sadly, at too many other venues - all of which naturally received coverage in newspapers across the land. Charles Green was acutely aware of the problem and no doubt had much to say to Henry about it, since there could have been a reputational and financial back-lash falling on Charles and the Georges, junior and senior. With this in mind, when Charles put an advert in, for example, the *Salisbury & Winchester Journal*, prior to his own forthcoming events, it included the following note.

'N.B. In consequence of the failures which have taken place at Devizes, Bath and numerous other places, by persons advertising to ascend in his name, Mr Charles Green feels called upon to appraise the Public, that he has no connection with any other Aeronauts.'

The *Hampshire Telegraph* report of the Portsea ascents, added the following to its text.

'Lest this intrepid individual [Charles] should be confounded with one of the same name who made a fruitless attempt to ascend in the early part of this week at Devizes, where the multitude assembled destroyed his balloon, under feelings of great irritation, it should be remarked that with this person [Henry] he has no connection whatever.'

It seems the Luddite-ish populace of Wiltshire was pretty keen on the pastime of casual mayhem, because it was later reported that a mob set about destroying Mr Goldsworthy Gurney's Steam Carriage when his revolutionary vehicle dared to pass through the county, carrying passengers from London to Bath! That incident prompted questions in Parliament about the need to sort out those barbarians in Wiltshire!

Charles' flight #117, advertised as taking place from Albion Place in Southampton on Wednesday, 29 July 1829, was quite uneventful. His 118th ascent was the second made from Southampton and accompanied by son George and local man Mr Whicher, they made a similar short trip to Lee near Romsey on 6 August.

It will not pass un-noticed that the number for Charles' event in Peterborough (below) is advertised as #149. This represents an enormous leap in his flight numbers - thirty - arising between his last trip in Southampton (#118) in August 1829 and Peterborough, his first flight in 1830 (#149). It is considered quite improbable for Charles' missing flights to have been overlooked in such a way by the British press - he was far too famous for such omissions.

LOG-BOOK PUZZLES

This year, the Green family flying season seems to have started in May 1830 and newspaper interest in them all is evidenced by coverage given in May to flights by brother George at Atherstone, Warwickshire (4 May) and Coventry (31 May) and even for Charles' other brother, James, who made an ascent from Ipswich on 25 May. With shades of his brother Henry's mishaps James, too, experienced problems with what he claimed as 'a new balloon,' when the valve-spring failed.

However, even at the rate that Charles made flights in his earlier years and still bearing in mind that the period in question includes winter months, such a large gap cannot be explained satisfactorily - or can it?

Careful scrutiny of newspaper reports clearly shows that Charles and his son George are now mounting joint events even if they do not always fly together. In 1830, son George clearly states that his two ascents from Barnwell, Cambridge on 8 May and 15 May, are his fortieth and forty-first flights. These are followed by Charles making two flights in Peterborough, advertised as his 149th and 150th ascents.

It cannot be mere coincidence that, if the sum of Charles' self-declared flights prior to that date (118 up to 6 August 1829) is added to the cumulative number of his son George's flights (41), it comes very close to Charles' latest total. Is the sought-after explanation for that anomaly in numbers, actually attributable to Charles adding together his own and his son's flights? What may be happening here is that Charles adds all his son's flights to his own and advertises that number; while his son still advertises his own flight total only.

What could have prompted Charles to adopt this bizarre method of counting his flights? He certainly had little to gain in reputational terms, since his already substantial number and his already substantial reputation, would hardly be further enhanced by falsifying his log-book. Could it be that now, in competition with his three aeronautical brothers - as well as other competitors outside the family - he wanted to be 'top dog?'

By 9 October 1830, Charles was claiming his 160th flight - made at Dewsbury - but at that time only ninety flights can actually be attributed to him. At this particular point in time, the balance of seventy is believed to be made up of fifty flights attributed to his son George, plus twenty random numbers unaccounted for since he started flying in 1821 and prior to his big 'number-adjustment'. However, brother George, his closest family competitor, was hard on Charles' heels since, by the same date, he had claimed eighty-seven flights - all of which appear to be 'genuine'. Was this competition, then, the reason for playing the numbers game? While Charles is using his 'creative' numbering scheme, unless he stopped flying or slowed down greatly, his brother George would never catch him up. Furthermore, another aeronautical competitor - George Graham - was by now also claiming around 100 (hydrogen) flights.

If this is the explanation then, of course, it throws a spot-light on the veracity of the final total of Charles Green's flights during his career - an oft-quoted figure of 525. Even at this point, it seems at least 100 flights over-stated. By the end of his flying career in 1856, it will be seen from Appendix 1 that, by Charles' own reckoning he had made 518 flights, but as has been pointed out, there are un-explained date and numbering discrepancies and furthermore, contemporary newspaper reports to support 183 of these numbers cannot be found – leaving a verified total of 335 flights. With a reputation such as Charles' and at this stage of his career, it is inconceivable that no newspaper in the land would carry even a few lines or an advertisement about his flights. Not that these findings are in any way meant to detract from his lifetime of aeronautical achievements, but it does give an insight to Charles' competitive streak and emphasises an historian's need to check facts in depth, rather than simply repeat unsubstantiated data.

LINCOLN 5 July 1830. #151 & 13 July 1830. #152

For the first manned balloon ascent in the city, the *Lincoln Herald* carried an advertisement in its issue dated 2 July 1830.

'At the request of the Mayor and Corporation of this City and from the consideration of public propriety, Mr C. Green has been induced to POSTPONE his Ascent from Lincoln (*on account of the lamented death of the King*) until MONDAY NEXT, JULY 5th.'

Midsummer Fair day in Lincoln dawned fine with blue skies and little breeze and on this occasion his son George, making his own forty-second flight, accompanied his father, Charles. Inflation of the *Coronation* balloon required 142,000 gallons (≈ 23,000 cubic-feet) of coal gas, a process overseen by Mr Needham the gas works manager. It began at 11.00 am in a paddock in Newland and could have been completed in as little as three hours but took longer due to Green's astute commercial desire to let as many paying customers as possible see the actual process for two shillings each. By the time of the launch at 5.00 pm, 800 visitors were in the enclosure being entertained by the Lincoln Band.

After a short speech from the crimson silk-covered car, the clock struck 5.00 pm and Charles cast off the last rope amidst loud cheers from all sides. These were echoed as the balloon rose gently over the heads of thousands of people watching from vessels on the river, its banks and along the whole brow of the hill from the asylum to the hospital. At 500 feet Green released a small parachute with a basket containing a cat, which landed safely in the paddock below. At first the balloon flew north, almost directly over the west end of the cathedral until, following the Brigg Road and still climbing, it encountered a current that swung it eastwards.

Now the aeronauts could see the whole panorama of the Lincolnshire coast before them, from the Humber to Skegness and into The Wash, with the Norfolk coast visible away in the distance. Over the bend in the river Witham, at Grub Hill, a fresh current took the balloon south-east and Charles was now hopeful of reaching Boston. Nearing Tattershall, at 12,000 feet altitude yet another change of direction set them north of east towards Horncastle and so, having been aloft for an hour and forty minutes and with the prospect of reaching the sea looming, Green began to vent gas for a descent.

It was 7.00 pm as many willing hands converged on the balloon, catching the grapnel and guide ropes to help bring it to earth in a pasture at Scrivelsby Park, residence of the Hon. the Champion Dymoke, where the gas was discharged entirely. In the absence of Mr Dymoke, his steward arranged a horse and gig to carry the two aeronauts and their balloon into Horncastle, 2 miles distant. Such was the warmth of the welcome and hospitality they received in Horncastle that their departure for Lincoln was delayed until midnight. It was 3.00 am next morning before they reached the city where, with but a few hours respite, they were again fêted at breakfast - heroes of the hour!

Prior to this particular flight, Charles Green encountered an obstructive response to his application to make the ascent from Lincoln Castle Yard. Despite his sponsors being County magistrates - who recommended approval - the Sheriff (custodian of the Castle grounds) refused permission and that was why the event was moved to Newland. In its reporting of the dispute the *Lincoln Herald* was both caustic and sarcastic about the Sheriff's attitude.

'We are happy to say that the Lincoln Gas Company has acted towards Mr Green in the most liberal manner and has so far redeemed the County and the City from the folly of the idle and absurd obstructions which had been thrown in his way by the magnates of office who happen to be the *Annuals* of the time.'

This spat with authority did not prevent Charles from staying on in Lincoln to make another ascent, his 152nd, on Tuesday, 13 July 1830. This trip was postponed from Friday, 9 July due to high winds and a lady, 'well known in the neighbourhood' who was billed to accompany Charles, changed her mind on the day so Mr J.B. Cuttill, in whose paddock the event was held, took up the offer of a flight.

It was to be another long day for the intrepid aeronauts. They took off at 6.30 pm and were carried northeast to land safely at Rothwell, 4 miles east of Caistor, after a journey of one hour and forty minutes. Sumptuous hospitality once again held them in Caistor and it was 6.00 am next morning when they arrived back in Lincoln. An aeronaut certainly needed plenty of stamina, a hearty appetite and a robust constitution in those days!

Charles devoted the remainder of the 1830 season to a tour of the north of England with his wife, son George - and the 'highly trained aeronaut pony', which was put on display with great success at all the venues. The tour began with son George taking command at Mansfield on 29 July for his forty-fourth flight, on which he carried Mr Simpson as passenger (landing at Humberley Moor, near Baslow). George junior took Mr Kelsall up from the White Cloth Hall in Leeds on 18 August, landing at Royston, near Barnsley. He made a second ascent from Leeds on 3 September, this time with Mr Snowdon and Mr William Russum as his passengers and they landed safely at Ings, near Wakefield. On 11 September, son George made a solo trip from Knaresborough, landing at Horne, 3 miles from Easingwold. The final venue of this short tour was Dewsbury, from where two flights were made. Son George made the first, with Mr Howarth as his passenger, to Heath Common, a couple of miles east of Wakefield. Charles Green made the second trip, advertised as his 160th ascent, with passengers: Mr Webster and Mr Brown and they landed safely close to the outskirts of Leeds.

With the end of the season approaching, Charles, his wife, his son and the long-suffering 'aeronaut pony,' made their way back to London via one final ascent made by George junior at Stafford. It was billed as his fiftieth trip and he carried Mr Dickenson, a grocer from that town, as passenger; landing safely at Landywood, near Churchbridge. Apart from the above mentioned 160th flight, this year Charles seems content to have left most of the flying to his son.

It was May 1831 before Charles and his son George began their new flying season in Cambridge, setting up an exhibition in the Barnwell district, a venue they had used in the past.

George junior made two ascents; the first, his fifty-ninth, was a solo effort on Monday, 16 May. It went well, despite having to take off an hour before the advertised time, due to damage to a small area of fabric that allowed gas to leak out. The loss of gas was not critical and he was able to reach an altitude of 10,000 feet before landing at Swaffham Bulbeck.

The damage was repaired and son George made a second ascent, his sixtieth, on 23 May with two passengers: Robert Hollond of Corpus Christi college and Thomas Frewen-Turner of St John's college. Hollond's name crops up later when, in 1836, he accompanied Charles Green on his great flight to Germany.

Meanwhile, Charles' brother George, began his own programme with two ascents (his eighty-eighth and eighty-ninth flights) in Chelmsford. The first was on 30 April, with Dr Forster as passenger, to Broomfield, while the second, on 12 May, saw him taking up the Misses E. and H. Kennett, two attractive young ladies from the town. They landed safely after a very short hop to Great Baddow. George senior then took his show on the road for a tour of central Scotland and the north-east of England that found him in Perth (2); Dundee; Dunfermline; Alloa (2) and Newcastle (3), the last of these flights being his ninety-eighth trip - so, in real terms, he was fast catching up with Charles.

Norwich was the next venue for the Charles Green & Son show. Charles' 190th aerial voyage - with another thirty conjured up, it seems as if he is almost plucking numbers out of the air now - was advertised for Thursday, 23 June 1831 from Richmond Hill Gardens in this fine city. The main event was preceded by some tethered ascents, with Mr Sparshall; Richard Crawshay and his two daughters, enjoying the experience. Later, Charles was accompanied by Richard Crawshay (1786-1859), a gentleman farmer of Honingham Hall near Dereham, for the first of many flights with Charles Green over the next couple of decades. They enjoyed a trip of seventy minutes before landing at Oby, a village near Acle, not far from Great Yarmouth. Charles made a second flight (#191) from Norwich on 2 July, this time carrying Alderman John Marshall as his passenger; landing safely at Hemblington near Blofield, 5 miles east of the city.

LONDON BRIDGE, 1 August 1831. #192

Charles and his son saw out the rest of this year by making flights from London. Charles became more involved with events at the Royal Gardens, Vauxhall and as a renowned and dependable aeronaut, he participated in festivities to celebrate several royal events in the city.

There would never be a more fitting start to his reign than when King William IV officiated at the grand opening of the New London Bridge on 1 August 1831. The existing bridge, which stood for 600 years, was unsafe and a hazard to those who lived and worked on it; those who crossed it and not least, those who navigated the river beneath it.

Designed by the Scottish engineer John Rennie the elder (1761-1821), his plans were submitted after his death to the new bridge design competition by his two sons, John junior and George. Amidst some controversy, Rennie's design was accepted and work began in 1824 on a new, five-arch granite bridge across the Thames, to replace the old structure. John Rennie junior was the engineer in charge of the project and received a knighthood for his efforts. Now, in 1831, that new bridge was complete and needed to be opened in the most-grand style by the Monarch himself. The King, with Queen Adelaide, arrived by state barge in a water-borne procession from Somerset House pier, disembarking at the northern end of the bridge. He and his entourage then opened the bridge by walking across it, before returning to a canopied area covering a large part of the bridge, for a state banquet with over 1,500 guests followed by more festivities. The sound of cannon and pealing bells combined with the noise from hundreds of thousands of people thronging the city, produced a cacophony of sound from dawn to dusk.

Apart from their Majesties, the star attraction of the festivities was none other than Charles Green - well, who else? He was in his element. Charles' balloon was inflated with gas from the Phoenix Gas Company, on a plot of open ground at the end of Tooley Street, 300 yards from the Southwark (southern) end of the bridge.

THE FLYING ADVENTURES OF CHARLES GREEN

Everything was timed for the inflation to be complete an hour before the King was due at the Southwark end. The balloon was then hauled by ropes, the short distance to the bridge itself where, at 5.05 pm, the King gave the signal for the balloon to lift off. On this most prestigious flight, Charles was accompanied by Richard Crawshay and they had an uneventful voyage of 29 miles, landing in Eight Acres Field, Charlwood.

Charles was back at the Royal Gardens, Vauxhall on 15 August as part of a gala evening in honour of Queen Adelaide's birthday (13 August), where he would make a night flight at 10.00 pm. Charles, with his son George on board, made his 193rd aerial voyage, a 90 minute trip to Parson's Green, Fulham.

On 22 August, Charles was part of a special programme of concerts, fireworks and extensive tableaux all lit up by myriads of coloured lights, that was laid on at the Vauxhall Gardens, this time in celebration of His Majesty King William IV's birthday (21 August). Attended by thousands of people, Charles Green's contribution was a night flight to Thornton Heath, Croydon, accompanied by his son George and Mr Adams. On a clear and calm evening, the flight and the landing were without problems and the travellers returned to Vauxhall by 12.30 am. A couple of days later, the proprietors of Vauxhall Gardens repeated these festivities and because he was becoming a lucrative attraction, they invited Charles to make another flight. Having had some intimation of this pending flight, following the Croydon landing Charles arranged for his balloon to be kept in its filled state and towed all the way back to Vauxhall - it must have been an impressive sight and no mean feat but, indeed, was successfully carried out. This meant that it needed very little gas top-up before his ascent (#195) at 7.30 pm on the 24th - another night flight, landing again in the vicinity of Croydon.

In a scene reminiscent of his very first flight back in 1821, Charles was engaged to make what was his 196th flight (by his counting) on the day of the coronation of King William IV on 8 September 1831. This time it was Charles who put forward the idea to the government and because the King was delighted with the London Bridge ascent, he approved the proposal. Word came down via HRH the Duke of Sussex, Ranger of Hyde Park, that Charles could make his ascent from The Ring in Hyde Park, between the hours of 1.00 pm and 3.00 pm - only. This time constraint appears to have been non-negotiable, so Charles declined to operate from Hyde Park because he deemed it impossible to complete his preparations and be ready in the time allowed. Consequently, he obtained permission to move his event to the Green Park, opposite Gloucester House - the venue of his first flight. Perhaps for this reason, Charles' subsequent flight - believed with his son on board - was not widely reported and the destination has not yet been identified. In contrast though, there was a great deal of press coverage for an ascent by the aeronauts Mr and Mrs Graham from a venue on Constitution Hill.

William IV's coronation took place fourteen months after he acceded to the throne on 26 June 1830. He was 64 years of age and shunned profligate pomp and ceremony. Unlike his predecessor, William was particularly keen that vast sums were not spent on his coronation; it was to be a low-key affair and some in the government even referred to it, sarcastically, as the 'half-crown coronation.' In the event, it is said to have cost just £30,000 (≈ £2,560,000 in 2023) compared to the £240,000 blown on George IV's coronation. With a tight budget, no real consideration was given to laying on public entertainment. The good people of London, therefore, had to settle for just a view of the regal processions between St James' Palace and Westminster Abbey and an evening firework display in Hyde Park - except of course for Charles Green and his wonderful balloon in Green Park. Accompanied by his son, he took off at 5.15 pm, and was last seen heading north-east.

It appears that this royal event was his last flight of the year 1831 and in common with the pattern of recent years, Charles did not venture into the air again until 16 May 1832. It is noteworthy that, not only did Charles Green inflate his balloons, but he was still inflating his flights, having claimed 196 while apparently making only 99! But who was going to argue such a point with him? His brother George, on the other hand, beat him into the sky by mounting what was advertised as his 100th ascent, which he made from the gardens of the Mermaid Tavern in Hackney, London on 14 May 1832.

Charles' ballooning pattern also changed this year. He made only one flight during the whole of 1832 - at Barnwell, Cambridge on 16 May, when he went up with his son George for the first ascent of the new season. This particular flight was reported as being made by George, his son and Charles appears to have gone along for the ride, together with another, fare-paying passenger, Mr James Hope of St John's College, Cambridge. They landed safely at Fowlmere, between Royston and Duxford but an irate farmer, into whose field they alighted, demanded £7 in compensation for the damage done to his crops by the horde of people who came to help the aeronauts control the landing and pack up afterwards.

In the absence of press coverage to the contrary, it can only be deduced that Charles was putting his efforts into supporting his son's aeronautical career. Barnwell on 16 May was George junior's seventieth flight and Charles claimed it as his own 197th.

Following his second ascent at Barnwell on 19 May, George junior went off on a solo tour of Coventry and Manchester after which he made no more ascents in 1832 and no press reports have been found to specifically indicate that Charles made any more trips in 1832 either. In respect of Charles, 1833 follows a similar pattern, since a thorough search finds him making just one ascent during that year, too. This is not to suggest that his balloon ascents were not being reported - far from it; it was just that Charles quite evidently was making no ascents under his own name. George junior was being reported upon and so was George senior - who was travelling the north of England during 1832 and 1833 and by late 1834, had completed at least 118 flights.

THE FLYING ADVENTURES OF CHARLES GREEN

In an age when steam-packet shipping was growing, Charles, billed as 'The Veteran Mr Green,' made his 198th ascent, in Southampton on Monday, 8 July 1833, as the main attraction of a regatta and various public amusements held in celebration of the grand opening of the new 900-feet-long Royal Victoria pier. This event was graced by the presence of Princess Victoria and her mother, the Duchess of Kent, who, watched by a crowd of 20,000 people, performed the opening ceremony. The landing site for this trip has not been established.

In 1834, Charles is believed to have made no ascents and only one flight that year can be attributed to George junior; that made on Monday 24 November 1834 in Stroud. Although this flight is reported as being made by 'Mr Green, the celebrated aeronaut,' it is considered this relates to George junior. If one looks at Charles' next flight number, it is reported as #199 and took place in London in 1835, which therefore supports the above deduction that he made no flights during 1834. In view of the fact that the *ODNB* 2020 revision claims that Martha Green died in 1834, this notable absence of flying activity by Charles during that year and a much-reduced programme in the preceding year, may well indicate that his wife had fallen ill, a situation that naturally would require Charles' full attention.

Chapter 9

A Mysterious Disappearance

In newspaper coverage of his first few flights in 1835, reference is made to Charles flying in 'a new balloon'. It is possible, therefore, that both he and his son George, were involved with the design and manufacture of this 'new balloon,' which should not be confused with the imminent arrival of the even larger *Royal Vauxhall* balloon in 1836. Since all this manufacturing work took place in London, it perhaps accounts for Charles' events being London-based in the immediate future.

Charles Green's 199th ascent - by his reckoning - was made on Monday, 25 May 1835. He had secured some events at the Royal Surrey Gardens, a pleasure garden opened in 1831, located in Newington, London, on the east side of Kennington Park Road, not far from the Oval cricket ground. Occupying about 15 acres, including a 3 acre lake, the main public attraction was a menagerie of animals assembled to compete with the London Zoo in Regent's Park.

Charles' first engagement there was on 25 May at a fete celebrating the sixteenth birthday of Princess Victoria. That afternoon Charles made an ascent from a raft floating on the lake, to which the London Gas Company had laid almost half-a-mile of pipes to supply gas for the balloon. The raft was used in order to give the maximum number of spectators a good view of proceedings. On this occasion, one of Charles' companions was a monkey named Jacopo, taken from the menagerie. Dressed in Spanish costume, Jacopo was secured in a small cage attached to a parachute, to be taken aloft and dropped over the side at a suitable altitude. Charles had carried animals aloft before, so a monkey was nothing extraordinary for him, but the public seemed to like the idea. In addition, Charles took up a passenger who, although un-named by newspapers at the time, is believed to be Mr Jephson.

All went well for aeronauts and monkey. Jacopo was duly tossed over the side by the passenger and floated to earth into the garden of a policeman in East Lane, Walworth. A label attached to the cage promised the finder a reward of £2 and free admission to the Zoological Gardens upon safe return of the monkey. Meanwhile, Charles' trip was uneventful and he landed safely at Brentwood in Essex. Although advertisements indicated ascents would be made on two consecutive days, no coverage can be found for a second flight and many reports state that despite Jacopo returning to earth intact, the monkey appeared quite upset by his experience.

THE FLYING ADVENTURES OF CHARLES GREEN

In view of his social status, Charles was eligible for jury service and in mid-June 1835, he found himself called to attend the Old Bailey for that purpose. He was listed as a member of the 'Fifth Jury' at the High Court, which meant he was a member of one jury among many that were each selected at random to adjudicate on a series of High Court trials. Charles managed to avoid being involved with cases that resulted in the death penalty but he sat in some theft cases on 20 June and 22 June that resulted in such penalties as prison or transportation, the latter being the fate of some defendants as young as 10, 14 and 17 years of age, who were transported - probably to Australia - for terms of seven to fourteen years. The law was harsh in those days. Another member of the Fifth Jury was George Rush, who later flew on several trips with Charles Green and it is believed they may have struck up a friendship during their time as jurymen.

Having found time to get married to Ann on 30 June, Charles' next flying event, at Royal Surrey Gardens, was - by his reckoning - his landmark 200th trip, made on Monday, 20 July 1835. He reckoned that by this date, he had flown a total of 240 hours and covered a total distance of 600 miles.

It was a holiday festival, described as 'a juvenile fete,' in the Gardens, 'attended by thousands of well-dressed persons' and during the day Charles made a number of tethered ascents from the raft while a band of the Coldstream Guards played and visitors gaped in awe at animals in the zoo.

At 7.00 pm, Charles made a solo flight that took him across the Thames to land between One Tree and Flamstead Hill in Greenwich Park, where he was mobbed on landing by some of the 20,000 crowd in the park. He had quite a job extricating himself from the folds of the balloon and from the hordes of over-zealous helpers, among whom one young man got too close to the gas valve and was carried away senseless from the effects of the fumes. He managed to return to Surrey Gardens at 11.00 pm.

This programme was repeated on Wednesday, 22 July for his 201st flight. Taking off at 6.30 pm, Charles was accompanied by a Mr Jephson and they travelled to near Staines Gas Works; 16 miles in about half-an-hour. After taking refreshment offered by a local gentleman the pair returned to the Gardens that same evening.

Having again proved his worth in the field of public entertainment, Charles was persuaded by the proprietors of the Royal Gardens, Vauxhall, London, to come and work for them on a more prolonged basis, rather than for *ad hoc* flights.

On the subject of working with animals, while at Vauxhall Gardens the well-known wild-animal trainer, Mr van Amburgh, suggested that Charles took a Bengal tiger into the air in his car. This attraction was actively promoted and thousands of spectator tickets were sold to the public. However, magistrates approached for a licence to stage the event refused to issue a permit, on the grounds of safety and the likelihood of the animal escaping. So, all the tickets had to be refunded.

A MYSTERIOUS DISAPPEARANCE

Always seeking a new attraction for the paying visitors, it is not clear who had the original idea, but his next venture was balloon 'racing.' Two balloons were to be employed, manned by Charles - who was reported as using 'a new balloon' - and one of his brothers. Sadly, none of the prolific quantity of newspapers carrying stories of these races thought to state the name of the brother involved, although one small clue has been found. This brother was described as younger than Charles and that this would be his forty-second trip. The quantity of flights and the use of the term 'brother' rules out Charles' son George, who had made nearly eighty by this time. The quantity of flights quoted (forty-two) also rules out brother George, who had made nearly 120. It is really only one of Charles' other two brothers, William Henry or James who would fit that measure of flights.

The first of these races was held during a 'one shilling' fete at Vauxhall on Thursday, 13 August 1835, on the occasion of Her Majesty Queen Adelaide's birthday. Charles agreed to take Mr Christopher Herbert Simpson as passenger, for the sum of 20 guineas. Better known as C.H. Simpson, he was employed as Master of Ceremonies at the Gardens and widely known as a flamboyant, immaculately-dressed character - but sometimes ridiculed for his affected airs and graces. When the time came for take-off, Mr Simpson thought better of his prospects and declined to remain in the car and so Charles went up for what he claimed as his 203rd flight alone - flight #202 has gone missing. In his brother's car, Mr Cave, who it was rumoured had paid 25 guineas, went up as the passenger. At 7.00 pm, upon a signal, both balloons rose into the air, Charles taking a slanting trajectory while 'the younger Mr Green' went straight up. Both balloons remained in sight for several minutes before their paths diverged and they were finally lost to view. First to land was 'the younger Mr Green;' at Barnes at 7.20 pm, followed by Charles who landed at Wandsworth at 8.00 pm. No winner appears to have been declared publicly.

For his 204th flight, the *Evening Chronicle* reported that Charles 'made his first nocturnal ascent in his new balloon.' This was on the occasion of a grand evening fete for the benefit of exiled Polish patriots, which was very well attended, including such notable personages as the Duke and Duchess of Sutherland; the Duke and Duchess of Somerset; Marquess and Marchioness of Clanricarde; Marquess of Douro; Marchioness of Salisbury; Marquess of Worcester; Earl and Countess of Chesterfield; Earl and Countess of Wilton; Lord Melbourne; Lady Dover and Lord Palmerston. It was quite a late affair, with the gates opening at 9.00 pm. For an admission price of four shillings, there was a programme of opera singers, illuminations and firework displays, but the main attraction was the solo night ascent by Charles, scheduled for midnight. All went very well, although the spectators had only the briefest view of the balloon before it was swallowed up by the darkness of the evening and last seen heading west.

A second balloon race was billed at Vauxhall for Thursday, 27 August, with the same arrangements as before. This would be Charles' 205th flight and he was accompanied by Mr Vivian, who was described as 'a young gentleman of fortune, who paid a liberal sum for his seat in the car.' Both balloon flights were uneventful; Charles, having reached 9,500 feet altitude at his highest point, landed one mile from Uxbridge and his brother - again un-named - landed at Northolt, where he was so well entertained that he did not return to Vauxhall until the following morning.

Always keen to conjure up a Royal theme, the Vauxhall Gardens announced an evening of celebrations in honour of King William IV's accession to the throne, which was a bit tenuous but it still drew in huge crowds who, as always, were keen to see Charles Green in action. The newspapers billed this as Charles' 207th flight, but there is no record anywhere of #206, so that's another hole in his log-book unaccounted for. Due to poor weather the date drifted from 8 September to Saturday, 12 September when the ascent actually went ahead during the afternoon. Charles was accompanied by Lord Dudley Stuart, son of the 1st Marquess of Bute; a Whig politician and staunch advocate of Polish independence, who was at this time MP for Arundel, but later held the seat for Marylebone.

VAUXHALL GARDENS, 17 September 1835. #208

By the mid-1830s Green's aeronautical reputation was unrivalled. but he had reached a stage in his career where he needed fresh challenges. His attention was drawn to high altitude experiments and long-distance flights, requiring an understanding of meteorology and in particular the patterns and use of air currents. However, there was still much to learn, usually by trial and error and often under the most hazardous of conditions. It was perhaps not surprising, therefore, to read in *The Times* of September 1835, the dramatic headline: 'Mr Green the Aeronaut Lost.'

Had fate caught up with Charles Green at last? This was the question on everyone's lips and as the newspaper put it:

> 'Considerable anxiety was on Friday [18 September] evinced by the public for the fate of this gentleman. Frequent enquiries were made of the proprietors of the Vauxhall Gardens, London as to where Mr Green had descended, to which no reply could be given, they [the proprietors] not having heard of him since his re-ascent at Walthamstow.'

Being, by now, something of a national treasure, Charles Green commanded this level of anxiety when his whereabouts caused concern. On this occasion though, Green himself had a considerable hand in creating an aura of mystery about this his latest aerial expedition in his *Royal Coronation* balloon.

A MYSTERIOUS DISAPPEARANCE

After some days the final story emerged and its outcome was clearly wrapped-up with his growing desire to undertake more adventurous balloon journeys. This one, his 208th, was to bring him, once again, to Norfolk.

That Thursday evening (17 September) saw Charles Green at the Royal Gardens, Vauxhall. It was the annual gathering of the Metropolitan Society of Florists for its Grand Dahlia Show and after the prizes were awarded, Charles was to entertain the crowd. His balloon was already inflated and the germ of an idea was no doubt already in his mind - for he was not a fellow to go off at half-cock. Chatting to a committee member of the Floricultural Society, he made a curious remark that he sought 'a gentleman of light weight but with a heavy purse' to accompany him on this flight. Bearing in mind it was already mid-September and approaching 5.30 pm, there would be little daylight remaining to complete much of a journey that day. However, his remark was taken seriously and immediately communicated to Mr Butler, a surgeon from Woolwich, known both as a gentleman of means and keen to undertake a flight, a combination seemingly less prevalent than might be imagined. Mr Butler must have been close by, for having been introduced to the aeronaut, to whom he offered the sum of 10 guineas (substantially below his usual fee level) for the privilege of a flight, the pair were airborne by 5.45 pm. To the accompaniment of loud cheering along its course, Green's balloon was carried north-eastwards on a gentle breeze. Crossing the Thames at Blackfriars Bridge, gaining height steadily, within half an hour it reached Walthamstow, with the city receding and countryside opening out below. It was at this point in the journey that events now took a curious turn.

Green brought the balloon to earth in a field on the north-east side of the town where a small crowd gathered, all keen to lend a hand in securing the balloon. According to Mr Butler's version of events, he was politely asked to get out of the car and make his way back to London. Mr Butler expressed his bitter disappointment to Mr Green at not being permitted to remain for the whole voyage and was told, 'It is quite impossible.' Upon enquiring why, Green replied 'I cannot tell you now but will on another occasion and you will be satisfied.' Pondering that assurance, the bemused Butler watched the aeronaut take on board a small quantity of sand ballast and promptly ascend again into the gathering dusk, still heading north-east.

No further news was heard of Mr Green for more than twenty-four hours during which time Mr Butler had returned to Vauxhall Gardens to recount his strange tale.

There was, naturally, much speculation as to Green's fate. It emerged that prior to his last balloon ascent he had told Frederick Gye and Richard Hughes, proprietors of the Gardens that, if the wind was favourable, he would attempt to cross the Channel and descend in France. However, his plan was thwarted at the last moment by a change of wind direction and he had to abandon the idea.

Listening to Mr Butler's story it was, in the opinion of these gentlemen, possible that Green decided to make another attempt at a sea crossing but wished to play down the matter in case of another failure. They knew that in the carriage was only a pint of wine and a few biscuits, surmising that such meagre provisions for a journey of any distance and having so keenly taken a companion, with whom he then abruptly parted company, indicated the possibility of undertaking a long journey was a sudden decision. This conjecture was reinforced by Butler adding that Mr Green had informed him they would land at Walthamstow 'for a particular purpose.' The conclusion reached by these anxious gentlemen was that if the all-important wind did not change, the course of Green's balloon must have been across Suffolk; Norfolk and the German Ocean (North Sea) to make a landing in Holland.

In the event, Charles Green was quite safe and sound and in no danger. There was great relief when he finally turned up at Vauxhall Gardens where he was able to give his version of events.

'On reaching Walthamstow, I informed Mr Butler of my intention to remain aloft all night. He was most anxious to remain with me to savour the experience but I did not deem this prudent. It was my opinion that in the event of being carried out to sea during the night it would be much more advantageous to have his weight in disposable ballast.

Having taken on board a fresh supply of sand I re-ascended and continuing northwards, passed over Bishops Stortford, Royston and Huntingdon. I encountered an air current which took me more to the east and it was by now quite dark. Below me, those towns lit by gas illuminated the atmosphere for a considerable distance and were easily distinguishable. I fired several Bengal lights [flares] during the night and from shouts reaching me from the darkness below, doubted not that their appearance must have created much astonishment.

I had reached a height of 11,000 feet and my view of the ground below was often obscured by fog. It was 6.00 am on Friday morning [18 September] when I decided to descend in the parish of Wimbotsham in Norfolk. Though it was an early hour I was soon surrounded by a large crowd, all anxious to render me assistance. In response to his kind invitation, I partook of an excellent breakfast at the residence of Mr J. Pike after which, as the sun's rays having evaporated overnight dew from the balloon and the gas once more expanded, at 9.30 am I rose into the air yet again.

I hoped to find either an inland current or one that would take me across the Channel. However, perceiving that I was going rapidly towards the German Ocean [North Sea], I allowed the gas to escape. At 10.30 am the balloon came safely down to anchor at North Runcton, within 8 miles of the sea [The Wash] and close to the town of King's Lynn.

While deflating the balloon and packing it up I received numerous congratulations, though upon hearing my story many people, I believe, were astounded by it and doubted my claim to have been in the air this past night. I am most grateful to Mr Francis Hulton Esquire for a sumptuous repast, after which I saw to the balloon

A MYSTERIOUS DISAPPEARANCE

being put in a carrier's van for conveyance to London. I then walked into King's Lynn where I was greeted most heartily and spent the rest of the day in that town. That evening I caught the *Red Rover* coach to London, travelling by way of Downham Market. At the Castle Inn in Downham, I was once more greeted most kindly.'

This latest Charles Green adventure was very widely reported, appearing in all the newspapers across the land from London to Limerick. Some reports, such as that which follows, offered a local slant on the basic story.[1]

'It appears that Mr Green's late trip produced alarm in the village of Stansted Mountfitchet. That little spot of quiet repose (gentle Stansted), shortly after nine o'clock on the eventful evening, was thrown into disorder by the daring voyager. The village blacksmith's wife uttered loud cries of "The world is at an end!" After she had been tranquillised, she gave the following account. Just before going to bed, she opened the door to look out and the candle in her hand was suddenly extinguished. Then the clouds opened and a voice from one who descended upon her exclaimed: "Where am I?" Fortunately, there were those nearby who succeeded in dispelling the poor woman's delusions. Mr Green's height here was not above 100 feet from the ground at the time.

Another scene occurred in Hockerill Street, too. About nine o'clock someone proclaimed that the "Comet was coming down!" "The gas was blowing up!" The world is at an end!" And so on. It happened that The Honourable J. Hook, who had just ordered two pairs of horses at the Crown Inn and was waiting for the second carriage coming up, to give some orders, made himself most praiseworthily active in quelling the fears of the timid, by assuring them all that it was Mr Green's balloon, which had that evening ascended at Vauxhall. Mr Green, in his late trip to King's Lynn, passed over the upper part of this street and his light, with some kind of small firework [a Bengal Light, perhaps] that he threw out, probably to attract attention, had caused the uproar. It appears he was sailing very low and very slowly, but in high spirits he could afford to be witty. "What county am I in?" inquired he. The above Honourable Gentleman answered, "Hertfordshire, but you will directly be in Essex. Why don't you descend?" "Because I cannot," replied he. "I wish I could."'

Upon his safe return to the Vauxhall Gardens in London, Charles cleared up the mystery which had surrounded his 'disappearance,' stating he remained in the air for fifteen hours overnight. He explained that his intention had been to cross to the continent but winds were eventually unfavourable. Instead, he travelled northwards, zig-zag fashion, for 130 miles and remarked confidently: 'from the trifling loss of power the balloon sustained during the whole of the expedition, I judge that I could have remained aloft for at least five days and nights.'

THE FLYING ADVENTURES OF CHARLES GREEN

UXBRIDGE. 6 October 1835. #209

Charles still hankered after making an aerial crossing to France and it was in his mind to have another crack at it when he lifted off from Mr Hancock's field adjacent to Uxbridge gas works on 6 October. Temporary pipes were laid and the gas was supplied by the gas works proprietor, Mr Stacy, free of charge. As with his earlier attempt, Charles had a passenger, Mr George Harman, a brewer from the town, with him but if he thought conditions were favourable, he could always land and drop him off. If nothing else, his plan was flexible.

Take-off was at 4.20 pm and the balloon took a north-easterly track, then veered to the east, which was looking promising. Passing over St Albans and north of Waltham Abbey, it was here that he decided to land and ask his passenger to step out so, at 6.30 pm, the balloon coming gently to earth 4 miles north of Epping. George Harman, no doubt reluctantly, stepped out of the car and Charles scouted around for a supply of sand as ballast to replace the passenger's weight.

At 7.00 pm, Charles took to the sky again but had difficulty finding the same favourable current and was drifting northwards. He decided to land again, this time at 10.00 pm near Good Easter, a few miles north of Chelmsford. Having been hospitably received by a group of ladies and gentlemen, Charles ascended yet again at 10.30 pm. Now he went for altitude, reaching 15,000 feet in the hope of catching a current to the east, but all this achieved was, instead, to remain almost stationary for 5 hours.

'I now abandoned all hopes of a more favourable current, which would either enable me to cross the Channel, or to visit my relatives in Nottinghamshire. I therefore commenced my final descent, which I effected at 4.45 am at Leigh's Hall, in the parish of Little Leighs, near Braintree, Essex, the home of Hugh Symons Esquire, at whose residence I was sumptuously entertained. From there I returned to London the same day and arrived at Uxbridge the following morning [8th].'

It was one of Hugh Symons' farm workers who raised the alarm. Going to work, he was dreadfully alarmed by seeing a balloon stationary on the farmland. He ran to the Hall, exclaiming, 'Master! Master! There's a cloud fell out of the sky!' When Mr Symons walked up to this phenomenon, he found that the balloon was safely anchored and Charles Green so fast asleep in the car that he was only wakened with some difficulty.

That brought Charles' flying season in 1835 to a close; a year which had seen him make long-distance flights, drop live animals by parachute from his car, make several night flights, let off fireworks in the air and introduce the spectacle of balloon racing to the public. But his fame was going to climb to even greater altitude during the coming year.

A MYSTERIOUS DISAPPEARANCE

Charles Green was indeed a famous person already, not just for his flying adventures but also for his technical knowledge in matters relating to the practical elements of aerostation. It was this expertise that saw him called upon during a civil court action: Macintosh versus Everington & Ellis, heard in the Court of Common Pleas at the Guildhall, London on 25 February 1836.

The plaintiff, Charles Macintosh (1766-1843), was a Scottish chemist whose name is forever linked to the invention of waterproof cloth that his fabric bonding process turned into weather-proof garments such as the ubiquitous 'Mackintosh' (the spelling usually associated with the garment). In 1823, Macintosh took out a patent on an invention for rendering a substance water- and air-proof, by the insertion of a flexible cement, composed of Indian rubber dissolved by coal oil, placed between two pieces of linen, cotton, woollen or other texture. He was suing the defendants, Messrs Everington & Ellis, for infringement of his patent.

In simple terms, in 1835 Everington was selling garments in his London shop that were similar to those made by Macintosh. However, these were not supplied by Macintosh because Everington had them manufactured to his own specification and sold them under his own brand as 'Fanshaw's Improved Patent Waterproof Cloaks.' Macintosh got wind of this and sent an anonymous buyer to the shop to ask for two of Macintosh's patent cloaks. The shopkeeper said he had none of Mr Macintosh's cloaks but he offered the secret shopper a cloak which he stated to be superior, of their own manufacture, having purchased the patent of a certain Mr Fanshaw, whose name appeared in the collar of the cloak. It was alleged there was no such person as Mr Fanshaw and when the Fanshaw garment was purchased and later put through a detailed examination by various eminent scientists on behalf of the plaintiff, he decided to lodge a complaint that Fanshaw's Patent Cloak constituted an infringement of his patent.

The defendants contended that Macintosh's was not a new invention, since a similar cement had been used for the same purpose prior to the date of Macintosh's patent. The defence called expert witnesses to support this claim and Charles Green, his son George and Charles' friend Edward Spencer - a solicitor who had both flown with him and assisted him in the manufacture of balloons - were among those who gave evidence for the defendants.

The case was reported widely and a particularly detailed version of events can be found in the pages of the *Mechanics Magazine* of 2 April 1836 (Vol 24; No.660). In this report in addition to the relevance to the court case, a number of facts emerged that throw useful light on some of Charles' activities in general. For example, there was always some question over what happened to Charles' first balloon, the original *Coronation* balloon, following his near-fatal experience in October 1821.

Giving evidence for the defendants, Charles made various claims about the use of his 'secret' cements, varnishes and his methods of working silk fabric during the manufacture of his balloons. The following are among some of the salient points he made.

'I have been in the habit of making balloons for a great number of years, solely under my own superintendence and that of my son. My first ascent was in 1821. I manufactured miniature balloons before that.

The upper part of a balloon should be flexible. I made it air- and water-proof by forming it of a double and treble texture, with a solution of India-rubber; some parts were double and other parts treble [ply]. The flexible cement for uniting this substance, I formed entirely of India-rubber dissolved in oil of turpentine. I used this cement in forming the seams of the balloon, without a stitch being put in it. A further substance [gum-mastic] was sometimes added to the solution depending on whether the fabric surfaces to be united were considered smooth or rough, since it is necessary to treat different surface textures differently.

Since the time I made that balloon in 1820, I have made two others. I made miniature balloons in a different way as a boy, but I made larger balloons, some of a double texture, for at least twenty-five years and during that time I have employed a flexible cement.

In May 1822, I constructed another balloon on the same principle. When I exhibited these balloons, if I was ever asked by the public about their construction, I explained the procedure [but] I did not tell [about] the cement I used or how I did it. No balloon was ever cemented together until I cemented one and only my son and I know how it is done.'

At some length, Charles outlined his procedure of varnishing and layering the silk of a balloon envelope and how his cement was applied where appropriate and the qualities it imparted. His son George, followed by Edward Spencer, added to the facts and this information was provided as evidence of the Macintosh-like process being known of and utilised prior to Mr Macintosh's patent. Charles Green continued:

> 'The pipes I use to carry the gas from the [gas] mains to the balloon, are of silk or linen, like this sample here. All the remains of the [original] *Coronation* balloon, which was destroyed in the sea off Beachy Head, I [used] where applicable for the purpose. The other fragments of the balloon that were not used as pipes, I cut into large pieces and - before I discovered they were useful for that very purpose - I used to throw them over my shoulders. I used a large one as a gig-cover and I gave several of [these pieces] to my friends.'

A MYSTERIOUS DISAPPEARANCE

His son; Edward Spencer and then another old friend, John Adams, all confirmed they had received pieces of the old *Coronation* balloon that had proved weather-proof and still effective all these years later. Further evidence was presented that fabric and garments with similar weatherproof qualities, had been found in use in some South American countries since the early part of the century.

The judge, Lord Chief Justice Tindal, summed up the arguments for the Special Jury and asked them to consider a verdict but it took only a few minutes discussion for the jury to find in favour of the plaintiff. However, the judge clearly had some misgivings because the plaintiff, Charles Macintosh, was awarded a trifling one shilling in damages and forty shillings costs.

Chapter 10

Foreign Expeditions

Having had his day in the limelight of the High Court, it was back to the business of flying and Charles returned to the Surrey Zoological Gardens for two ascents in May 1836.

The first of the new season took place on 23 May at a fete, in honour of Princess Victoria's birthday. The location was again from a raft on the lake, around which a crowd estimated at 22,000 people gathered to watch the famous Mr Green. With take-off at 7.00 pm Charles, accompanied by his friend Edward Spencer, made a trip of 28 miles over Vauxhall Gardens and Hammersmith Bridge - reaching 11,000 feet - before landing in Weston Park, near Guildford. Returning to the Zoological Gardens by 3.30 am next morning, Charles went up again in the evening of 24 May, watched by another crowd of 20,000, with Richard Crawshay as his passenger. This time, after travelling a similar distance, the travellers descended safely near Charlwood, between Reigate and Crawley. Charles claimed these flights as #211 and #212, but some newspapers reported them as #212 and #213.

The *Morning Post* (7 July 1836) reported Charles' next flight, made from the Royal Gardens, Vauxhall on Tuesday, 5 July, as his 214th ascent, therefore since the Zoological Garden flights, one more flight number becomes unaccounted for. This latest trip, his first of the season from Vauxhall, was unremarkable and took him to Hertford Common, near Hertford on the northern outskirts of London. He flew alone on this occasion, although his (second) wife Ann asked him to take her up. He declined to do so because the weather signs suggested a thunderstorm was brewing and rain would affect the lift, so he erred on the side of caution about safety and payload. It would not be long before Mrs Green got her wish, though. John Widdicombe, the proprietor of the Black Lion Inn at Hoddesdon, provided Charles a very warm welcome and refreshment and later arranged for a chaise and four to convey him and the balloon back to London by half-past midnight.

Balloon racing was back on the programme and a series of two-balloon races was arranged at Vauxhall Gardens that summer. Speaking to the newspapers about this novel idea, Charles took the opportunity to impress their readers with some scientific 'spin.' He said his objective in ascending with two balloons was:

FOREIGN EXPEDITIONS

'To prove to the scientific world that different currents of air existed in the upper regions. Though, it is my opinion that beyond the action of the clouds, by concurrent causes upon the elements, there are in our latitude, currents of air which, like the trade winds [for sailors], have their periodical courses. I have invariably found that the higher I rise - and I have attained an elevation of three miles and three-quarters [20,000 feet] - the existence of a current from the north-west; which induces me to conclude that at a distance of six or seven miles [31,000 to 37,000 feet] from the earth's surface, there is a continued current from the north-west.'

It seems Charles had recognised the meteorological phenomenon that we, in modern times, refer to as 'the jet stream.'

The first of the races took place at Vauxhall Gardens on Saturday, 23 July 1836. One of the balloons was crewed by Charles and his wife and the other by William Green and his wife (whose first name is not reported). We are treated, however, to a rare glimpse of Ann Green when, for example the *Evening Chronicle*, London, describes her as:

'a very pretty brunette, wearing a blue silk dress and a satin bonnet of the same colour; who took her seat in the car with the greatest self-command.'

Stormy weather caused a postponement from Tuesday, 19 July to Saturday, 23rd. Preserved posters and handbills together with many contemporary newspaper reports for all three race days, announced that the second crew was Mr and Mrs W. Green. This seems straightforward enough to enable one to draw the conclusion that it refers to Charles' brother William Henry, of whom we have heard before. However, it is frustrating to find that many newspapers, have failed to identify clearly this relative of Charles. Nevertheless, the first race was watched by 6,000 spectators in the Gardens, including such notables as the ambassadors of Russia; France; Sweden; Persia and Turkey with their families and entourages, together with a host of British peers and noblemen.

Take-off at 6.15 pm saw Charles' balloon tracking towards the Tunbridge Wells Road, while his brother drifted over the Isle of Dogs towards the Maidstone Road. A little past 7.00 pm, William landed about a mile-and-a-half from Eltham. Observing this, Charles landed a few minutes later at St Paul's Cray, near Orpington both balloons coming down safely.

The rector of Paul's Cray, Reverend Simmonds, having said a prayer for the travellers, entertained Charles and his wife with the utmost cordiality and rather touchingly, presented her with a book of testament before they parted company. The rector whistled-up a chaise and four for the couple and their balloon to return to London. On the road back, the race continued apace, when Charles' chaise caught up with and overtook that carrying his brother and wife back to Vauxhall. It was reckoned that Charles had landed 3 miles further on than his brother but again, no winner was publicly declared.

The tone was set for the second race on Tuesday, 2 August 1836 and once again, the second balloon crew was publicised again as Mr and Mrs William Green (*Morning Chronicle*: 3 August). On this occasion, Mrs Green was ready to depart with her husband for his 217th ascent, when word came that the Irish peer, the Marquess of Clanricarde, wished to take a flight. A request from a Peer of the Realm could not be ignored so Ann graciously gave up her seat to His Lordship. It was not recorded whether any monetary inducement was involved.

In his car, Charles used his new invention, a friction-collar designed to spring-release a bight of the final restraining rope when its operating lever was moved. Both balloons moved upwards simultaneously, just 20 feet apart. At a height of 1,000 feet, the two envelopes bumped and rubbed together - without damage or dismay - then began to go their separate ways, one to the east and one to the south but, as time wore on, their paths crossed several times.

It was reported that a short while into the flight, Lord Clanricarde suggested they open a bottle of wine and drink several toasts to The King and Queen; Lady Clanricarde and others. One newspaper says it was sherry, while another said it was champagne. Whatever it was, perhaps, having reached an altitude of 12,300 feet, 50 minutes in the air and half-a-bottle of bubbly, His Lordship came over a bit queasy, since he suggested to Charles that maybe they should land soon because he 'was aware that the Marchioness felt anxious about his safety' and he was keen to get back to her. Charles duly obliged and made a good landing in a field one mile east of Farningham. Willing helpers were quickly on the scene, the balloon was emptied and packed up. Both men were invited by local gentry to take refreshment but this was declined as His Lordship was anxious to return to London as soon as possible. A ubiquitous chaise and four was obtained and His Lordship, Charles and the balloon reached Vauxhall Gardens by 10.40 pm that evening. Charles' brother landed in the parish of Orpington on the estate of Sir Percival Dyke, interrupting a cricket match whose players helped to restrain the balloon and pack it up. After refreshments, the second crew returned to Vauxhall by midnight. This time, it was reported that bets had been wagered on which balloon went the greatest distance.

These races were proving to be a good money-spinner for the Vauxhall Gardens owners and a crowd of 10,000 people attended the third event on Tuesday, 9 August 1836; Charles' 218th ascent.

A flood of thirty applications came in for seats in the car. Both aeronaut's wives gave up their places to two 'scientific' gentlemen for this race. Mr Charles Wrottesley flew with Charles while Mr Collett flew with his brother. Charles' companion was the son of the famous astronomer, Sir John Wrottesley FRS FRAS (1798-1867; 2nd Baron Wrottesley), owner of a splendid observatory in Blackheath but, as far as Mr Collet(t) is concerned, nothing more is known.

In the Gardens, the substantial crowd again included many notable British peers and 'other fashionables.' Among these was the flamboyant and immensely wealthy emigré Duke of Brunswick, who made it widely known that he was keen to make a flight and attempted to induce both the above gentlemen - unsuccessfully - to give up their seat.

Take-off was at 6.30 pm, and the trip was uneventful. Charles and Mr Wrottesley landed in a meadow belonging to Jacob Ellery Esquire, near Crawley, where it took them quite a time to find transport and did not return to Vauxhall until 4.00 am the next morning. His brother and Mr Collett landed close to Epsom Downs, from where they were able to return to town by 10.00 pm that evening.

His Highness Karl II, Duke of Brunswick-Wolfenbüttel got his way and was the centre of attention when Charles Green prepared for his next two-balloon race, held on Tuesday, 16 August. But all did not go to plan. The Duke was given to displaying false bravado and was a bit of a 'diva,' so it was perhaps inevitable that he might clash with the implacable Charles Green.

Charles planned for take-off at 7.00 pm and 20,000 people descended on Vauxhall Gardens on that basis, first drinking in a multitude of wondrous attractions, such as the Ravel Family; musicians; singers; vaulters; cosmoramas; dioramas and walks with statuary fountains and clockwork displays. Inflation of the balloons began early that morning, with a signal-gun announcing completion at 6.30 pm.

At 6.00 pm, the Duke of Brunswick informed the proprietors that he wished to take his seat now and begin the flight. He was told that the flight was programmed for 7.00 pm, and having been announced to the public by newspaper and handbills, it was impossible to alter the time. The Duke declined to start an hour later, observing that when he landed it would be dark. In a fit of pique, he refused to wait and left the Gardens. In many polite circles, the courage of the good Duke was a subject of some speculation!

Of course, there was no shortage of takers for a place in the two cars. Charles took Mr W. Hodges and his brother took Mr G. Patrick. After a pleasant trip of about two hours, Charles landed at Plaistow Marshes and his brother's balloon came down at Charlton, Kent.

The final race of the 'season' took place from Vauxhall Gardens in front of a crowd of 20,000 spectators on Tuesday, 30 August 1836. Mrs Evans, a lady said to be about 30-years of age and residing in Dover Street, Piccadilly, paid 25 guineas for the privilege of flying with Charles while his brother was accompanied by Dr Benjamin Arthur Kent, a physician resident at 20 Harley Street, Cavendish Square, London. James Green was identified by name three times in an article carried by the *Morning*

THE FLYING ADVENTURES OF CHARLES GREEN

Advertiser of 31 August, while the *Globe* persisted with the name of William Green - each newspaper reporting the same event. Dr Kent wrote an account of the ascent, published in the *Globe* of 1 September.

Charles landed near Romford and his brother near the Maypole on the edge of Hainault Forest but their respective chaises met up in Ilford, from where they returned together to Vauxhall Gardens at 11.00 pm that evening.

His earlier overnight voyage from London to the shores of The Wash served to convince Charles Green that his future and that of the science of aeronautics, lay in long-distance flights and facilitating scientific research into the mysteries of the upper atmosphere. His current balloon served him well but, even though it had well-proven capabilities, he believed he now needed one with much greater powers to achieve these aims.

Having drawn up his specification and plans, Charles estimated the cost of the huge new balloon would be in the order of £2,100 (≈ £197,000 in 2023). Unable to finance the manufacture of this new Leviathan himself, he turned to his hosts at the Royal Gardens, Vauxhall for support. His pulling-power for their audiences, together with the potential revenue value of his ambitious future plans, was enough to sway the proprietors, Gye and Hughes, to commission the construction at their expense. To the proprietors, the principal attraction of Charles' idea for such a large balloon was that it would be capable of carrying many passengers - possibly ten or even twelve - into the air at a time. Furthermore, these would be fare-paying, which meant a handsome income per flight at the prices being considered. Charles got the machine he wanted but, as a result, he was beholden to the wishes of Gye and Hughes for the next four years.

To be known as the *Royal Vauxhall*, dimensions of this new balloon were often reported in a confusing or contradictory way, but some key statistics issued by the proprietors during August 1836 are as follows:

70 feet tall (80 feet including car and suspension ropes).
50 feet diameter.
157 feet 'equator' circumference.
70,000 cubic-feet capacity for coal gas - nearly four times the size of his existing craft.

It was estimated that it could lift up to 4,000lbs, of which 1,000lbs was its own weight plus that of its accessories, including: hemp-netting weight: 300lbs; fabric of the envelope weight: 700lbs. The car is made of wicker basket-work and a grapnel (or anchor) would be carried, attached to a hemp rope with an India-rubber shock-absorber (from the factory of Mr Sievier) joining these two components. When ballast in the region of 350 to 400lbs was carried it was expected it could take at least eight to ten people aloft.

FOREIGN EXPEDITIONS

Publicly displayed in the Rotunda of the Vauxhall Gardens, the original car for the new *Royal Vauxhall* balloon was described by the proprietors as follows.

'Its dimensions are fully treble the size of an ordinary car. It is covered with crimson silk and lined with yellow silk. Over the top is suspended a splendid drapery of purple velvet with a gold fringe. Round the ring, to which the ropes are attached, is a tasteful drapery of sky-blue silk, ornamented with a deep gold fringe. At each end of the car is the representation of the neck and head of an eagle, beautifully gilt. On the whole, it is the most splendid car ever manufactured.'

Believed to have begun in late-1835, construction of the 8,000 square-feet envelope surface area was achieved with forty-four alternate crimson and white segments or 'gores', each measuring roughly 150 feet in length; 44 inches at their widest point, tapering almost to a point at each end. It consumed 2,000 yards of the finest imported Italian silk, dyed by Mr Jacques and woven by Messrs Soper of Spital Square, in one of the small factories for which the Spitalfields district of London was famous. The proprietors of the balloon requested several sample patterns of silk cloth to be sent to them from Lyons (France) to be considered for the construction of their balloon. None were found either in strength or fine-ness to be equal to that manufactured by the Spitalfields weavers and in consequence, the extensive order was awarded to Sopers. The unusually-large width of the silk (44 inches) required all the looms to be made expressly for this purpose and 'none but the strongest and most experienced of the workmen could accomplish the task.'

The finished crimson silk was priced at 12-shillings-and-9-pence per yard and the finished white at 13-shillings per yard. The raw silk was said to have cost around £700 (≈ £65,700 in 2023); the finished fabric being oiled and laminated by the processes described earlier in this book to make it gas-tight and water-proof. Part of Charles' original specification was that the seams of the gores were not to be sewn but would be 'cemented' using a bonding glue 'of such tenacious adhesion,' invented and developed in conjunction with his son George and proven to be very successful in his earlier balloons. There is clear evidence (see below) that Charles changed his mind and added strength to the joints by having them not only cemented but sewn also. (*Globe*; *Morning Advertiser*; *Sun, et al*: 25 August 1836). There is no doubt, too, that the durability and longevity of Charles' bonded-construction process is amply proven by the fact that the *Royal Vauxhall* had a working life of almost forty years. It was reported in various newspapers:

'In the workshop of the [Vauxhall] Gardens, an immense balloon is in preparation which, it is understood will be completed in a few weeks. When complete, Mr Green [expects] to take up with him eight or ten aspirants for the upper air [passengers].'[1]

'The seams of the edges when joined together, [are] first cemented by a solution of India-rubber prepared by Mr Green himself, and to give extra strength are firmly sewn together, about which several women are at present employed in Vauxhall Gardens.'[2]

'Every seam has three rows of needlework which, without the attention to the ornamental character of the work, is done with equal nicety with the work that is bestowed upon the shirt collars of the most fastidious in dress.'[3]

Charles himself estimated that no fewer than 619,000 stitches would be required!

Initially, the car was a relatively small, ornate boat-shaped design, measuring about five feet long by four feet wide. However, after the balloon's first flight, it was immediately evident that the payload could be very substantially increased and so a far more-roomy, oval-shaped car, 9 feet in length by about 4 feet width, was used thereafter. Across the centre of the car was a one-foot wide thwart to which various apparatus could be attached, or it could be used as a seat or table. The car was attached to the balloon by ten ropes securing it to a 6 feet diameter hoop made from a double layer of ash wood. Payload, in the eyes of Charles and Messrs Gye and Hughes, meant more paying passengers and thus more income.

Right from the outset, this considerable investment in the *Royal Vauxhall* balloon yielded a handsome return for Gye and Hughes, because Charles Green's balloon ascents - particularly after his German adventure - provided a huge attraction for visitors to the gardens. Furthermore, they proved be a real money-spinner in the sale of tickets for passengers to travel in the balloon's car, not only on tethered 'flights,' but also on real flights out of London. On 21 September 1836, Charles Green made the second ascent in his new balloon, with ten passengers in a new and larger car and the fares for those passengers had been set at 20 guineas (£21.00) for gentlemen (≈ £1,900 in 2023) and 10 guineas (£10.50) for ladies – quite a bit below the sums Charles used to charge for that privilege. However, it was a more attractive price for a budding customer and there were many more seats up for grabs. Passenger flights were also offered as lottery prizes at the Gardens, with lottery tickets selling for one-shilling each.

The maiden flight for the new balloon was on Friday, 9 September 1836 from the Royal Gardens, Vauxhall. It was announced in the newspapers of the time:

'On no previous occasion in the annals of aerostation has public curiosity been so strongly excited as on that of the ascent of the stupendous *Royal Vauxhall* balloon, which took place from the fashionable [Vauxhall] Gardens.'

Although admission price was raised to two-shillings-and-sixpence for this great occasion, long queues awaited the opening time of 1.30 pm. Inflation of the balloon

FOREIGN EXPEDITIONS

began at 11.10 am and it had already reached enormous proportions as the spectators entered the grounds. At 2.00 pm it began to rain and blow, continuing unabated for the next three hours but the crowd seemed quite unperturbed. When the rain finally gave way to brighter skies, the final stages of preparation for the flight commenced.

Such was the buoyancy of this behemoth that initially 5 x 56lb iron weights were attached by ropes to the netting to hold it down. As the balloon swelled, more weights were attached until 41 x 56lb weights surrounded the sphere - and even these were lifted three feet off the ground. Thirty-six constables of the Lambeth Police Division took charge of the weights and adding their own weight to the mix, they had to wind their truncheons through the ropes to avoid cutting their hands. This was still not enough, so twenty workmen from the Gardens team were called upon to add more muscle. With a further 300lbs of rainwater adhering to the fabric, there was nigh on three tons of restraining power being exerted on the balloon now.

Charles took his time adjusting the wet securing ropes of the car; removing the sodden purple velvet covering and discarding the gilded eagle-heads to reduce weight. 24 x 14lb bags of ballast sand were stowed in the bottom of the car and a thermometer, barometer and a cage containing six carrier pigeons were also stored on board. All was now ready to load the passengers for this grand maiden voyage.

At 6.20 pm in front of an estimated 30,000 people, Charles Green - about to embark on his momentous 221st flight - asked the following persons to step into the car:

Mrs Ann Green, CG's wife.
James Green, brother.
Captain Currie; believed to be Army officer Robert William Currie of 3rd Dragoon Guards and a frequent flyer with Charles Green and other contemporary aeronauts.
Robert Charles Hildyard, barrister (later QC, MP).
Edwin Gye, son of Vauxhall proprietor.
William Hughes, son of Vauxhall proprietor.
Robert Hollond. Desperate to make this momentous flight, Hollond took his seat only because he proffered such a large sum of money that Thomas Hughes (the proprietor's other son) was persuaded by his father to vacate his seat.
Miss Mary Ann(e) Green, Charles' niece.

Due to the particular attention given to the production of the gas by Mr Hutchinson, engineer for the London Gas Company, the buoyancy of the filled balloon was much better than Charles anticipated. His experience told him that the rate of ascent would be very rapid therefore, given that he could fit no more people in the car, he decided to valve-off about 15,000 cubic-feet of gas - around twenty per cent of the £70-worth of gas supplied - before risking lift-off. Then, to the musical strains of

THE FLYING ADVENTURES OF CHARLES GREEN

God save the King and thunderous cheering and applause, the last rope was let loose. They were off!

Charles found the rate of climb was still rapid but well under control and in five minutes the balloon left behind the dull cloud below to find brilliant sunshine at 13,000 feet above the city. With the gas now heating up and expanding in the envelope, he was satisfied with the performance but considered it inadvisable to climb further. It was time for a glass of sherry to be taken, with the inevitable round of toasts and one thoughtful person had even brought along some walnuts to accompany the wine. Who says in-flight cabin drinks and nibbles are a modern invention?

Now with the onset of dusk, in the vicinity of Gravesend, he let out more gas to begin a controlled descent. This all went well and the grapnel on its long rope first took hold on a common near the village of Cliffe, 2 miles from Rochester in Kent. After dragging somewhat, it suddenly snatched tight. The balloon hoop to which it was secured snapped in two, leaving the grapnel and its rope on the ground in its wake. The balloon drifted a further 100 yards while Charles, awake to just such a situation, pulled the gas valve wide-open, rapidly collapsing the sphere and bringing it to a halt. The car remained upright during this disturbance and no-one was hurt.

It was a little after 7.30 pm when they landed. Charles was well satisfied with the way the voyage had gone and said later:

> 'All my companions expressed the greatest delight during the voyage and enjoyed themselves very much. Indeed, so loud was their mirth several times, that I had some difficulty in making my instructions audible, for I assigned a duty to each, such as watching the rise and fall of the mercury in the barometer and thermometer, throwing out ballast etc. Being forced to take such a large quantity of ballast, we found the car too small, but a new one, much larger, will be constructed for the next ascent.'

A farm cart was procured and Edwin Gye and Robert Hollond were instructed to proceed immediately to Gravesend and arrange for a chaise and four to be procured and a man to take it to the balloon landing site. Gye and Hollond then found another chaise and returned to Vauxhall by midnight, to let everyone know that all was well. In darkness now and with no suitable transport available, Charles and the other six passengers found accommodation in the village of Cliffe and having travelled to Gravesend next morning, carriages were found for the party to reach Vauxhall at 10.00 pm the following evening.

This maiden ascent of the *Royal Vauxhall* was commemorated by a piece of embossed plate that was presented to Charles Green by Robert Hildyard, one of the passengers on that occasion. Mr Hildyard invited a party to meet the aeronaut at his chambers in the Temple where, after a sumptuous meal, the memento was

FOREIGN EXPEDITIONS

presented to Charles. The next ascent was scheduled from Vauxhall for Wednesday, 21 September, when it was intended to use the new, larger car.

Charles reckoned that the weather on 21 September could not have been better for an aerial voyage and 7,000 people flocked to the Gardens, with many thousands more in the streets outside. Inflation, supervised by Mr Hutchinson of the London Gas Company, went very well and was completed in four-and-a-half hours and then Charles took the opportunity to find out what he called 'the power' of the balloon with its new, enlarged, car.

He had scrupulously weighed all the components:

Silk and valve	338lbs.
Netting	224lbs.
Car	200lbs.
Hoop	85lbs.
Liberating iron and ropes	30lbs.
Grapnel and rope	120lbs.
Total	997lbs.

While safely anchored, Charles invited as many gentlemen as the car would accommodate, to step aboard and nineteen men took up his offer. Charles then sat on the edge of the car, to make it a total of twenty persons. Conservatively calculating each person at 140lbs in weight, made a total of 2,800lbs which, added to the 997lbs of equipment, gave a grand payload of at least 3,797lbs. Allowing the tethered balloon to rise 20 to 30 feet, it was clear to Charles that there was ample power to lift that weight – and, he thought, possibly even two or three more people.

Well satisfied, he restrained the balloon, cleared the car and invited his eleven passengers for the flight to take their places. Having loaded sand ballast of 780lbs, Charles threw his liberating lever and began his 222nd flight at 4.50 pm. In addition to his usual instruments, this time he carried a simple climb and descent indicator. This device was constructed by a Mr Burton to Charles' specification and consisted of a lightweight fan, the spindle of which was connected to an indicator that showed in what direction the balloon was rising or falling and at what rate it was moving up or down.

In order to offer a good view to those on the ground, Charles maintained an altitude of only 4,000 feet throughout the flight, which passed very well and a safe and gentle landing was made one hour later in Dr Scott's meadow on Clay Hill, in the parish of Beckenham, Kent. Coincidentally, it was the same field in which Charles landed with his pony six years earlier.

Helpers by the score were quickly on the scene and as if on cue, the Beckenham stagecoach galloped up the hill as the landing was completed. Leaving John Adams behind to take care of the balloon, Charles commandeered the stagecoach to carry himself and the other passengers back to Vauxhall Gardens by 9.40 pm, with Mr Adams arriving with the balloon in a cart shortly before midnight.

Tuesday, 27 September was the date of the next ascent of the *Royal Vauxhall*. The weather was fine but grey clouds made for a gloomy scene, which probably accounted for the much smaller crowd. There were no problems, however, and the balloon left the ground at 4.05 pm with Charles, eight passengers and 1,000lbs of ballast on board. In the Gardens prior to the ascent, two young ladies were overheard to offer £30 (total) to the proprietors for two seats but were refused and told politely that this was 'quite insufficient.'

Tracking over the Tower of London; the East End; the Lea reservoirs and Hainault Forest, 36 miles and 55 minutes later, the balloon came to land between the village of Writtle and Chelmsford in Essex. The travellers made their way into Chelmsford where they were greeted by a brass band and a huge ecstatic crowd.

Charles' next ascent on 9 October 1836, his 225th, was a similarly successful flight, although heavy rain and low cloud put a real dampener on the attendance - only 1,000 - in the Gardens. In torrential rain, few takers queued up for seats this time but, by the time for take-off Charles had drummed up seven passengers. For their comfort, as part of his 'customer service' policy, he took the precaution of knocking a small hole in the floor of the car to let the rainwater out! But they all still got a ducking in flight, from the rain running down the balloon fabric due to surface tension and dripping on them in the car. An uneventful voyage was followed by a safe landing in the parish of Denham, 2 miles from Uxbridge and they were all back at Vauxhall by 10.15 pm.

Poor weather brought the ballooning season at Vauxhall Gardens to a close with a final public ascent on Monday, 17 October 1836. With a cloud base around 500 feet and thick mist swirling across the Gardens, it was damp and uncomfortable for the spectators.

On this, his 224th trip, Charles took the opportunity to try out another piece of new apparatus: two copper tanks of 5 gallons capacity each, secured to the outside of the car, containing water as an alternative to sand ballast. The tanks gave more space inside the car and it was thought they might allow the release of ballast to be more-finely tuned. It was a nice idea, but they were not a success, as one of the tanks sustained damage during take-off.

Fortunately for all on board, inside five minutes they were above cloud and basking in sunshine when Charles levelled off at 5,000 feet. Taking a northerly track, after a pleasant trip of two hours, Charles brought the balloon down safely 2 miles north of Leighton Buzzard, Bedfordshire and they were all back at Vauxhall Gardens by midnight. It is interesting to find both Robert Hollond and Thomas Monck Mason on board, as these two were preparing for their 'big adventure.' In respect of this ascent, the writer Monck Mason waxed lyrical, submitting a very long and somewhat flowery article to the newspapers about this flight - a practice-run, perhaps, for his next big adventure.

FOREIGN EXPEDITIONS

GERMANY. 7 & 8 November 1836. #226

Now 50 years of age, from 1836 Charles Green turned his efforts to a number of scientific and exploratory balloon journeys during the next decade. Using *Royal Vauxhall*, these included long-distance flights in Britain and on the continent; altitude records; flights in adverse weather conditions and involvement with the ill-fated parachute experiments of Robert Cocking. Charles' sights, though, were firmly fixed on his dream of making a voyage across the English Channel to the Continent of Europe.

It was the sixth voyage of the *Royal Vauxhall* balloon that saw Charles Green achieve his dream, when he launched from Vauxhall Gardens in the afternoon of Monday, 7 November 1836 and by the evening of the next day, had flown into the record books and stamped his mark forever on aeronautical history. Accompanied by two avid enthusiasts of aviation: Robert Edward Hollond (1808-1877), a successful lawyer, entrepreneur and from 1837, MP for Hastings and Thomas Monck Mason (1803-1889), writer, publisher, musician and theatre impresario, Charles flew *Royal Vauxhall* from London to Weilburg in the province of Nassau in North Germany, a track distance of just over 500 miles in only 18 hours. A true demonstration of the concept of air travel.

Although the exact sequence of events is unclear, the idea for an aerial expedition seems to have unfolded during 1836 as a result of two factors: (a) the obvious potential of the *Royal Vauxhall* and (b) Frederick Gye and Richard Hughes' wish to stage a balloon exhibition in Paris. Mounting such an expedition in the month of November might be regarded as flawed planning, especially concerning the weather - indeed a valid view. However, the reason was simple; Charles, Gye and Hughes and not least the *Royal Vauxhall* balloon, were far too busy with operations at the Royal Gardens to consider undertaking such a venture prior to the end of the Garden's season. The loss of income would have been unacceptable and so this somewhat speculative venture - albeit strongly endorsed by the proprietors - had to wait until late in the year.

Charles was keen to experiment with long-distance flights and when the idea for a show in Paris was mooted, at some point he discussed this matter with Robert Hollond. Somehow the balloon must be transported to Paris so one - or both - of them proposed that it should be flown there. Simples! Robert Hollond said he was happy to finance such an expedition on the understanding that he would accompany Charles on the trip. When presented to Gye and Hughes, they saw the whole concept had distinct advantages and agreed to it while, on their part, expressing their willingness to back it by allowing the use of *Royal Vauxhall* free of charge and paying for the gas to fill her up in London and Paris (£63 and £120 respectively). It was further agreed between all the parties involved that this flight would be conducted as a private and not a public venture - so none of the usual advertisements in the press - and it would not be conducted as a direct money-making scheme. The basic idea behind the proposed flight from England, therefore, was that Charles would aim to land as near to Paris as possible; carry out the single flight in Paris, then return to England - and if the latter could be achieved by air, that would be better still. If the track of the balloon was pushed northwards, then they were happy to adjust their plans to take in the Belgian capital.

There was more than enough potential for an immense future benefit to be gained from the prestige factor that success would bring to each individual involved - and because they would become the first Englishmen to fly across the Channel, there was prestige for the nation.

With the only Channel crossing by air being in 1785, when Blanchard and Jeffries flew from Dover to Calais, there were many in the know who expressed surprise, shock, or even disbelief, that Charles intended to take off from London, let alone try to reach Paris. Charles, though, was unconcerned about the distance, since he had no doubts about the qualities of the balloon; frequently avowing that it was quite capable of staying in the air for weeks.

As captain of the craft and the professional aeronaut, Charles controlled all technical aspects and decided to limit the number of people on board to three. Robert Hollond had, in effect bought his place and his task was to keep the log of the voyage, noting such things as time; distances; compass course and barometer readings. Hollond had long been convinced about the viability of balloon flight, ever since he was taken aloft twice while a student at Cambridge and twice more-recently in the *Royal Vauxhall*. In the 1860s he would become one of the founding members of the Aeronautical Society of Great Britain (AeS), later adding Royal to its title. He was a wealthy man and when he and Charles discussed the possibilities, it was Robert who agreed to finance the project stipulating, not unreasonably, that he wanted a place in the car. The son of a wealthy government official in Bengal, Hollond was educated in England. After graduating from Corpus Christi, Cambridge, he qualified as a barrister although, as one newspaper (erroneously) put it: 'possessing an ample fortune, he does not practise his profession.' It was not until March 1837, after the German expedition, that he became an MP; acquiring the seat for Hastings upon the resignation of Howard Elphinstone. His expenditure on the voyage is said to have been in the order of £300 (≈ £28,100 in 2023) and covered such things as provisions, utensils, clothing, living expenses and ground transportation.

As for Thomas Monck Mason, the reasons for his selection are less clear although he, too, was known to be a great advocate of aerostation who had flown on several occasions. It is believed one of his contributions was that he could speak French and German, which was felt likely to come in very handy. At one time Mason ran the London Italian Opera House, where he staged orchestral concerts, opera and ballets and is credited with bringing both French and German opera to the London stage for the first time. Unfortunately, his company went broke and he was declared bankrupt in 1832, but he had by this time developed a great taste for balloon trips and flew with the Grahams as well as Charles Green. Thomas Monck Mason also had literary talents,

Right: Mezzotint print of Charles Green, engraved by George Thomas Payne (active 1832-1855): 'from an original painting by John Hollins, in the possession of Robert Hollond MP' – to whom the plate is dedicated by Hodgson & Graves, publishers. Published by H&G on 6 June 1838. (Public domain image)

Below: Marriage certificate of Charles Green and Martha Pope, 8 February 1807; bottom right in marriage register of St Leonard's church, Shoreditch, London. (Ancestry.co.uk)

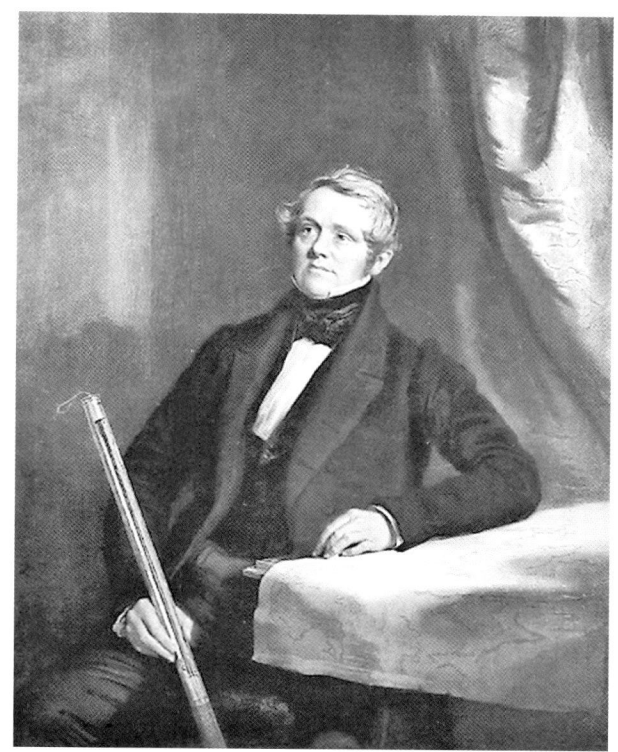

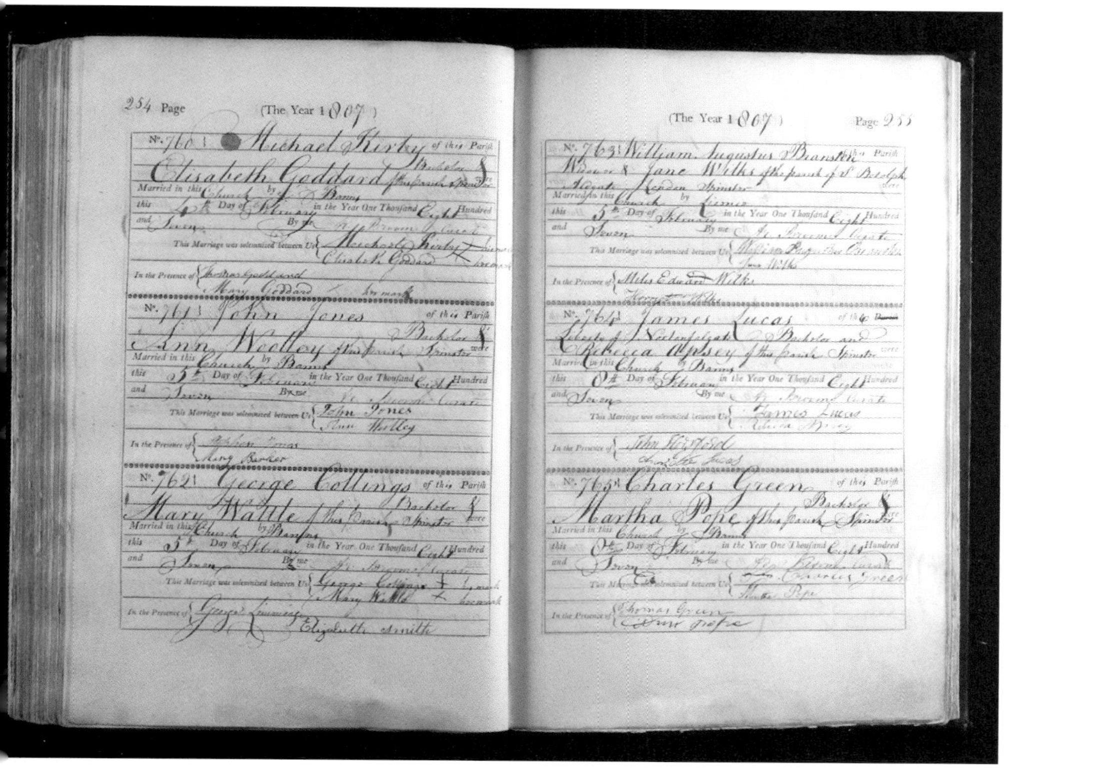

254 Page (The Year 1807)

No. 760 Michael Kirby of this Parish Bachelor & Elisabeth Goddard of this parish Spinster were Married in this Church by Banns this 4th Day of February in the Year One Thousand Eight Hundred and Seven By me
This Marriage was solemnized between Us Michael Kirby, Elisabeth Goddard
In the Presence of Thomas Goddard, Mary Goddard

No. 761 John Jones of this Parish Bachelor & Ann Wootley of this parish Spinster were Married in this Church by Banns this 5th Day of February in the Year One Thousand Eight Hundred and Seven By me
This Marriage was solemnized between Us John Jones, Ann Wootley
In the Presence of

No. 762 George Collings of this Parish Bachelor & Mary Wattle of this parish Spinster were Married in this Church by Banns this 5th Day of February in the Year One Thousand Eight Hundred and Seven By me
This Marriage was solemnized between Us George Collings, Mary Wattle
In the Presence of Elizabeth Smith

(The Year 1807) Page 255

No. 763 William Augustus Branstock of this Parish Widower & Jane Wilks of the parish of St Botolph were Married in this Church by Licence this 5th Day of February in the Year One Thousand Eight Hundred and Seven By me
This Marriage was solemnized between Us
In the Presence of

No. 764 James Lucas of the Parish Bachelor and Rebecca Apsey of this parish Spinster were Married in this Church by Banns this 8th Day of February in the Year One Thousand Eight Hundred and Seven By me
This Marriage was solemnized between Us James Lucas
In the Presence of

No. 765 Charles Green of this Parish Bachelor & Martha Pope of this parish Spinster were Married in this Church by Banns this 8th Day of February in the Year One Thousand Eight Hundred and Seven By me
This Marriage was solemnized between Us Charles Green, Martha Pope
In the Presence of Thomas Green

Above: Basin in The Green Park from where Charles Green made his first ascent in 1821. Westminster Abbey in background. (Public domain image via Ackermann's Repository of Arts, Vol 4, Plate 22, page 245; London, 1810)

Below: Print dated 19 July 1823 depicting Charles Green's *Coronation* balloon in the sky above King George IV's 1821 coronation walkway from House of Lords to Westminster Abbey. (US Library of Congress, Washington; repro no. LC-DIG-ppmsca-02637)

Right: Advertisement with programme details of Green's seventy-ninth ascent, at Vauxhall Gardens, Manchester on 10 August 1827. (Author's collection)

Below: State opening of the new London Bridge on 1 August 1831. Charles Green's balloon is shown in the sky above the bridge. (US Library of Congress, Washington; repro no. LC-DIG-ppmsca-02629)

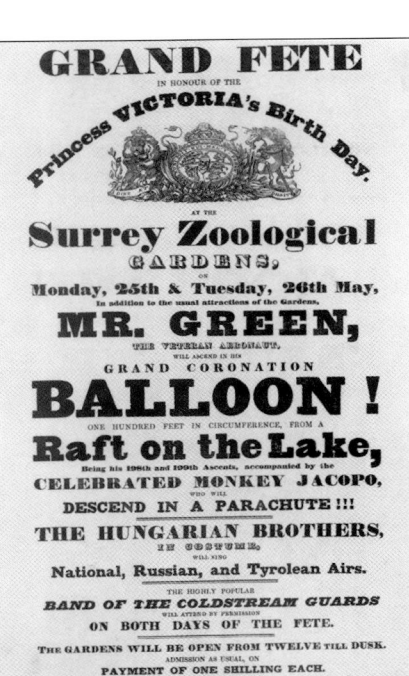

Left: Advertisement for two Charles Green ascents, with Jacopo the monkey, at the Surrey Zoological Gardens in May 1835.

Below: A print of a view of the Surrey Zoological Gardens with Charles Green's balloon overhead, in celebration of Princess Victoria's 17th birthday in 1836. (US Library of Congress, Washington; repro no. LC-DIG-ppmsca-02630)

Right: A depiction of the *Royal Vauxhall* balloon making its first ascent on 9 September 1836, carrying Charles Green and eight passengers from Vauxhall Gardens, London to Cliffe in Kent. (Author's collection)

Below: Engraving by John Henry Robinson, of the planning meeting prior to the great continental air expedition on 7 November 1836. Standing left to right: Walter Prideaux, lawyer and friend of Robert Hollond; John Hollins, artist; Sir William Milbourne James; standing on right: Thomas Monck Mason; seated left: Robert Hollond; seated right: Charles Green. (US Library of Congress, Washington; repro no. LC-DIG-ppmsca-02224)

Above: Green, Mason and Hollond flying at night over the iron furnaces of Liege and Namur in Belgium, *en route* to Germany 1836. (Courtesy of Linda Hall Library of Science, Engineering & Technology; Kansas City, USA)

Below left: Lithograph print of Joseph Louis Gay-Lussac, the eminent French chemist, physicist and aeronaut. (Public domain, via chemistryland.com)

Below right: Handbill advertisement for Charles Green's second balloon ascent, with *Royal Vauxhall/Nassau,* in Paris on 9 January 1837. (US Library of Congress, Washington; repro no. LC-DIG-ppmsca-02613)

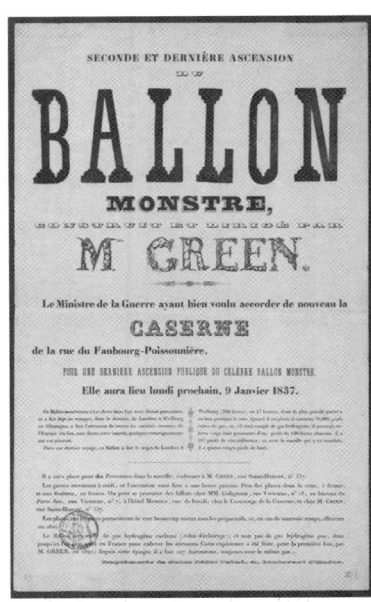

Widely described as *Nassau* over River Medway in Kent, *en route* to Germany on 7 November 1836. However, since the original states '1837' and there are more than three people in the car, it more likely depicts a flight by Green and six passengers on 30 May 1837, from Vauxhall Gardens to Wormshill in Kent, which also crossed the Medway. (Courtesy of Linda Hall Library of Science, Engineering & Technology; Kansas City, USA)

Above: Lithograph print, published in London by Gabriel Tregear, depicting Robert Cocking (centre) and his ill-fated parachute descent on 24 July 1837. Left panel shows Cocking in his parachute, being carried aloft beneath the *Royal Vauxhall/Nassau* coal-gas-filled balloon, manned by Charles Green and Edward Spencer. Right panel shows the collapsing parachute carrying Cocking to his death near Lee Green, Kent. (Wellcome Collection/Public Domain mark CC-BY 4.0: Image 36318i.)

Below left: Lithograph print of Edward Spencer, a friend of Charles Green who accompanied him on several flights, including the Robert Cocking parachute incident on 24 July 1837. (US Library of Congress, Washington; repro no. LC-DIG ppmsca-02265)

Below right: Lithograph print of Charles Green dressed in a heavy cloak, drawn from life by and published by G.P. Harding FSA (1783-1853), London, 1839. (Public domain image)

The Charles Green Salver. Originally presented to Charles by Richard Crawshay for their ascent from Norwich on 16 October 1839. This salver is now the British Balloon & Airship Club's premier international award for outstanding achievement in the sport of ballooning. (Courtesy of British Balloon & Airship Club)

Print depicting an ascent from Norwich on 24 September 1840, with *Royal Nassau* carrying: R. Crawshay; F. Crawshay; E. Crawshay; N. Bacon; W. Andrews; W. Shalders and Charles Green. (Author's collection)

Above: Lithograph print of a view looking northwards from Weymouth promenade, Dorset, depicting Charles Green accompanied by Captain R.W. Currie, flying in the coal-gas balloon *Albion*, on 12 August 1842. (Wellcome Collection/Public Domain mark: Image 36444i)

Below: Ascent of Charles Green in *Albion* balloon from Cremorne Gardens on 22 August 1842. (The Metropolitan Museum of Art, New York, USA: Anonymous painting in public domain.)

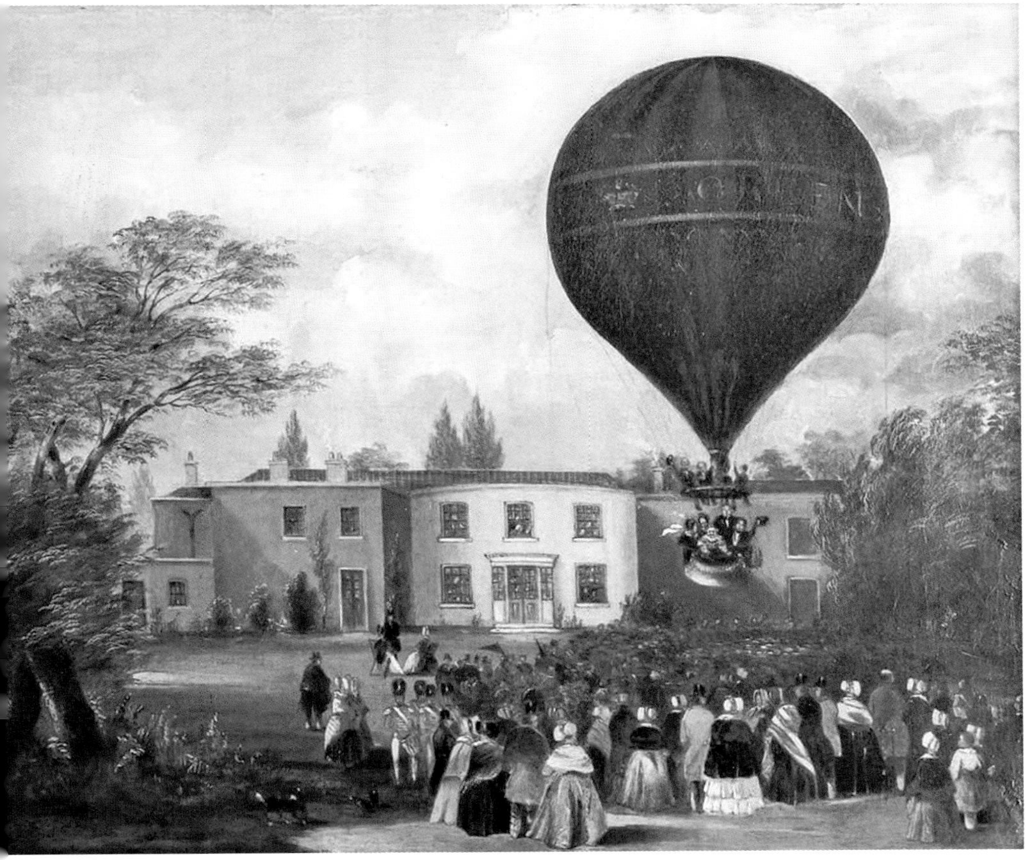

Above: Ascent of *Nassau* balloon from Cremorne House Gardens, Chelsea, London on 28 July 1845. Charles Green with twelve passengers including the popular theatrical entertainer Thomas Matthews, seen here in the car dressed in clown costume. Several passengers are seated precariously on the hoop. This image is from a painting, circa 1850, by an unknown artist. (Courtesy of Peter Woodward of 3details Art & Design)

Right: Advertisement for special railway travel to see Charles Green and balloon *Victoria* in Colchester on 17 May 1848. (*Chelmsford Chronicle*, Friday, 12 May 1848, page 3)

CHEAP EXCURSION
FROM
Ipswich and Hadleigh,
TO COLCHESTER AND BACK.

GREAT ATTRACTION!

NASSAU

BALLOON ASCENT!!

On Wednesday, May 17th,

EXCURSION TRAINS will leave IPSWICH and HADLEIGH, for COLCHESTER, as under:—

IPSWICH	1 30 p. m.
Bentley	1 50
Manningtree	2 5
Ardleigh	2 18
Colchester	2 30
HADLEIGH	1 20 p. m.
Raydon	1 27
Capel	1 36

The Train will return from Colchester in the Evening, at Seven o'clock, for Ipswich and Hadleigh, calling at all Stations.

Fares in Inclosed Carriages:—

From Ipswich and Bentley to Colchester and back 2s.
From Hadleigh, Raydon, & Capel, to Colchester, and back .... 2s.
From Manningtree and Ardleigh to Colchester and back .... 1s.

☞ First Class Carriages will be attached to the Trains if required, Tickets 3s.

N. B. Passengers producing an Excursion Ticket will be admitted to the Botanic Gardens at Half Price (6d. each), which will enable them to witness the celebrated Mr. GREEN ASCEND in his VICTORIA BALLOON.

A GOOD BAND WILL ATTEND.

JNO. S. MARTIN, Superintendent.

Ipswich Station, May 1st, 1848.

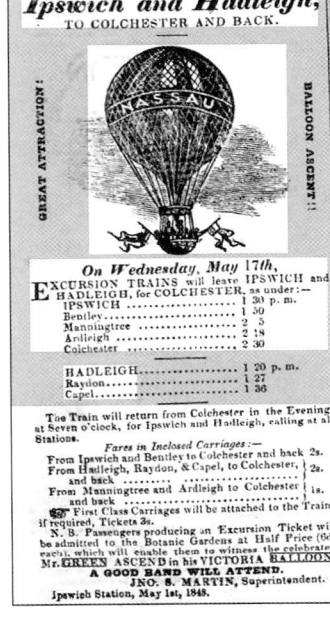

Above: Print of Charles Green's balloon *Royal Victoria* and passengers, being prepared for a night ascent in front of a large audience in Vauxhall Gardens, London in 1849. A coal-gas supply pipe is in the foreground. Engraving by Dalziel Brothers published in 1878. (Wellcome Collection/Public Domain: Image 36384i)

Below: Charles Green, with brother Henry, flying their coal-gas balloon *Royal Victoria* over the Liverpool Fancy Fair, in Prince's Park on 9 or 10 August 1849. The scene is viewed from the top of Park Nook House, home of Rev James Martineau, looking west towards the river Mersey and Wales. On the left is St Paul's church on Belvidere Road (demolished 1975) and Prince's Park Mansions are on the right edge. The image is from a lithograph print produced by John Raphael Issac; derived from a watercolour by William Gawin Herdman (1805-1882). (Wellcome Collection/Public Domain mark: Image 36443i)

The *Royal Nassau* balloon crash-lands in the Thames estuary on 29 June 1850, with Charles Green and George Rush on board. Rush is on left, in water holding on to the hoop; Green is in bow of boat, holding a boathook. (Source unknown)

The second scientific flight for British Association for the Advancement of Science at Kew. Engraved print from a Daguerreotype photograph taken by John Mayall prior to flight #498, made by *Royal Nassau* balloon on 27 August 1852. From left: Richard Nicklin, John Welsh, separated by their instrument-table from Patrick Adie: standing outside the basket and Charles Green seated right. (Wellcome Collection/Public Domain CC-BY-4.0: Image 36390i)

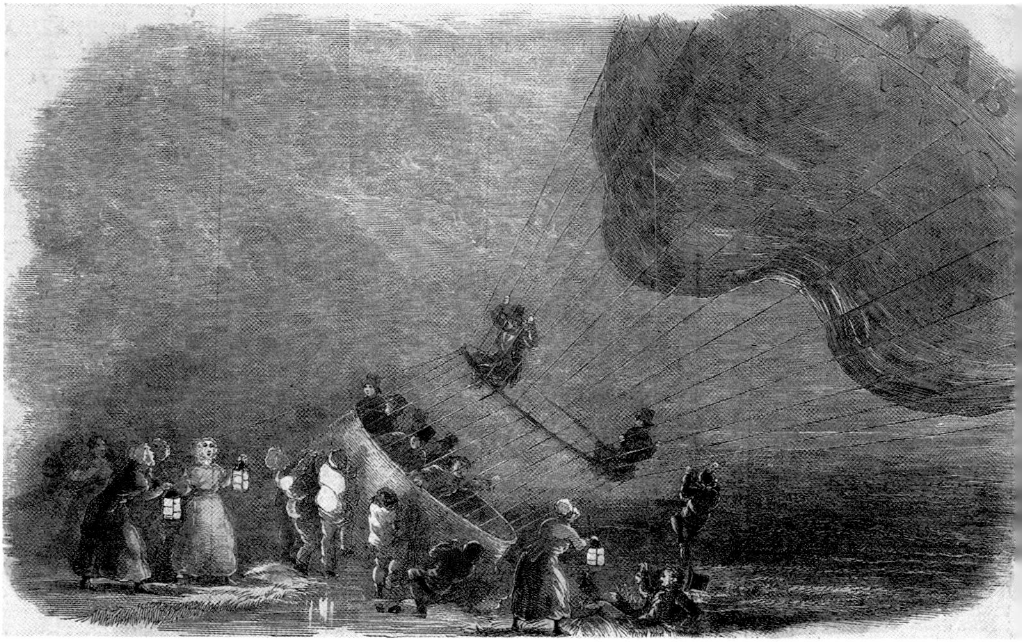

Above: Advertised as Charles Green's 500th flight, made from Vauxhall Gardens, London on 8 September, 1852 in the *Royal Nassau* coal-gas-filled balloon. In this wood-engraved image, depicting the perilous landing on Pirbright Common, Surrey, part of the name: '*NAS*' can be seen on the balloon at top right. (Wellcome Collection/Public Domain CC-BY-4.0: Image 36315i)

Below: Marriage register entry, top right, for wedding of Charles Green to Jane Culling at Islington parish church, London, on 22 May 1865. (Ancestry.co.uk)

Page 182

1865. Marriage solemnized at the Parish Church in the Parish of Islington in the County of Middlesex

No.	When Married	Name and Surname	Age	Condition	Rank or Profession	Residence at the time of Marriage	Father's Name and Surname	Rank or Profession of Father
363	22 May 1865	John Tingey	Full Age	Bachelor	Bricklayer	1 Parkfield St	John Tingey	the same
		Mary Ann Harding	D°	Spinster	—	D°	James Harding	Gardener

Married in the Parish Church according to the Rites and Ceremonies of the Established Church, by or after Banns by me,

This Marriage was solemnized between us, John Tingey, Mary Ann Harding; in the Presence of us, James Massey, Sarah Harding

1865. Marriage solemnized at the Parish Church in the Parish of Islington in the County of Middlesex

No.	When Married	Name and Surname	Age	Condition	Rank or Profession	Residence at the time of Marriage	Father's Name and Surname	Rank or Profession of Father
364	22 May 1865	Henry Cooper	Full Age	Bachelor	Paper Hanger	46 Britannia Row	William Russell Cooper	the same
		Anna Kelsey	D°	Spinster	—	D°	John Kelsey	Turner

Married in the Parish Church according to the Rites and Ceremonies of the Established Church, by or after Banns by me,

This Marriage was solemnized between us, Henry Cooper, Anna Kelsey; in the Presence of us, Joseph Randall his X mark

Page 183

1865. Marriage solemnized at the Parish Church in the Parish of Islington in the County of Middlesex

No.	When Married	Name and Surname	Age	Condition	Rank or Profession	Residence at the time of Marriage	Father's Name and Surname	Rank or Profession of Father
365	22 May 1865	Charles Green	Full Age	Widower	Gentn	Tufnell Park Rd	Thomas Green	Hatter
		Jane Culling	D°	Spinster	—	D°	Isaac Culling	Farmer

Married in the Parish Church according to the Rites and Ceremonies of the Established Church, by or after Banns by me,

This Marriage was solemnized between us, Charles Green, Jane Culling; in the Presence of us, H Bilby

1865. Marriage solemnized at the Parish Church in the Parish of Islington in the County of Middlesex

No.	When Married	Name and Surname	Age	Condition	Rank or Profession	Residence at the time of Marriage	Father's Name and Surname	Rank or Profession of Father
366	22 May 1865	Charles Moore	Full Age	Bachelor	Block Cutter	Willesden	Thomas Moore	Surgeon
		Susan Bowyer	D°	Spinster	—	10 Everilda St Hemingford Terr	George Bowyer	Butcher

Married in the Parish Church according to the Rites and Ceremonies of the Established Church, by Licence or after by me,

This Marriage was solemnized between us, Charles Moore, Susan Bowyer; in the Presence of us, George Searles, Elizabeth Franklin

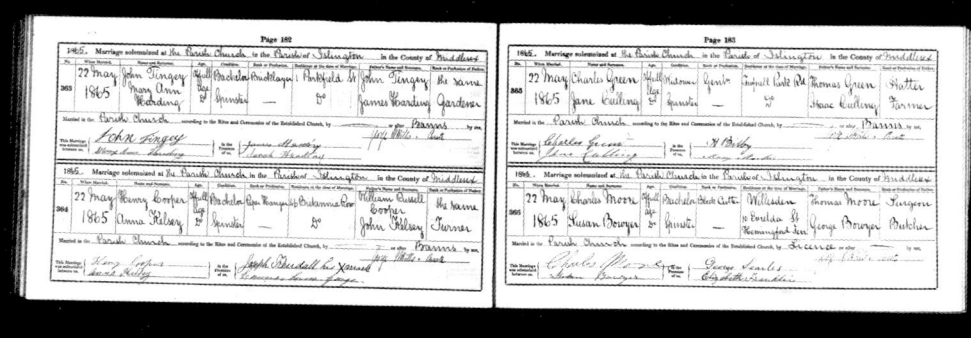

Print, dated 1865, of the French aeronaut, Wilfrid de Fonvielle, who visited Charles Green in 1868. (Source unknown.)

THE LATE MR. CHARLES GREEN, THE AERONAUT.

An engraved print, believed derived from a photograph, of 'The Old Ethereal Pilot' Charles Green, shortly before his death in 1870. (Public domain)

Grave memorial stone of Charles Green, Aeronaut, in Highgate (East) Cemetery in 2021. (Courtesy of Simon Edwards; CCA-SA 4.0; public domain)

which came in very useful since a prodigious amount of persuasive correspondence was required to put the logistical arrangements in place. For several weeks prior to departure, he was, for example, exchanging letters with the proprietors of a number of gas works in Paris to discuss costs for the supply of gas for the proposed exhibition in the city. One company in Paris apparently quoted a price per cubic foot that worked out to a total of £870 to fill the balloon - clearly unacceptable. So, with 'snail-mail' involved, it took some time to sort this item out, but eventually Mason found someone with a much cheaper rate. Furthermore, correspondence was necessary to obtain clearance for this foray over foreign territory, coming in the form of passport letters from the French and Dutch Embassies and indeed to take possession of a letter intended for the King of Holland from Mr J.W. May, the Dutch Consul-General in London - should the track of the balloon deposit them much further north than intended. Monck Mason was invaluable in this way and later made copious notes during the journey and wrote them up for publication. Mason published a small book about the voyage very shortly after their return, then he re-wrote and extended the scope of that book in 1838.

Well in advance of departure, Frederick Gye (proprietor) travelled to Paris to receive the voyagers and prepare the way for their arrival. The day before the departure of the balloon, the proprietors' sons: Frederick Gye junior and William Hughes set out for Paris, also to be on hand to assist with preparations for the ascent in the city. During their time in Paris, the English expedition would be greatly assisted by the efforts and patronage of Monsieur Jean-Francois Depuis-Delcourt, himself an aeronaut and a future founder of the Aerostatique and Meteorology Society of France. Well, at least everyone seemed optimistic about the outcome.

Although it was anticipated that the intended voyage should not take more than a couple of days, such a journey into the unknown called for some degree of caution and none more so when it came to victuals. While it was clear that, over land, within reason a landing could be made almost anywhere; if the wind were to carry the balloon out to sea - be it the North Sea or down Channel to the Atlantic - then food and water would be vital and 125lbs of stores were stowed on board.

12 chickens (45lbs; cooked).
2 tongues (cooked).
8 dozen (96) biscuits.
2 dozen (24) penny bread rolls.
1 large piece of cold, boiled beef.
1 large piece of cold ham.
Preserves.
Sugar.
2 gallons of coffee, ready-made (to be re-heated as required).
1 gallon of sherry, 2 quarts of brandy.
2 x 4 gallon kegs of drinking water.

A barometer, telescope and compass were of course essentials. With the close proximity of coal gas to the car and its occupants, it was vital to avoid the use of naked flame. The utensils carried therefore included a Davy Safety Lamp of the type used by Charles on a previous voyage. For heating up coffee, they packed a small piece of apparatus that used slaked-lime as a heat source, on which coffee or water, could be warmed up in a pot. Flares were carried, but it was intended to ignite these only in an emergency and then attached to the end of a long line trailed below the car. Cloaks, warm clothing and gloves were necessities for the time of year and for an over-night flight at altitude.

Some modification was made to the interior of the car. The centre thwart was removed and in its place was fixed a much stronger timber board with an opening over which a small windlass was secured. Between 150 and 200 fathoms (a fathom being 6 feet suggests around 1,000 feet) of rope was wound on the windlass drum and it passed through the timber plank, down through a hole in the floor of the car, to trail free below it. This was the epitome of Charles Green's famous 'guide- or trail-rope;' his low-altitude, height-regulating device. However, it could also be used - with a leather bucket tied to the end - as a water-lifting device to replenish the drinking water or top up the small water-ballast containers fixed to the outside of the car. The latter were in addition to the sand ballast carried. There seemed to be a certain amount of wishful thinking with regard to this water-replenishment idea. The total ballast weight, including men, food, equipment, sand and water, was about one ton (2,240lbs) and there was not a great deal of space left over for the intrepid aeronauts.

All was ready, then, for a voyage into the unknown.

'The tentative plan was to lift off from the Gardens on a morning when the wind was favourable for a Channel crossing and to reach Paris, or as near to the French capital as the winds would allow.'[4]

That morning came on 7 November. Inflation, started at 7.00 am, was complete by 1.00 pm. Weather conditions were uncommonly good for the time of year, with light clouds but the wind was from a favourable direction. Charles made the decision to go and it was with good humour and an air of confidence that the three men shook hands with their friends, bid them farewell, then took their seats in the car.

At 1.30 pm, Charles released the balloon and before a moderate breeze from the north-west, it ascended steadily, heading towards Kent. Its trajectory remained quite low, since the idea was to keep in this air current for as long as possible, climbing only very gently, so as not to lose it. Now we can refer to Robert Hollond's log notes for an outline of the journey.

FOREIGN EXPEDITIONS

'Monday, 7 November.
All times are London time.

1.30 pm.	Ascended.
2.48 pm.	Crossed the Medway, 7 miles south of Rochester.
4.05 pm.	Passed 2 miles south of Canterbury.'

Over Canterbury a letter attached to a parachute was dropped in greeting to the mayor.

4.15 pm.	Saw the sea.

Another letter dropped for the Mayor of Dover.

4.48 pm.	Left England, 1 mile east of Dover Castle.

It began to get very dark about ten minutes after we were over the sea, but we did not lose sight of the lights of Dover until we were nearly over France.

5.50 pm.	Over France, 2 miles east of Calais.
9.10 pm.	Barometer: 21.7 inches.
9.20 pm.	Barometer: 21.3 inches.
9.20 to 11.30 pm.	Passed over several large lighted towns. Altitude varying from a mile to two miles [5,300 to 10,600 feet]. Occasional flashes of lightning.
11.30 pm.	Over a populous district, lighted with numerous furnaces, thought to be near Namur and Liege.
12.00 midnight.	Very dark, the earth hidden from view by an unbroken mass of cloud. Stars very bright above and show extent of darkness below.

Tuesday, 8 November.

1.36 am.	Barometer: 21.0 inches
2.30 to 3.30 am.	Earth again obscured by clouds.
4.00 am.	The clouds dispersed. Saw extensive plains of mist immediately on the earth, giving appearance of water. Rustling of forest leaves produced sound like waves of the sea. Confident that we are going in an easterly direction.
5.00 am.	There is a slight appearance of daybreak.
5.10 am.	We are at our greatest altitude. Barometer: 20.0 inches.
5.20 am.	Daybreak began to dim the stars on the eastern horizon. Morning star shining brightly about 25 degrees above.
6.15 am.	Daybreak now beyond everything magnificent. We have not descended above a quarter-mile (1,300 feet) from our greatest altitude (12,000 feet).
7.30 am.	Descended.

We have had a delightful excursion and have been most hospitably received. They have lent us the military riding school [to store] the balloon.'

THE FLYING ADVENTURES OF CHARLES GREEN

It is not intended here to reproduce in detail the story of the voyage, since that can best be enjoyed by reading Monck Mason's account on one of the many internet sites where both his books (1836 & 1838) can be found. One amusing incident, however, is worth repeating.

It was approaching midnight; prior to arriving over the recognisable built-up area of Liege, Charles thought it prudent to haul in the guide-rope (trail-rope) until they were clear of the city, when it could be re-deployed again. He also wanted a little more height to keep well above the extensive buildings and factories. Reaching the city, the balloon appeared to dip a little - only slightly - but Charles, wanting to fine-tune the stability, thought he would do this by dropping just a little ballast. He decided to dump the lime that that had already been used in the coffee-heater appliance. It could then be re-charged with fresh lime. Charles picked up the appliance, rested it on the edge of the car and opened the little door of the lime-chamber preparatory to pouring it out over the side. Calamity! The coffee-heater slipped from his grasp and plummeted to the ground - hopefully without hitting anyone! No more hot coffee and when the temperature fell below freezing as the night wore on, the coffee and other potable delights froze into murky, un-appetising liquids - but at least the brandy wouldn't freeze.

Deprived of this most valuable comfort, there was now no need for the lime on which it was dependent and there was quite a lot of it left in the car. It was now just useless - but potentially volatile - ballast in a stout barrel. The lime itself was poured overboard and lost to the winds but the barrel was a problem. You couldn't just toss a heavy wooden barrel overboard without really knowing what - or who - was below. The dilemma was overcome by attaching a small parachute (they carried several with which to drop letters) to it and then tossing it out.

Now clear of the city, the guide-rope was let down again and the altitude reduced accordingly. Being only about 1,000 feet up, the travellers believed they could hear the sound of voices below and keen to make contact - even as a cry from the darkness - they shouted through a speaking-trumpet, yelling greetings in French and German, as the balloon flew silently on!

The intrepid aeronauts crossed the English Channel; France; Belgium and Germany and after passing over the prominent river Rhine, Charles decided they should attempt a landing. He had in mind the prospect of drifting on towards the *steppes* of Poland and beyond to Russia, or 'quitting while he was ahead' and landing in a reasonably populated area that would allow him to meet his commitment in Paris. He wound-up the trail rope - proven overnight to be very effective in its intended role as a safety measure - which was found to be an awkward and knuckle-scraping task because the windlass was 'of poor construction and imperfect in action.' Having completed that task however, he cast the grapnel over the side and let it down to the extent of its 120 feet-long cable. Now for the landing!

The first attempt was aborted rapidly when trees and steep hills threatened - it needed a quick heave-ho of a half-hundredweight bag of sand ballast to soar clear.

FOREIGN EXPEDITIONS

The second attempt in another valley met with similar difficulties resulting in more ballast dumping – while also putting the fear of God into two peasant-women who were spotted emerging from a wood to find this gargantuan monster towering above them. Then, after eighteen hours of flight, the third attempt was successful in gaining an anchorage with the grapnel on the end of its rope. The balloon was brought safely to a halt. As usual, help was quickly on hand but there were cries of disbelief when the travellers announced they had left London only the previous afternoon. 'Wheels' were duly 'oiled' by dispensing liberal swigs of brandy from the on-board stock and the party and balloon were well cared for. They had arrived at a location that was quite precisely identified by Thomas Monck Mason as:

> 'A field in the valley of the Elbern, close to a mill named Dillhausen in the commune of Niederhausen, about 6 miles from the town of Weilburg, in the Duchy of Nassau. Longitude 7.52 East, Latitude 50.16 North; 32 miles west-north-west of Frankfurt.'

Weilburg is situated about 30 miles east of Koblenz (spelled Coblenz prior to 1926) and the (meandering) track distance flown was at least 500 miles, at an average speed of 28mph. The distance flown by the *Royal Vauxhall* balloon stood as a record in Europe until 1907. The approximate track flown from Vauxhall Gardens in London to their destination is as follows:

> Eltham; Bromley; Foots Cray; Rochester; Canterbury; Dover; Calais; Cassel; Ypres; Courtray; Lille; Oudenaarde; Tournay; Ath; Brussels (the field of Waterloo); Namur; Liege; Spa; Malmedy; Koblenz.

A number of letters were hastily dispatched to various friends and newspapers in England acquainting them of the happy completion of the voyage. Charles, for example, dashed off a note to his friend Edward Spencer.

'From Weilburg, 8 Nov.

Dear Sir,

After a pleasant – but exceedingly cold – voyage of eighteen hours, we effected our descent near the above town, which is in the duchy of Nassau, in Germany, distant from London 480 miles. We left the English shore about one mile east of Dover at ten minutes before five on Monday, and after crossing the channel to France we passed over [the coast] about one mile to the east of Calais at ten minutes before six the same morning. In haste for the post.

I remain, dear Sir, yours very truly,
Charles Green.'

The *Royal Vauxhall* was packed up and taken to the Military Riding School in Weilburg for safe-keeping, while the travellers waited for letters from Paris. The next ten days were one continuous round of balls, dinners, concerts and amusements, held in honour of the adventurers by the civic dignitaries of Weilburg and nobility of Nassau. The town had seen nothing like it since Monsieur Jean-Pierre Blanchard landed his hydrogen balloon there fifty years earlier. Charles, of course, did not let this adoration go to his head. Well aware of his forthcoming exhibition in Paris, he spent much of the daylight hours shaking out the balloon fabric to allow the air to dry it both outside and in, examining it carefully for signs of wear and damage. Now was the time, too, to check over all the accoutrements and the car, so that there were no slip-ups later.

On the day prior to the party's departure for Paris, during an elaborate ceremony laid on by the nobility of the Weilburg area, the balloon was 're-christened,' For this, Baron de Bibra, Grand Maitre des Eaux et Forets and Colonel the Baron de Preen took the role of godfathers, while the Baroness de Bibra and Baroness de Dungern acted as godmothers for the 'christening.' The balloon was inflated with ambient air so that it filled the Meeting Hall, whereupon Charles, accompanied by eight young ladies ducked inside the giant sphere and Mademoiselle Theresa, the attractive daughter of Baron de Bibra, bestowed it with the name: *The Great Balloon of Nassau*. This was followed by:

> 'a copious libation of wine and the ceremony was concluded with a collation consisting of the remains of our stock of provisions that were un-consumed at the time of our descent.'

That same evening, at the largest inn of Weilburg, all the civic dignitaries assembled for a final grand supper. Speeches and toasts were exchanged until, with a final flourish, a crown of laurel was ceremonially placed on the head of Charles Green and his health and that of his two companions, was drunk most heartily. Charles then presented the two flags, carried in the car during this journey to Baron de Bibra to forward to His Highness the Duke of Nassau, to be preserved in the archives of the Ducal Palace in Weilburg. It is believed these are still on display in the town to this day.

PARIS, 19 December 1836 & 9 January 1837. #227 & #228

On 20 November 1836, when the festivities had subsided, Charles Green, Robert Hollond and Thomas Monck Mason left Weilburg to make their way overland, with the balloon and all its accoutrements, to Paris where Messrs Gye and Hughes had arranged for Charles to make an ascent from the city. Having travelled by air the 500 miles from London to Weilburg in just 18 hours, the journey from Weilburg to

FOREIGN EXPEDITIONS

Paris took six days and nights on the road and was uncomfortable in the extreme. The weather was atrocious with heavy rain turning roads into quagmires and the cold penetrated to the very bones – but it was, after all, November!

Having set off on the morning of 20 November, after an uncomfortable journey in a waggon, they arrived in Koblenz that evening. Robert Hollond had pressing business to attend to and by agreement with his companions, travelled overland from Koblenz to London alone. In Koblenz, Charles and Thomas purchased a chaise for their onward journey, deeming it to be a great improvement over the waggon. The balloon, however, was far too big to be carried atop the coach and so the pair decided to remove the bodywork and mount the balloon car on the carriage suspension springs. Their intention was to fix a plank of wood as a temporary seat across the car and then rig a waterproof oilskin shelter that could be raised and lowered in the manner of a *landau* hood. These modifications proved tricky and took a few days to complete, so it was 24 November before they could press on once more.

The new carriage was an unusual sight to behold and caused much curiosity at each of the places they stopped to change horses. Intended to be somewhere for them to rest and sleep beneath, the landau cover proved quite useless. Experiencing torrential rain at times, the fabric was found to be far from waterproof and leaked like a sieve. The wind made it billow and rip and the best the travellers could do was to de-mount it and stretch what was left across the car, secure the edges and crawl into the car beneath it, where they spread some straw for respite. To make matters worse, during the first day on the rough, pot-holed roads, the seat broke and deposited them in a bedraggled heap at the bottom of the car.

Stopping overnight in Thionville to escape the rain, they bought wood to repair the seat and over the next few miserable days did their best to cope with or ignore the awful weather. While sorrowfully comparing the delight of their journey by air with their snail-like plodding through the mired roads of France, they were heartened by joyful anticipation of new hospitality awaiting them in Paris.

It was 31 November when Charles and Thomas finally reached Paris, where they were greeted by Frederick Gye and Richard Hughes and their two sons: Edwin Gye and William Hughes.

The first ascent was advertised for Monday, 19 December 1836, from the military barracks in the Rue Du Faubourg Poissonniére in Paris. Gye and Hughes had planned to mount only one flight in the city but circumstances gave rise to a second ascent. The balloon was partially inflated on Sunday afternoon and by evening dominated the sky-line above the barracks. Working in teams, it took many soldiers and massive iron weights to hold it down. The weather had been poor for a few days and with the arrival of dawn on Monday, it was clear it was still dull, foggy and rainy. Gye and Hughes were urged to postpone the ascent but refused to disappoint all the spectators who had braved the elements to watch. By mid-morning the remaining gas was piped in and the result was a truly magnificent sight as the *Royal Vauxhall/ Nassau* towered above the roof-tops.

At the appointed hour, five adventurers joined Charles in the car for what was billed as his 227th ascent. One of these was no less a celebrity than Joseph Louis Gay-Lussac, the famous scientist and aeronaut from the French Academy of Sciences. Charles Green - having lived with Gay-Lussac's Law all his working life - could not have wished for a more fulfilling moment than when he and Gay-Lussac - two giants of the aeronautical world - met and flew together.

Final adjustments were made and several bottles of champagne were carefully stored and it might just be that this was when Charles confirmed his taste for champagne, as it began to feature in so many of his later voyages. Lift-off was delayed in expectation of the imminent arrival of His Royal Highness the Duke of Orleans but, after half an hour, word came that the duke was regrettably unable to attend.

Finally, at 2.15 pm, Charles released the balloon and it rose gracefully amid much cheering from the crowd. The spectacle was short-lived though, because within two minutes the balloon was obscured by fog and low cloud. Fortunately, the cloud layer was thin and after a few more minutes the travellers emerged from the cold and dampness into bright sunshine at 500 feet, where the thermometer soon climbed to 87 degrees F. In warmth and sunshine, this intrepid group saw off the champagne with numerous toasts to themselves and those below as they cruised gently along for about an hour, before an uneventful landing was made near Vitry, 5 miles south-east of Paris city centre.

It was the intention of the balloon proprietors and Charles Green to return to London after making one ascent in Paris. However, due to very poor weather curtailing the spectator view of the ascent on the 19th, it was agreed that, if the same venue could be retained, Charles would mount a second ascent on Monday, 9 January 1837. In the days prior to this second ascent, the weather improved a little and the sun even appeared on the day itself. Spectators were slow to arrive but by the scheduled time of departure, a good crowd filled the streets and queues of carriages in the boulevards had great difficulty in making it to the gates of the barracks in time.

Seven passengers accompanied Charles on this trip. When the balloon rose, it twice drifted sideways and the car hit a chimney, dislodging some bricks but Charles quickly tossed out ballast and the balloon soared upwards away from danger. Charles could be seen waving his flag to reassure those below that all was well. Once again it took just moments until the balloon was lost in cloud, through which it soon gained altitude and burst into the warmth of the sun. The rest of the 50-minute flight was uneventful and a safe landing was made near Claye-Souilly, 15 miles east of Paris.

Now it was time to return to England. Charles was particularly anxious to return since he had received word while in Paris that his mother was dangerously ill at his home.

Chapter 11

Parachute Disaster

Charles Green, Monck Mason and the *Royal Vauxhall/Nassau* arrived in London on Monday, 16 January 1837; a quiet affair, although many newspapers carried a few lines about it. Hollond and Mason returned to their own occupations and do not seem to have ventured aloft again. Robert Holland commissioned the Vauxhall Gardens resident artist, E.W. Cocks, to paint seven small scenes from sketches made during the expedition. These paintings are believed to have been for his own private collection. Hollond is also thought to have commissioned a limited-edition bronze medallion (made by William Joseph Taylor) to commemorate the voyage. Only seven or eight of these bronze medals are known to exist in public and private collections throughout the world. Charles Green received no grand public title or medal for his efforts and appears to have been satisfied to bask in the public adoration that worldwide publicity brought him for the rest of his life.

Suitably recovered from his triumphs in Germany and France, Charles was now obliged to turn his attention to helping Gye and Hughes earn a good return on their capital invested in the *Vauxhall/Nassau* balloon. This meant that Charles was duty bound to spend a great deal of his time in London, although this would be no hardship, since he could spend more time at his Highgate home than he had done for many years.

His first engagement of the new season was on Whit Monday, 15 May 1837 at the Royal Gardens, Vauxhall. With so many holiday attractions all over the city, the crowd in the Gardens, although described as 'respectable,' could have been better. However, six passengers accompanied Charles, who took off at 6.30 pm, the balloon being borne smartly along by a strong wind from the north-east.

Despite the strength of the wind, the flight went very well with the balloon passing through clouds at 5,000 feet into glorious sunshine. They made a safe landing on Mr Stacey's farm at Nutfield, east of Redhill, having flown 25 miles in only 23 minutes (65mph). It was necessary to make an equally swift return to Vauxhall, because Charles was scheduled to make another ascent the very next day (16 May).

The new day dawned with brilliant weather, the Gardens within and the Kennington, Wandsworth and Stockwell roads without, bustled to the animated sound of thousands of visitors. Vauxhall Bridge was congested by carriages and cabriolets, while hundreds of men and women on horseback mingled with vehicles of every description. Peers, knights and gentry in their finery graced the balloon enclosure along with 7,000 spectators in the Gardens. Sir George Cayley, regarded as the father of English heavier-than-air aeronautics, was one of those spotted in the crowd on this auspicious occasion. But Charles was the man of the moment and when all the great and the good had been presented to him, he called his eight passengers together for the flight.

With the wind again from the northern quadrant, upon the firing of a gun at 6.30 pm the balloon lifted off and landed safely at 7.35 pm, in Charlwood Park, Horley after a trip of 26 miles. Six of the passengers managed to find passage back to London on the *Times* Brighton coach while Charles and the rest travelled back with the balloon next day.

Flights from Vauxhall Gardens now came thick and fast for Charles Green and all were completed safely. He took six passengers aloft on Tuesday, 30 May 1837 and made a good landing at Wormshill in Kent where, after seeing most of his companions off to London, Charles and two passengers stayed to deal with the balloon. They were entertained by the Reverend R. Dolling, who gave them supper and a bed for the night. Having travelled into Maidstone next morning, Charles saw the balloon put aboard a boat to be transported back to the city, after which they caught the post coach to London in time to meet the vessel.

Airborne again on 16 June, Charles took seven passengers and they all landed safely in a turnip field on Offley Hole Farm, 3 miles from Hitchin.

In the gap between these last two engagements, Charles had the pleasure of attending the baptism of the first child of his very good friend, Edward Spencer; standing as godfather to Charles Green Spencer, born on 30 May and named in his honour. Charles Green Spencer (1837-1890) went on to establish a famous balloon manufacturing company that spanned the turn of the century.

The following week saw a spell of fine weather and Charles was airborne from Vauxhall Gardens on Friday, 23 June with seven passengers, making another safe descent in Westcroft Park, the seat of Thomas Dyer, a mile and a half from Chobham in Surrey.

For a change, Charles took the *Royal Vauxhall/Nassau* to Cheltenham for its first trip from a venue outside the capital. It was Race Week in the town where, arriving on Saturday, 1 July, he was in good time for his ascent from Montpellier Gardens on Monday, 3 July.

Mr Thomas Spinney, lessee of the Cheltenham gas works, was in charge of the inflation process, which began on Sunday evening and completed about 12 to 14 hours later. Taking off at 5.25 pm, even with six people and 900lbs of disposable ballast on board, the balloon quickly passed through a dense layer of cloud, bursting out into sunlight and pleasant warmth. Cruising along, the travellers drank a toast to the health of the new Queen Victoria, every now and then glimpsing the ground through holes in the cloud, noting, for example, that they passed over Charlton and Pittville

PARACHUTE DISASTER

Lake. A new current took them over Birdlip and into more cloud which, when the temperature tumbled, prompted Charles to decide it was time to land. Tossing out the grapnel on its rope, it snaked around in the airflow and suddenly entwined the long, trailing gas filler-tube. Made of proofed linen, the tube was ripped away at a seam just below the 'south pole' of the balloon, so that now the interior of the balloon was quite visible to the passengers. There was little escape of gas, since air pressure forced it generally upwards in the sphere and they were on their way down, anyway, so nothing to worry about.

The balloon touched down first in a corn field just within the Gloucestershire boundary. In order to avoid damaging the crop, Charles instructed two passengers to hop out then, duly lightened, he allowed it to drift to a grass field a short distance away. It was 6.50 pm and they were down safely near the village of Ashton Keynes, a mile from South Cerney. A cart was found for the balloon, and the travellers obtained a carriage from the Plough Inn, arriving in Cheltenham at 11.15 pm.

Now halfway through his flying career - one might say: 'at its highest point' - Charles Green encountered the most dangerous flight of that long career, when he carried a parachute and its inventor Robert Cocking into the air from the Vauxhall Gardens on 24 July 1837. In the air, there was nothing he could have done to avert the tragic death of Robert Cocking and it was only through his own professional skill that he managed to avoid his own death and that of his companion and friend, Edward Spencer.

But first, who was this Robert Cocking, that everyone was getting worked up about?

Described as a gentlemanly person of short stature, Robert Cocking was a professional artist specializing in water-colours and landscapes, who also had a passionate amateur interest in science. His main claim to fame arose from his single-minded pursuit of an ideal design for a man-carrying parachute, an obsession that went back to the time he witnessed the one and only parachute descent in England made by the Frenchman, André-Jacques Garnerin, in 1802 in London. Garnerin's descent was successful, but Cocking felt there were flaws in his design and was convinced he, Cocking, could do better. The fundamental difference in design was that Garnerin's was based on a flexible, dome-shaped canopy - not unlike a modern parachute - while Cocking's was an inverted, semi-rigid, hollow cone; much larger in diameter and much heavier than Garnerin's. His obsession would be the death of him.

At the time of his death, Cocking was 61 years of age and lived at 1 South Island Place in North Brixton, London. Having, after many years, come up with what he considered his perfected design, he wrote to Frederick Gye, one of the co-proprietors of the Vauxhall Gardens, prior to 1835, offering to make a parachute descent in his invention as an attraction for the Gardens. Despite Cocking applying many times, Gye did not take up this offer, claiming he did not see the merits of the invention. On one occasion, Gye visited Cocking at home and found the parlour festooned with pictures of balloons and parachutes. It was plain to see he was engrossed with the subject. At this time, Gye and his partner, Hughes, did not have a balloon vehicle of their own and the weight of Cocking's invention - or contraption - put it beyond the performance limit of Charles Green's existing balloon and anyway, when approached, Charles expressed grave doubts about Cocking's concept. He was unconvinced by the peculiar design and could not see a practical use for it.

In September 1835, when he became aware of the massive *Royal Vauxhall* balloon being constructed, Cocking wrote to Frederick Gye again, saying: 'Now you have an opportunity of letting me go up with my parachute.' He was, according to Gye, so insistent and persuasive that he began to think there might be something in the idea. Since they now owned the *Royal Vauxhall* and Charles Green was 'their' aeronaut, Gye and Hughes again put the proposal to Charles, but he remained adamant in his opposition to this particular parachute drop from the new balloon piloted by himself - Charles was probably the only person around able to handle this new Behemoth, too.

Despite Charles' opposition, Gye and Hughes succumbed to Cocking's pressure and set a date for the event. No doubt they were moved by Cocking's threat to take his invention to their competitors at the Surrey Zoological Gardens or elsewhere - although it is doubtful he would have found a balloon capable of handling his contraption. On several occasions Charles was asked to give Robert Cocking assistance while he built the parachute device, but he always refused to interfere and even suffered Cocking's anger for not backing the project. Charles was, however, in a difficult position. When Gye and Hughes made a formal arrangement with Cocking to undertake his ascent with his parachute beneath their *Royal Vauxhall* balloon, Charles (speaking under oath at the subsequent inquest) said he did not feel at liberty to refuse to fly it, because by doing so he would forfeit his connection with the balloon, which was his livelihood. When the die was cast, though, he made the best of it and took steps to ensure his own safety. Charles insisted he would not be responsible for the final release of the parachute and so a trigger-rope was set up from the balloon 'liberating-lever' to the parachute basket, so that Robert Cocking could release himself. Charles also constructed a rope pulley arrangement so that Cocking could be hauled up to the safety of the balloon if, at the last moment, he did not wish to make his leap. Frederick Gye had asked his workmen to make a rope ladder for this purpose, but Charles recommended that it was changed to a pulley-tackle, so that he and Edward Spencer could haul Cocking up, rather than Cocking being left to climb a precarious vertical ladder himself, possibly while in a very nervous state.

Charles neither sought nor received any special payment for making this ascent; he was paid his usual, contracted ascent-fee and because there were no fare-paying passengers aboard, he would not even receive his usual cut of those fares. His friend Edward Spencer, freely volunteered to fly with him when Mr Hildyard, who was to

PARACHUTE DISASTER

have gone up, declined to do so. Extracts from the contract between Messrs Gye & Hughes and Robert Cocking that follow, make interesting reading.

Construction of the parachute would be done by Cocking, but it would be paid for by Gye & Hughes and become their exclusive property. In return, they would bind themselves to Cocking and employ only him to make subsequent jumps with the parachute. Robert Cocking undertook to make the first descent without any recompense, except for the cost of carriage to recover it to Vauxhall Gardens on that and subsequent occasions. He would not be charged in any way for the use of the balloon. After the first descent, Gye & Hughes would pay Cocking 20 guineas for each of the next two jumps and £30 for each descent thereafter, as often as Gye & Hughes wished him to do so - fair wind and weather always being considered. Robert Cocking agreed to work solely for Gye & Hughes and to make descents elsewhere in England or on the continent if required to do so, also for the sum of £30 per descent. Basically, it was a case of: 'prove it works, then we will take you on and pay you.' The parachute took about three weeks to make in the Vauxhall Gardens workshop and it cost Gye & Hughes £40 (≈ £3,700 in 2023).

The inverted-cone shape of the parachute was built up from three hoops, the largest and uppermost, being 107 feet in circumference, the smallest and lowest being 20 feet in circumference and just above the parachutist's head as he stood in the basket. The hoops were made of tin tube of about 2½ inches bore. The three hoops were inter-connected by ten light spars around their circumferences, further strengthened by a series of cord-lines stretching from the top hoop to the bottom hoop, again placed around the circumferences. Significantly, to save weight, there were no cross-pieces to keep the circles rigid. This framework was covered by a fine cloth made up of twenty-two gores, each measuring 50 inches at the upper hoop, tapering down to 11 inches at the lower hoop. This results in a structure of about 6 feet in depth; with an upward angle of 30 to 35 degrees from the horizontal and a cone-surface area of 124 square-yards. A wicker basket, in which the parachutist would stand and remain there during the whole descent, is attached to the lower hoop by ropes; allowing the basket to remain upright even if there was movement of the inverted-cone canopy. The weight of the apparatus was given as 223lbs, to which was added 170lbs for the weight of Mr Cocking; a total of around 400lbs. It was expected that the parachute would descend at the rate of 10 feet per second. At the inquest it was suggested the structure weighed in at nearer 500lbs and that one of the tin tubes, damaged prior to ascent, was repaired by a splint of laths and sash-line.

Thousands flocked to the Vauxhall gardens and surrounding streets to witness this exciting spectacle.

Inflation began at mid-day and was completed by 5.00 pm Charles tested the buoyancy for his intended load and had to offload 650lbs of ballast before he was satisfied. Now he allowed the balloon to rise to about 40 feet so that the parachute could be attached by the release rope to the balloon. During this lengthy process, the gas cooled down and Charles was obliged to dispense with another 100lbs of ballast. For this he used a 50-foot-long canvas tube that allowed him to cast out ballast so that it missed the parachute.

Around 7.00 pm, Robert Cocking exchanged his coat for a light jacket; took a glass of wine with his friends; shook their hands and stepped into the parachute basket. At 7.35 pm, Frederick Gye gave the signal to lift off and the balloon, rising gently but steadily, took an easterly course. It was agreed with Robert Cocking that Charles would try to attain an altitude of 8,000 feet for the release, but upward progress slowed due to a combination of the parachute weight and its large span having a great resistance as it was dragged upwards through the air. Charles instructed Spencer to shake a 20lb bag of sand down the tube; then another bag; then yet another. They were flying over the Surrey Zoological Gardens, but only at 2,000 feet, when the ballast tube, waving about in the airflow, broke free.

Green and Spencer were able to have a shouted conversion with Cocking, since they could see each other through the lower hoop central aperture. Charles told Cocking they would have to put the sand into small bags (6lbs) so that it could be thrown well clear of the parachute; then they set about doing that task. Meanwhile, darkness was approaching.

Another 400lbs of sand went over the side. Now they struggled towards 5,000 feet and approaching Greenwich, with darkness approaching, Charles told Cocking he could not coax it any higher. Cocking shouted back:

> 'Let me know when we are at 5,000 feet and I will liberate her, as the country appears well open.'

Charles replied:

> 'I say, Cocking, how are you now?'

The answer came:

> 'I am very well and never was more comfortable in all my life.'

Green:

> 'Well, then, we are at 5,000 feet. If you will not make use of the [escape] tackle, I wish you goodnight and a pleasant descent.'

In the vicinity of Blackheath, Cocking calmly replied:

> 'Goodnight Green; goodnight Spencer.'

Just before Cocking's farewell, Charles ordered Spencer to crouch down in the car, hold on tight and take a firm grip of one of the vent-ropes while he, too, crouched down and took a strong grip of the other.

PARACHUTE DISASTER

As soon as Charles saw the liberating-lever fly open; felt the shock of release and the violent upward surge of the balloon seeking its freedom, he and Spencer hauled on their lines and gas poured out of the upper (3 feet diameter) and lower (2 feet diameter) vents. They were going up like a rocket!

To avoid asphyxiation in the cloud of gas, Charles had taken the wise precaution of loading a large, proofed-silk bag, pumped full of atmospheric air and with two, stoppered, breathing tubes attached to it. Now, crouching down, blinded by noxious gas all around them, for about nine minutes they sucked life-saving air through their tubes as the balloon went higher and higher; the gas rushing noisily from the vents. They were unable to see what happened to Cocking.

The ascent slowed. Then seemed to stop. Close the vents!

Spencer's vision cleared enough to see the barometer showing about 13.2 inches, indicating they were at 23,300 feet. However, the trajectory must have peaked even higher because, by that time, they had already been descending for several seconds. Later, Charles had time to do some rough calculations and reckoned he had valved-off 30,000 cubic-feet during the headlong rush upwards.

To bring the descent under control Charles, having now fully regained his senses and vision, emptied ballast-water from the tin vessels. The rate of descent remained rapid and with the barometer at 17.5 inches - indicating 16,600 feet altitude - and the temperature at a chilly 28 degrees F, Green and Spencer began to take stock. They were going down towards huge banks of dark cloud with only a distant glimpse of the setting sun. The loss of so much gas and the downward plunge, forced the balloon to take a hollow-dome shape inside its netting, with its lowest part more than 50 feet above their heads. It was now 8.45 pm and although it was light above the clouds, Charles realised it would be darker below and difficult to see the ground for a landing. Passing through cloud, at about 300 feet altitude Charles and Edward, thinking they were in a wooded area, frantically threw overboard every loose article they could move in an effort to stabilise the craft; sand, ropes, empty ballast-bags, cushions and the like.

After shouting out for some time and hanging out the grapnel on its rope, they heard voices in reply and unseen people below hauled on the rope to draw the balloon to a safe place for landing. This proved to be close by the village of Offham, near Town Malling, 7 miles west of Maidstone in Kent and they had been in the air for 80 minutes.

'The balloon was packed and conveyed in a cart to Town Malling, where we were hospitably treated and provided with beds by the Reverend Money who, strange to relate, informed me he was the son of Major Money, the aeronaut who, on 23 July 1783, ascended in a balloon from Norwich and landed in the sea 20 miles off Lowestoft!

At 10.30 am next morning [25th], we left Town Malling and it was only when we arrived in Wrotham that I enquired if there was any news of Mr Cocking and was acquainted with the unexpected and melancholy result of his experiment. Both Spencer and I were deeply harrowed by this news. Throughout the whole of our voyage, Mr Cocking displayed the greatest courage and fortitude and his features light and joyous, manifesting his great satisfaction that a theory to which he had devoted his last twenty-five years, was about to be triumphantly put to the test.'

Robert Cocking's parachute was found in a broken heap in a field near the village of Lee Green, three-quarters of a mile from the Eltham Road. John Chamberlain, a shepherd of Burnt Ash Farm, found the crumpled body of Robert Cocking, breathing his last gasp. At the inquest, he said he witnessed the parachute parting from the balloon and of its descent, said it 'came down with a noise like thunder.' The basket with the man inside hit the ground first then the parachute collapsed on top of him. Lifting the wreckage, Mr Chamberlain saw the man, up to his chest in the basket with his head on the ground. He heard a groan but saw no movement. No imprint whatsoever, was left upon the parched, stone-hard ground.

Thomas Grisdale, footman to Mr Norman of Burnt Ash Park, on whose land it fell, also saw the descent and said he 'heard a great crackling and the parachute seemed closed up.' He helped to remove the body from a tangle of ropes and carry him on a hurdle panel to the Tiger's Head Inn, in Lee where, although four medical men attended, it was quite clear Robert Cocking was dead.

Among the witnesses called at the inquest was Professor (later Sir) George Biddel Airy (1801-1892), Astronomer Royal at Greenwich, who had followed the progress of the balloon through a telescope. He saw the parachute detach and said although it oscillated from side to side as it fell, it did not turn over. He was aware it had already been stated the parachute kept its shape for forty or fifty seconds, but he was sure it did not retain its shape for more than four seconds before the sides folded up and flickered backwards and forwards as it fell. In his opinion, the parachute was flawed in design; 'very badly constructed and inferior in many respects to parachutes of the old construction.'

At the inquest, Frederick Charles Finch, a surgeon who conducted the post-mortem, read out a sad litany of injuries sustained by the deceased. Falling so freely from a few thousand feet, the impact on hard ground had broken just about every bone in poor Cocking's body.

Joseph William Carttar, coroner for West Kent, seemed very thorough in drawing out the facts of this sorry episode. Furthermore, when Charles was called to describe his involvement, the coroner gently reminded him that he need not say anything to incriminate himself, although it was evident from his clear and detailed statements that Charles' conscience was entirely clear. The coroner, however, found harsh words for the heartless, money-grabbing antics of Thomas Seares, landlord of the Tiger's Head Inn, where the inquest was held. The remains of the shattered parachute

PARACHUTE DISASTER

were brought to the Inn, where Seares seemed to regard it as his property, charging sixpence a person for the privilege of peering at the wreckage in one room and at Robert Cocking's body in another. After 45 minutes, the jury reached its verdict.

'We find that the deceased, Robert Cocking, came to his death casually and by misfortune, in consequence of receiving diverse severe injuries in falling from a parachute of his own invention and contrivance, appended to a balloon. The parachute is declared a deodand and is forfeit to the Queen.'

The coroner then addressed Charles Green and Frederick Gye, saying that he and the jury were perfectly satisfied with the manner in which they had acted throughout the whole of the unfortunate transaction.

It might, however, be reasonable to wonder that, if Gye and Hughes held misgivings - as Gye claimed he did, right up to the fateful morning - why did he not revoke the use of their balloon and order the event not to take place under the auspices of the Vauxhall Gardens. He had gone so far as to declare he was even prepared to return all ticket money for the ascent day, if Cocking called it off. Cancellation would have then released Charles from his obligation to pilot the craft. But hindsight is a wonderful thing.

It was 2.00 pm on 30 July 1837 when, watched by several hundred people, the funeral cortege of Robert Cocking left the Tiger's Head Inn, Lee and wended its way to St Margaret's Old Church-yard, on Belmont Hill. Here, the Reverend G. Lock conducted a burial service with family mourners, Charles Green and Edward Spencer, at the grave-side.

The sad affair was closed with a Fete at Vauxhall Gardens on 9 August, organised by Gye and Hughes, with all proceeds for the benefit of Robert Cocking's widow and family. Charles Green was engaged to take up the *Vauxhall/Nassau* balloon and donated his earnings, while the balloon was inflated free of charge by the Vauxhall gas works; this having a benefit of £50. Furthermore, no less a person than Queen Victoria herself gave the widow a gratuity of £50. Charles' 236th trip was straightforward, with six passengers. A young lady approached Charles for a seat on this flight, but he declined to oblige her and it is reported that she did not conceal her vexation at his refusal! After 50 minutes, the landing was made at Laleham, near Staines and everyone was back at the Gardens by midnight.

Henry Green's last flight on behalf of his brother was again from the Yorkshire Stingo tavern on 14 August. It turned out to be quite an entertaining day for the population of London, too, because on the same day, Margaret Graham went up in her balloon from The Rosemary Branch Gardens; landing near Kilburn, while Charles Green ascended in the *Royal Vauxhall/Nassau* balloon from Vauxhall Gardens. In a bit of lively competition, a gathering of 7,000 people was tempted into the Gardens by the reduced entrance price of one shilling each.

THE FLYING ADVENTURES OF CHARLES GREEN

Accompanied by five passengers, Charles took-off at 6.15 pm, for an uneventful cruise through a clear blue sky at a relatively low altitude. Charles' barometer, damaged during the Cocking flight, was still under repair and he did not want to venture too high without his trusty instrument. The landing was, however, far from uneventful. Lowering the grapnel, Charles prepared to land at Isleworth, but the field was devoid of potential helpers. A chance gust of wind, on an otherwise calm evening, wafted the balloon towards Hounslow, where the huge lawn in Osterley Park, the seat of Lord Jersey, was his target. Unfortunately, the grapnel snagged firmly in a large tree and the deflating balloon became fixed, like a gigantic nest, among the top branches. Mr Trumper, Lord Jersey's steward and some local gentlemen rallied to try to get the passengers safely to ground from their precarious perch, 80 feet up in the tree. Much to the amusement of all, after several attempts, Charles, Gye and Hughes managed to clamber down, followed later by Captain Polhill, but the other gentleman required a ladder before he made it down to earth, amid rousing cheers. The landlord of the Rose & Crown in Hounslow thoughtfully sent a post-chaise to convey the travellers back to Vauxhall Gardens by midnight.

Charles was back in the air on Monday, 21 August 1837, with six passengers, landing at High Ongar in Essex after a flight of 41 minutes. Upon landing, passenger Doctor Simon took Charles' pulse and found it to be 112 beats per minute. Perhaps it was not just due to the exertion of landing but that a Mr Palmer came to the site to claim £3 from Charles and berate him for damage to his corn crop!

Charles and *Royal Vauxhall/Nassau* were kept busy, with flights at the rate of one a week for the rest of the season. He also managed to pull in one flight in his own *Coronation* balloon for himself and an un-named passenger, for a fund-raising fete held on 12 October at the Surrey Zoological Gardens for the benefit of exiled Polish refugees.

Earlier that week there was much speculation when the newspapers got wind of a story that the proprietors of the Vauxhall Gardens were working on another Grand Expedition.

'Another voyage of discovery by a select party of gentlemen, who have agreed to pay the expenses of the voyage and the return of the intrepid aeronauts. It is expected that the ascent will take place in a few days and will be similar to the Continental trip of last year, the destination, weather permitting, being Scotland, instead of the land of the stranger. Mr Green is anxious to reach the extreme part of Scotland.'[1]

When the Vauxhall Gardens finally ended its season, Charles was called upon to make what turned out to be three flights from the Gas Works located behind the Lamb Inn in Salford, Manchester. An advertisement for the third of these stated it was Charles' 254th ascent, but that is at odds with his opening flight of his 1838

PARACHUTE DISASTER

season on 25 June, being advertised as his 250th. These Salford flights ought to be numbered 246; 247 and 248.

Charles made the first Salford flight with the *Nassau* only two-thirds full and due to a mishap, took up only one passenger: Charles Taylor, who had flown with Charles once before and once with Charles' son, George. There was nearly a nasty accident when the balloon fought free prematurely from the handling-party, comprised of a group of soldiers - quite useless for the job as it turned out - as well as a small number of Vauxhall-men. Without time even to load the barometer, refreshments or cloaks and with two more passengers in the very throes of handing over their 20 guineas fare-money, the balloon shot up, taking one of the handlers, Mr Carpenter, up with it, dangling on the end of his rope. Being a former 'British Jack Tar' though, Carpenter made light work of shinning up his rope into the car. In just his shirt-sleeves, he was in for a very cold ride but Mr Taylor lent him his greatcoat and Carpenter thoroughly enjoyed the rest of his free trip. Charles was probably very peeved about the loss of two fares, though. They landed safely at Poynton, near Hazel Grove.

Making his next ascent on 23 October in very unfavourable weather, he claimed in his later published report of the flight it was his 253rd ascent. The balloon was quickly lost to sight and with cloud-base at 800 feet and tops at more than 6,000 feet, it was a wet and uncomfortable flight. Reluctant to press even higher through the dense cloud; with no warming sun to be found, Charles and his companions found inner warmth by drinking hearty toasts to 'our most gracious Queen;' 'the Ladies' and 'all friends below,' before landing at Wintersett, near Wakefield.

Bad weather, cold, fog and rain continued to mar the Salford tour, causing postponement of a flight advertised for 30 October (said to be #254) until Saturday, 4 November. This day brought better weather but, when Charles and the seven passengers burst through the clouds into glorious sunlight, they found the peak temperature of 63 degrees F was infinitely warmer than on the ground.

There were plans to move on to Liverpool and Dublin but with the prospect of poor weather, it was deemed time to call it a day and return to London.

Chapter 12

Adventures with *Albion*

Charles was still tied to Vauxhall, where he and his flights in the *Royal Vauxhall/ Nassau* balloon continued to be a great money-spinning attraction. It is recorded in the Royal Garden accounts for 1838 that Gye and Hughes paid Charles £980 (≈ £89,300 in 2023) for the total of his per-flight-fee income. Excluding the Paris flight in January, Charles made 14 other flights for Gye and Hughes that year, indicating that his fee is £75 a flight. His earnings were supplemented by receiving the season's income from the sale of tickets for two seats in the balloon car - another £588 (a gentleman's ticket cost 20 guineas) in 1838. Although this sort of level did not occur every year, 1838 would have given him a total income of £1,568 (≈ £142,900 in 2023) - a tidy sum indeed - but, let's face it, despite his undoubted skill, he was putting his life on the line each time he flew. For Charles, this represented a comfortable, steady living without all the rigours of his old touring regime. Any remaining passenger seat-revenue went to the proprietors but, on many occasions, the passenger list did not fill the car to capacity and the proprietors and/or their sons were 'frequent flyers,' so it is unlikely that they paid for their seats. However, almost all the passenger lists indicate Charles would at least have received his 'two-seat' payment.

It is clear that the Garden's income, stimulated by Charles Green, with his regular flights, night-flights, balloon races and the prices charged for passenger flights was, in no small measure, responsible for keeping the Royal Gardens, Vauxhall in business when many other pleasure gardens were failing. For example, for the fourteen balloon events held during 1838, the account-book shows total income as £6,446 whereas it was only £5,544 for all the other fifty-nine ordinary entertainment nights put together.[1]

However, despite the undoubted financial and prestige success that Charles Green generated for his employers, Messrs Gye and Hughes sank into financial difficulties and in 1839 were declared bankrupt. Although the Royal Gardens, Vauxhall continued to operate for a short period under new ownership, in the 'fire-sale' auction that followed, Charles Green took the opportunity to buy the *Royal Vauxhall/Nassau* balloon. He became his own man once again.

The big event in 1838, of course, was the coronation of Queen Victoria on 28 June. On the Monday (25 June) prior to the big day, Vauxhall Gardens held a grand fete at which Charles took up the *Nassau* balloon for the first time that year and it was, by his counting, his 250th trip. It was also the first time that coal gas generated by the Vauxhall Gardens' own gas works was used to inflate the *Nassau*. A landing was made in the parkland of Denham Court, near Uxbridge, said to be one of the most splendid mansions in England. It was the home of Sir William Ellis, who entertained some local noblemen to supper and cordially invited Charles and the four passengers to join them.

Upon his return to London, Charles collected his wife and left almost immediately for Cambridge, where he was engaged by the University to make an ascent from Midsummer Green, as part of the coronation day festivities on Thursday, 28 June 1838. Prior to the event, newspaper reports widely suggested Charles Green would make an ascent in the *Vauxhall/Nassau* from Hyde Park in London on coronation day - and Mrs Graham would go up with Captain Currie in her balloon from The Green Park. For reasons that are not entirely clear, Charles neither flew in London nor in the *Nassau* on coronation day. However, Mrs Graham did indeed fly in London that day and came a cropper, too. She had to land prematurely among the dense housing of Marylebone Lane and a bystander was killed by falling masonry. The *Nassau* balloon would have been operated out of Vauxhall Gardens, if at all, but there was a newspaper story circulating that the proprietors did not open the Gardens - in contrast to other such London venues - because the government 'only' offered them £450 to do so and Gye and Hughes demanded £750. They did not get it and the Gardens remained closed. This may be why Charles took his own *Coronation* balloon to Cambridge on coronation day.

Charles flew his trip from Cambridge accompanied by his wife Ann and after drifting to and fro, they landed safely at Fulbourn, not far from the city. Mr William Ekin, mine host of the Hoop Hotel in Jesus Lane, followed the balloon in his gig and was immediately on hand to take Mrs Green back into Cambridge, while Charles dealt with packing it up. The *Cambridge Chronicle* reported this as his 251st ascent.

Charles was back at Vauxhall Gardens for its grand coronation gala on Monday 2 July. The Duke of Nassau and several foreign ambassadors who attended the coronation, watched intently as the *Vauxhall/Nassau* balloon rose into the evening sky. With five passengers on board, it tracked north-east towards Essex, but the landing place has not been identified.

Further trips came thick and fast. On 10 July: seven passengers to Sandon, near Chelmsford. On 17 July, watched by the renowned French Marshal Soult - Nemesis of the Duke of Wellington - seven passengers to Kelvedon, in Essex. On 24 July, seven more passengers to Oxted, Surrey where, upon landing Charles was grossly insulted by a farmer who tried to extract £10 from him for alleged damage to his crop - damage not only in a different field, but done by local villagers. Charles gave him short shrift!

It will be recalled that Margaret Graham had a mishap with her balloon on coronation day, 28 June, when dislodged parapet stones killed a person in the street below. The inquest on the victim, John Flay, held in the boardroom of the Middlesex Hospital, concluded on 27 July. Charles Green was a witness called by the coroner. Another witness produced 3 yards of balloon fabric he claimed was torn from the balloon and left behind on his house. Although admitting her balloon was torn, Mrs Graham said she did not think any fabric was left behind. Disingenuously, she said the fabric produced by the witness must be from Mr Green's balloon. Charles asked to see the silk and on inspection, declared that the fabric was not from any of his balloons. The jury wished to question Charles, so he was sworn in and stated that, in his opinion, the specimen produced as part of Mrs Graham's balloon was entirely unfit for such a purpose, the silk being of too flimsy a nature. Questioned further, Charles said he would not have allowed his wife or anyone belonging to him to have gone up in such a balloon and that hydrogen gas of an impure nature (as used by Mrs Graham) would be likely to render a balloon speedily unfit for use. The jury returned a verdict of 'accidental death' with a deodand of £1 on the balloon. Prior to 1846, a deodand (from the Latin *'deo dandum'*: given to God) was an ancient common law that could be applied in a situation where an animal or object, deemed to be the immediate cause of the death of a human being, was forfeited to the Crown or a fine levied in its place, to be used then for what were called 'pious purposes'. In this case it was a fine but in the Cocking case, it was the object of the parachute.

George Rush was a wealthy farmer; a frequent flyer and keen amateur scientist who, on 4 September 1838, hired Charles and the *Nassau* to undertake an attempt to fly higher than had ever been attained before. He invited Edward Spencer, Charles' good friend and a reliable aeronaut, to accompany them on this trip. The altitude attempt from Vauxhall Gardens was to be part of a two-balloon show, with Charles, Rush and Spencer in the *Nassau* and Henry Green and a Mr Stevens in Charles' *Coronation* balloon.

With over 700lbs of ballast aboard, the *Nassau* lifted off at 6.40 pm, climbing steadily into the cold evening sky. It was swiftly followed by *Coronation* but gradually their two courses diverged, with *Nassau* heading north-west then veering east while, at a lower altitude, *Coronation* went to the west. The latter came down near Edgeware - rather confusingly, with several newspapers reporting Henry Green as taking off but James Green as landing!

In the *Nassau*, Charles, Rush and Spencer managed to reach 19,000 feet - not the highest by any means - but the weather conditions were against them. At 11,000 feet, snow fell in large quantity, covering the balloon top - and adding weight - and the aeronauts' clothing with a thick layer. Then into a warmer current, where the snow melted, running in torrents off the fabric; saturating their clothes and everything else in the car. It was clear to Charles that the balloon had reached its peak, so he made a rapid descent, to land safely near Debden, 3 miles south of Saffron Waldon in Essex. Coincidentally, the site was just 5 miles from George Rush's home at Elsenham Hall.

ADVENTURES WITH *ALBION*

The breakthrough came on Monday, 10 September when Charles made a second attempt, flight #264, with only George Rush as his companion. With no half measures this time, the *Nassau* was filled to capacity, its original small car was attached and 1,700lbs of ballast squeezed on board. Take-off from Vauxhall Gardens was at 6.30 pm and the craft rose steadily, heading south. Going ever higher, they passed through clouds and snow showers. The cold became intense, numbing Charles' hands and feet while the thermometer fell to 5 degrees F or 27 degrees below freezing point. In anticipation of reaching a very high altitude, George Rush had commissioned a splendid new precision mercury barometer specially for this trip. Made by that most eminent of instrument makers, the mathematician Thomas Jones FRS FRAS (1775-1852) of 62 Charing Cross Road, London, this instrument was finely calibrated and could provide much lower readings than Charles' usual barometer. It proved its worth when its reading at the highest point of the flight showed a mere 11 inches. They had reached an altitude of about 27,500 feet, but their barometer and temperature readings would be scrutinised by Thomas Jones, whose task it would be to calculate the precise altitude attained. Upon landing, Charles confirmed that he and his companion had experienced no breathing difficulty at the highest altitude.

Meanwhile, they had to return to Mother Earth. Charles had a feeling they were somewhere close to the south coast and breaking through the cloud layer, found the balloon in the vicinity of Lewes. It was a bit of an anti-climax, thereafter, to make a straight-forward, safe landing at Southover, near the home of the Reverend Henry West, who entertained the travellers and helped them arrange transport. Mr Simmonds, owner of the landing field was rewarded with a gold half-sovereign coin for himself and a whole sovereign to buy communal beer for his labourers who packed up the balloon. Having arranged for Mr Shoesmith, a carrier, to convey the *Nassau* back to the city by Wednesday, where it was needed for Charles' next engagement on 14 September, Charles took a coach to London. George Rush travelled down to Brighton, where his wife and family were staying with some friends.

It was Charles' belief that *Nassau* could have gone even higher but, with his feeling that they were nearing the coast, he chose caution as he did not wish to risk a landing in the sea. When Thomas Jones completed his intricate calculation, he verified that Charles, George Rush and the *Nassau* balloon had reached an altitude of 27,145 feet; they could justifiably claim a world altitude record for flight in an aerial vehicle - and one that would not be beaten for twenty-five years.

There was an element of 'from the sublime to the gor-blimey' about the Vauxhall proprietors' plan to have Charles take Mr van Amburgh, a noted animal trainer, aloft with what was billed as 'a ferocious Bengal tiger,' in the car on 27 September. Quite how that would have worked is a bit of a mystery but, fortunately for Charles, in the interests of public safety the local magistrates refused to licence the event - and anyway it rained incessantly on the day planned, so it would probably have been a non-starter for that reason alone.

THE FLYING ADVENTURES OF CHARLES GREEN

Long-distance flying remained at the forefront of Charles' and Gye and Hughes' agenda and brought an un-announced flight by Charles and six gentlemen in *Nassau* on 2 October 1838. Following the van Amburgh fiasco, *Nassau* was kept inflated for a whole week in the hope of putting on a flight that would aim for Bonnie Scotland, but that scheme was thwarted by a persistent gale from the north-east. Instead, with suitable clothing, provisions and ballast taken aboard, Charles determined to make a lengthy trip and settled for heading westwards hoping, perhaps, to reach Plymouth. In the event the travellers had to cast overboard all the said clothing, provisions and ballast in order to gain height and seek out an air current that would stop them from going out to sea. And, as if that was not enough, as the balloon neared Guildford, with Charles flying low in order to try out the trail rope, 'a ruffian out for sport' took a pot-shot at the balloon with his shotgun. Pellets only just missed Frederick Gye's face; several struck his oilskin cap and others rattled loudly on the taut balloon fabric!

In the end, it was not possible to reach Plymouth and they had to settle for a landing at Bishop's Waltham, 8 miles north of Fareham. With everything packed up they all headed off to Portsmouth for an excellent dinner at the Crown Inn. So much for the Scottish adventure - it never did come off.

On the matter of wind-currents, Charles wrote to the Meteorological Society of Great Britain, where his letter was read out at its first meeting of the season, held at the Mechanics Institution in London on 14 November 1838. Commenting on the variety of currents over England, he expressed the opinion that, at a great altitude - from 3,000 to 14,000 feet - a current from the north-west generally prevailed throughout the year, without reference to what the wind was doing nearer the earth. He found this constant upper current carries his balloon at the rate of 6mph, while a lower-level current will carry him at 30mph. Charles informed the Society that during one of his ascents from Liverpool (in 1827), he entered the constant current at an altitude of 14,000 feet and descended into a lower, south-east current at a height of 12,000 feet; the former carrying his balloon at the rate of 5mph and the latter at the rate of 80mph. The greatest speed he had ever travelled was 97 miles in 58 minutes (100mph) and his speed has often been from 60 to 80mph.

At this time, air balloons were rightly considered state of the art technology, but there was a new, rapidly emerging, technology on the ground and this came in the form of the steam railways. Charles was quick to embrace this form of transport, in order to help him move around the country more quickly, particularly after his descents. From now on, if at all possible, Charles made use of the railways - rather than coach and horses - to both take him to and from venues. The first time this scenario appears is after his flight in *Nassau* from Cheltenham on 23 April 1839.

George Rush had again hired his friend Charles and the *Nassau* for this trip and the pair, with Richard Hughes junior also on board, covered 100 miles on a zig-zag track in about 4 hours. The reason for George Rush organising the trip was reported as:

'The scientific gentleman [Rush] who accompanied Mr Green is now trying an experiment preliminary to the establishment of a line of balloons between Cheltenham and London, so as to supersede (if possible) every mode of travelling.'

In what is almost certainly the world's first attempt to establish a passenger-carrying airline, they landed safely at Hazeley Heath, near Hartford Bridge. It was 2 miles from Hartley Row (now Winchfield) station, the interim terminus of the London and Southampton Railway Company's line. The railway originated at Nine Elms, London and by the date of this flight had reached Hartley Row/Winchfield. Its next section towards Southampton opened in June 1839.

A quite sublime story now unfolds. George Rush first obtained a chaise from the White Lion in Hartford Bridge and with the packed balloon, the party drove to Hartley Row station. Having seen the balloon coming down near his station, the stationmaster despatched a person hotfoot to inform Mr Green that 'he would have engine power ready to convey him, his companions and balloon to London.' This splendid offer was duly accepted and paid for by Mr Rush and an engine and carriage conveyed them the 39 miles to Nine Elms station - the London terminus - which, being a stone's throw from Vauxhall Gardens, they reached after a journey of just an hour-and-a-quarter. The rate of travelling by balloon was 22mph and the rate by railway was 32mph. But what a great way to travel!

Around this time, John Hampton was still treading his own accident-prone aeronautical and parachuting path with his *Albion* balloon and despite financial difficulties, managed to keep going until 1850. Hampton was declared insolvent in a debtor's court in London on 2 March 1840, although having been in prison since November 1839 anyway, he was ordered to be discharged. We shall see later that Charles bought Hampton's balloon *Albion*, but Hampton acquired another and returned to his aeronautical occupation.

With the exception of Charles Green, it was not only aeronauts who found themselves in choppy financial waters. During the summer of 1839, the writing was on the wall for Gye and Hughes at Vauxhall Gardens. It can be seen that from August 1839, Charles stops flying *Nassau* and makes his ascents from other venues using his own *Coronation* balloon. Gye and Hughes continue operating at Vauxhall until 5 September, then they are declared bankrupt. The Gardens continued to operate, but in the hands of a series of lessees, although they still continued to lay on balloon events, which remained a popular attraction for the public.

For Charles, the year 1839 closed with a trip from Norwich with Richard Crawshay of Honingham Hall, Norfolk, who became a staunch friend. Arriving in Norwich on 8 October bad weather delayed the flight until 16 October, when the pair set out in *Coronation*. The trip was quite uneventful, apart from a cat being dropped - rather appropriately - over Catton in a basket with a parachute attached. They landed safely at Trunch, on the north Norfolk coast, 1 mile from the sea. Mr Crawshay commemorated the trip and showed his gratitude to Charles, by commissioning a silver salver to be made and presented to him as a gift. This salver was beautifully engraved with scroll patterns, a depiction of the balloon and the inscription:

> 'Presented to Mr C. Green by his friend Richard Crawshay to commemorate their ascent from the City of Norwich, October 16th 1839.'

This very salver has become highly prized by the modern aeronautical world. It passed by bequest to the Royal Aeronautical Club (RAeC), which was formed in 1901. In the mid-1980s it was, along with some other silverware, about to be declared surplus to requirements and sold off to raise funds for the Club. However, the renowned balloonist and constructor, Don Cameron, who represented the British Balloon and Airship Club (BBAC) at the Royal Aero Club, proposed that it should be put to a much better use as a trophy for ballooning achievement. The RAeC Council agreed and sold it to the BBAC for £1,000 which was less than half its true value. Since then, the Green Salver - as it became known - has been the premier award of the BBAC and given only for exceptional flying achievements or services to ballooning. First presented in 1988, its inaugural recipients were Per Lindstrand and Richard Branson for the first crossing of the Atlantic by a hot-air balloon - a feat dreamed of by Charles Green but one which, sadly, he was unable to achieve.

During November 1839 newspapers across the country[2] reported that Charles was planning and making calculations for a new, huge balloon with which he could cross the Atlantic from New York to England. From his experience, gained while making 275 ascents to date, he said that if this balloon reached sufficient altitude, it would enter a continuous current of air from the north-west that would carry it over a great distance. Furthermore, he expressed the opinion that, in relation to his German flight and long distances: 'had it not been for the need to have the [*Nassau*] balloon in Paris by a specific date, I could have proceeded to Turkey on that course.'

It was in the context of his theory about the winds of the upper atmosphere that brought about Charles' lectures at the Polytechnic Institution at 309 Regent Street, London in March 1840. The demise of Gye and Hughes returned to Charles what might be called 'his freedom' to be his own man again and 1840 seems to have been a time for reflection on what he wanted to do in the future. Under the titles: 'Novel Experiment in Aerostation'[3] and 'London Exhibitions, The Polytechnic Institution'[4] were published fascinating articles outlining Charles' theories and touching upon his trans-Atlantic idea - in which he considered such a journey, possibly of 4,000 miles, might be achieved in a flight of four days. The articles describe in simple detail Charles' use of 3-feet-diameter model balloons incorporating miniature clockwork-operated machinery in the car, driving fans (two-blade propellers - that would equate to 6 feet in length on his proposed Atlantic balloon), by which the direction of flight could be changed in the vertical and horizontal planes. They go on to describe how this both worked and could be applied to long-distance flight. Tantalisingly, there is also one passage that states: 'Mr Green has kept a regular log of all his numerous voyages,' Would that the log could be found!

The year 1840 also saw the Gye and Hughes bankruptcy laid bare in court between May and November and in advertisements for the sale of assets at the Gardens. Among all the large sums being bandied about, even Charles was mentioned as being owed £56-9s-6d. What was much more significant, however, was the auction of the Great *Nassau* Balloon, which took place at the London Auction Mart, St Bartholomew's Lane on 17 July 1840. After a spirited bidding competition, it was knocked down to Charles for £500 (≈ £41,900 in 2023).

From a flying point of view, 1840 was quiet for Charles, with him making only three ascents that year. The first of these was from Cremorne Gardens and marked the beginning of a few years' association with this popular pleasure ground. Although in modern times the gardens of Viscount Cremorne's London house are just a sliver of their past grandeur, located around the original ornate gates in Lots Road; in the 1840s they extended north from the Thames bank at Chelsea to the King's Road. In 1831 the Viscount's estate was sold to Charles Random, who styled himself 'Baron de Berenger' and he turned it into a commercial sporting club venue. In 1845 the site again changed hands, being acquired by Thomas Bartlett Simpson, who sub-let it to James Ellis who, in turn, opened up the house and gardens as Cremorne Gardens in the style of a typical - in those days - pleasure garden complex, presenting public attractions such as concerts, restaurants, firework shows, dancing, walks in the beautiful gardens - and balloon events.

Charles did not begin his flying year until 17 August 1840, when he went up from Cremorne, in his *Coronation* balloon with Richard Graves MacDonnell. MacDonnell was the honorary secretary of the Friends of Poland section of the London Literary Association and the event was a Fete with proceeds for the benefit of Polish refugees. The trip was not without incident. A very high wind bowled them along at 60mph; the grapnel snatched viciously on landing, smashing the hoop to which it was secured and the car slammed hard into the ground time and again over a distance of a mile-and-a-half. The two occupants held on for grim death, smashing their way through bushes, fences and over ditches. Gradually the escape of gas slowed the brute down and they could finally emerge from the car, close to Rainham in Essex. Mr MacDonnell suffered bruises and cuts to his hands, but Charles was badly knocked about. Both men were able to organise the packing up and return to London, where Charles admitted to taking some hard knocks, but praised his companion's courage. Through the newspapers, he hastened to assure the public that his injuries would not prevent him from continuing his chosen

THE FLYING ADVENTURES OF CHARLES GREEN

career. In a letter to the *Morning Post*, Mr Duckworth Nelson, the surgeon who attended Charles said:

> 'He is not so seriously hurt as first thought; the whole amount of his injury being a dislocation of the first and second bone of the sternum, with a simple fracture of two ribs on his right side which, after the perilous exploit of yesterday evening, is as trifling an accident as could well have occurred.'

They were tough in those days!

Recovered from his injury, Charles took the *Nassau* first to Norwich for another trip with Richard Crawshay and five of his friends on 24 September 1840, then he made an ascent on 6 October from the Commercial Gas Works in Ben Johnson Fields, Stepney, with Thomas Monck Mason and two Naval officers. They landed safely at Mereworth, near Tonbridge.

During 1841, Vauxhall Gardens re-opened under new management for a summer season that included six big fetes. Charles Green was engaged for some of these and he only made flights from Vauxhall that year. All, bar one, of these were in *Nassau* and he took several members of his family aloft that summer. His first trip was on 12 July 1841 and among the passengers was Mrs Green, his daughter-in-law - presumed to be George junior's wife. George junior accompanied his father and other passengers on 26 July and again on 30 July when Charles' brother (un-named, but possibly Henry) was also among the passengers. On 23 August it was the turn of Ann Green, Charles' wife and his father, Thomas - who was in his 70s - to take to the skies. The flying season ended on 30 August with passengers that included Ann Green again and a lady named Joanna Forrest, described as a portrait painter from Bloomsbury. Captain Robert Currie, who was making his own thirty-third ascent, Doctor Locock, Mr Dally and one unidentified gentleman made up the party and they landed safely at Navestock, near Brentford. The men had to hike 6 miles to the nearest Post House, but the ladies gave up after a couple of miles and sought shelter in a wayside cottage. They were very rudely received and told to 'be off.' Fortunately, the reception at the next house was infinitely more hospitable and they were fed and watered in front of a blazing fire to await the return of the men and a chaise. A couple of months later, on 23 October, there was a report of a case in the Crown Court in Chelmsford. William Millbank aged 23, a labourer was prosecuted for the attempted theft of 7 yards of cotton velvet; 7 yards of blue calico and 7 yards of tasselled fringe - the property of Charles Green, taken from the balloon car when it landed at Navestock. It is thought that Charles attended court and maybe put in a good word for the defendant, because the court accepted that Millbank had no felonious intent and being of previous good character, the jury acquitted him.

ADVENTURES WITH *ALBION*

It was on 30 August, in a newspaper advertisement, that the Vauxhall lessees: 'respectfully announce that this long-celebrated scene of entertainment, will close for ever in the course of the ensuing week and on Friday the Vauxhall will positively close its doors for ever.' This turned out to be untrue, but management of the Gardens changed hands frequently thereafter.

For some time, the good people of Dublin had tried to persuade Charles to make a balloon ascent in the city but were unsuccessful. On 2 September 1841, Mr Steele of Dublin, reported to the newspapers that he had received a letter from Mr Green in which he said it was impossible for him to visit Dublin this season. Charles said he was keen to try out the *Nassau* and its trail rope, on a journey from Dublin, across the sea and as far as possible over the Continent. The reason for his reluctance to visit Dublin was that neither of the two Dublin gas companies could offer him sufficient quantity of gas for the inflation of the *Nassau*. He travelled to Dublin in May 1843 to investigate what might be possible but although some hydrogen balloonists - e.g. Richard Gypson - made flights there, there is no evidence of Charles Green making ascents from that city.

His final ascent of 1841 was to take place from the Citadel in Hull in *Coronation*, on 28 September. Temporary pipes were laid from the gas works, across the river to the Citadel, but the pressure was poor and inflation proceeded very slowly. So slowly that it was not ready at the appointed time and the weather deteriorated. High winds and a heavy rain storm blew in. Thirty hefty men tried in vain to hold the bucking monster but it tore from their grasp. The balloon was impaled on buildings and battered incessantly until all the gas escaped and the fabric and netting lay in tatters. The event was cancelled and what was said to be ascent #284 did not count. Newspaper reports are not entirely clear about the final state of *Coronation*, but she appears to have been very badly knocked about.

The demise of this most recent incarnation of *Royal Coronation* seems to be confirmed, since she does not feature in Charles' subsequent flights. His next event was not until 27 June 1842, when he flew *Albion* for the first time, solo from the Albert Saloon in the gardens of the Royal Standard Tavern, in Hoxton, London, to Crayford. The *Albion* balloon was previously associated with the aeronaut John Hampton - who made thirty flights with her - but he got into financial difficulty and was in debt. Although there is no clear evidence, it seems likely that Hampton put *Albion* up for sale to help clear some of his debts and that Charles Green took the opportunity to buy the balloon from him. The precise date of acquisition by Charles is not known, but could have been during 1841, since he made his first flight in *Albion* in June 1842. The intervening period can be explained by a newspaper snippet of Charles' ascent on 4 August 1845, which stated that the balloon used was: 'formerly Hampton's *Albion*, but Mr Green considerably enlarged it to hold 25,000 cubic-feet of gas and [it measures] 50 feet in height.'

This latest flight was billed by Charles as his 'first and only ascent this season, in preparation for his intended voyage across the Atlantic Ocean in *Nassau*.' So, Charles still nurtured his grand aim but, in the event, he could find no financial backers. It also transpired that it was not Charles' only ascent that year.

The supply of a sufficient quantity of coal-gas for Charles Green's *Royal Vauxhall/Nassau* balloon - which had a capacity for a stupendous 70,000 cubic-feet of gas - presented difficulties to several towns that craved a visit by this magnificent aerostat. Weymouth was one venue where Charles used his smaller, 25,000 cubic-feet *Albion*, a balloon of 113 feet circumference and 50 feet tall from basket to peak, for that very reason. Charles and his companion for the event, Captain Robert William Currie, late of the 3rd (Prince of Wales' Own) Dragoon Guards, travelled by railway train from London to Southampton, then by coach to Weymouth, arriving in the evening of Thursday, 4 August 1842. His balloon and accoutrements had arrived a few days earlier, having been carried as cargo aboard the Weymouth & Southampton Steam Packet Company's paddle steamer *Rose* (Captain Thomas Harding), which docked in Weymouth from Southampton on Tuesday, 2 August. The balloon ascent, the first ever seen in Dorset, was to take place on Friday, 12 August, the day after Weymouth Races finished.

The original take-off enclosure was sited in front of Pulteney Terrace, but Charles' tests found the pressure of gas in the 3 inch main pipe at that point to be quite inadequate for filling *Albion*. The enclosure was therefore moved to a site adjacent to the town gas works in Westwey Road, where temporary pipes were laid from the gasholder to the balloon.

Supervised by the Gas Works Chief Engineer, Mr Bowman, extra gas was generated from 5.00 am and inflation of the balloon with coal-gas began at 2.00 pm, with take-off being scheduled for 4.00 pm. Admission to the inner *sanctum* to watch the inflation process cost one shilling (≈ £5 in 2023) and 1,500 people squeezed in to see this technological wonder of the age. Meanwhile, at least 200 vehicles/carriages had passed through the turnpike toll and it was estimated that at least 8,000 people were milling about the streets of Weymouth, eagerly anticipating the ascent.

In sunshine and to strains of the town band playing '*God Save The Queen*,' the balloon lifted off at 4.55 pm, drifting across the bay towards Holworth cliffs. Fifteen minutes later it was lost to sight as it climbed above the clouds, heading North-East. During their 15 mile passage inland, the aeronauts had the first aerial view of the White Horse of Osmington, a hill figure depicting King George III on horseback, carved into the chalk. The heat of the sun having helped to expand the gas, the balloon reached a maximum altitude of 10,000 feet before the two aeronauts descended safely 1½ hours later in the valley of the River Piddle, a few miles south of Bere Regis. Upon landing, the travellers were entertained to 'a sumptuous dinner' at the home of the Reverend Richard Waldy, rector of Affpuddle, whose generous hospitality extended to providing a carriage into Wareham. Green and Currie reached Dorchester by 1.00 am next morning and after fresh horses were found, were back in Weymouth by

8.00 am Charles Green even found time to relax a little by watching a friendly game of cricket between teams from Dorchester and Weymouth, before returning first by coach to Southampton and then boarding a train service on the recently completed railway line between Southampton and London.

1843 saw Charles making ascents from a real mixture of venues. It was not really a tour, but took him from Brighton to Belfast via Birmingham, from a quite late start in July to just the first week of September. It was at the end of the flight from Birmingham to Coleshill on 17 July 1843, the first trip of the season in *Nassau*, that we find Charles using the railway to return to Birmingham. Having packed up everything after landing, the 13½ hundredweight (cwt) bulk of *Nassau* and car was taken to Coleshill station on the Birmingham to Derby Railway from where it was forwarded to the city by the 'luggage train' next morning. In the meantime, Charles and his four passengers procured a chaise and four in which they returned to Birmingham by 11.00 pm on the day of ascent.

From 1843, the Cremorne Gardens were briefly owned by Renton Nicholson (1809-1861) a businessman, theatre impresario and editor of *The Town* and other magazines, who also opened, in 1842, the Garrick's Head and Town Hotel, in Bow Street, London. Nicholson was pretty free with his money - a trait that would see him in financial trouble before long - and arranged a lavish three-day fete at Cremorne: 'Nicholson's 1,000 guinea Fete' at which Charles was a star attraction in *Albion* on 1 August. He still liked the idea of trying to cross the English Channel, too, if the wind was favourable, but was thwarted on his ascent from Stepney gas works on 12 August and again when he went up from Brighton on 17 August - both trips with *Albion*.

Now, it was across the Irish Sea to Belfast, but by land and sea rather than balloon. The gas works storage could not handle the requirements of *Nassau* but could manage *Albion* and Charles made two ascents from the Botanic Gardens, one on 2 September 1843 and the other, one week later. The first trip was made solo and did not go far, landing near Craigavad House on Belfast Lough. The second trip went very little further and had a local man, Mr Montgomery, as passenger but both trips were otherwise safe and unexciting.

Only one flight was made in 1844, this being in *Albion* on 25 September with two passengers from Stepney to Horton, near Epsom and reported by several newspapers as Charles' 300th ascent. This is believed to be incorrect and is a further example of the way in which the flight numbers, around this period, have become a bit of a mess once again. The data in Appendix 1 will help provide some semblance of order.

In sharp contrast, 1845 was a very busy year indeed for Charles, during which he made seventeen flights from the Cremorne and Vauxhall Gardens and the Albert Saloon, but he was only able to achieve such a high number of ascents by operating from London venues alone. It is also recorded at this time that 'the aeronaut Charles Green lived at Naomi Cottage, North Hill [Highgate] in 1844/45.'[5] The use of the words 'cottage' and 'Highgate' might tie-up with a visiting card found, printed: 'Mr Charles Green. Aerial Cottage, Highgate.'[6]

In 1846 he flew on no less than twenty-three occasions in various parts of the country as well as in London, but this was an exceptional tally. This is why - in relation to the 500 flights Charles claimed to have been made in total - it has been pointed out before, that he would need to have made an average of sixteen flights every single year of his thirty-one-year career - but there is no evidence that this happened. It should also be borne in mind that the window for making flights was often just five or six months in any given year, with very few exceptions. Coupled with pure logistics and the discrepancies that continue to be uncovered in the numbering scheme, it does little to diminish the feeling that the claim for a total of 500 flights is going to be questionable. Coming immediately after the claimed flight #300, for example, Charles told reporters that his very next flight, on 5 May 1845, was #305. Yet, three months later, after six more flights, he again told reporters that his flight on 4 August 1845 was, guess what - #305!

Nevertheless, the trips came thick and fast that summer and the actual milestone 300th flight took place on 23 June 1845, from the Albert Saloon of the Royal Standard Tavern in Hoxton. Charles took W. Selwyn Morris a surgeon from Wye in Kent along for the ride in *Albion* and they landed safely at Brooks Meadow in the parish of St Paul's Cray.

Having turned 60 years of age, Charles had taken many a hard knock during the course of his flying career and he could clearly display quite stoic personal qualities when the need arose. For example, on 7 August 1845 (#306) he gave one of his many aerial-firework displays from the Cremorne, solo in *Albion*. When the fireworks - suspended on a wooden frame well below the car - had finished, he continued the flight, landing in a turnip field on Mr James Russell's farm, 2 miles from Farningham in Kent. On this, his twenty-first night flight, take-off was at 10.45 pm, and the landing sometime around midnight. Naturally at that hour there was no one around to lend a hand, so Charles wrapped himself up and slept the night away in the car. Waking bright and early, he walked to Mr Russell's house to arrange help and transport. Mr Russell gave him a hearty breakfast and saw him on his way back to Cremorne, which he reached at 3.00 pm, the next day. Another typical example of Charles' demeanour can be seen on the trip from Cremorne in *Nassau* on 28 July 1845. The gas quality was so good that he was able to take twenty-one paying passengers aloft for tethered 'flights,' before setting off on the 'away' flight with no less than twelve passengers aboard. Among these was Thomas Matthews, a popular theatrical clown in the mould of Joseph Grimaldi, who was allowed to belt-out some of his best-loved comic songs, while Charles held the balloon finely balanced above the heads of the crowd. Renditions of the comic ballad '*Hot Codlins*' and other popular airs, floated from the car before it, too, floated upwards into the evening sky. As part of the 'on-board hospitality' Charles always carried a supply of wine and he had grown rather fond of champagne, since it crops up in the reporting of many of his post-Paris flights. How better to make several boisterous toasts to HM Queen Victoria; Prince Albert and many other worthies, than by cracking open a few bottles of bubbly at a great height on this trip - Charles certainly had style, too. This flight landed on Tottenham Marshes following which, all the travellers were hospitably entertained to a hearty meal by Mr H.L. Small, a director of the Northern & Eastern Counties Railway Company, whose mansion was close by.

He always remained conscious of his duty to the paying public. Many are the times he made flights in weather conditions that were both uncomfortable to him in the extreme or, quite frankly, dangerous. But the show must go on and yet he seemed to relish coping with discomfort and taking on the elements in a calculated risk. He certainly earned his reputation as the best in the business. Despite being begged not to go; anxious to satisfy the drenched crowd, Charles set off at 10.00 pm on a solo flight from Cremorne in *Albion* on 18 August 1845, in the midst of a torrential rain storm. With a display of bravado, he waved an umbrella with one hand and his hat with the other, as the balloon rose into a leaden sky. With water streaming from the balloon into the car, after an hour in the darkness he used his safety lamps to help him to what, miraculously, turned out to be a safe landing near Harrow. His clothing was sodden and he reckoned a ton of water had poured from the balloon fabric during the voyage, filling the car, submerging his instruments and making his food and wine completely unfit for consumption!

Charles had certainly used up seven of his proverbial nine lives with close encounters with the Grim Reaper and the latest of these occurred on 20 August 1845, with *Albion* in high wind conditions. Again, he went ahead because he did not wish to disappoint the public. His trip began at the Royal Gardens, Vauxhall, London where he was booked to put on an aerial firework show - and indeed it was judged by all to be a great firework display. He published the following account of his latest brush with death.

'When I left the Gardens, the wind was blowing west-by-south and the balloon went almost due east. The wind continued in the same quarter during the whole of my voyage. I crossed the Surrey Zoological Gardens and then bore away towards Greenwich, Charlton and Woolwich. The balloon then carried on across the river [Thames] to the opposite shore, in the direction of Purfleet. I could then have made a landing several times had the wind dropped and had I had assistance but, knowing that if I attempted a descent with such a boisterous gale and no help at hand, I should have been carried on to the river. The balloon continued its course until it arrived at Gravesend Reach. I kept at very low altitude; in fact, at times, I was close to the shore and near to the water's edge. On arriving at a place which I think is marked on my map as Osterland, [a hamlet between Lower Stoke and Allhallows on the Hoo peninsula, near the Medway estuary] I endeavoured to descend, but the balloon dragged along the land for at least 3 or 4 miles, the wind still blowing with great violence from the west.

At length, the car got into a deep dyke and I thought I should be enabled to empty the gas. I opened the valve and then got out of the car, but no sooner had I set my foot on the banks of the dyke, than I became entangled in the netting. A gust of wind suddenly drove the balloon out of the ditch and I was dragged along the ground until eventually the car became secured in another, deeper dyke. All this time, I was endeavouring to dis-entangle myself from the netting. For the first time in my life, I became alarmed for my safety. I thought of my knife, and happily found it in my pocket. I then began cutting away with the greatest vigour but, because the cordage being of peculiar fabric, I experienced the greatest difficulty in liberating myself. The oscillation of the balloon was frightful but I held on firmly knowing, from the escaping gas, that its ascending power was gone and that it would only drift by the wind. At length, becoming exhausted, I let go my hold and the balloon went away; car, grapnel, barometer and all my other meteorological instruments seemed to be disappearing in the direction of Queenborough [Isle of Sheppey]. It was dark, but I could clearly see the balloon make three or four halts before it became invisible.

I then made my way along the banks of the river, towards Gravesend without meeting a soul or finding a house open, a distance of 18 or 20 miles from the spot where I parted company with the balloon. I arrived at Gravesend at about half past six o'clock and to prevent being annoyed by the questions of strangers, I preserved a strict *incognito*. The balloon has since been discovered off the flats at Cliffe, 8 miles from Gravesend, torn to pieces.'

Charles and the balloon returned to London by river steamer. Rumours of his death were greatly exaggerated and the story was dictated to a reporter who visited Aerial Cottage in Highgate. Here, he found Charles in bed with a severe cold, his hands bandaged and with multiple bruises, claiming not to be injured but 'being affectionately attended by Mrs Green.'

The balloon was very badly damaged and the wreckage, described as 'a mass of rags,' was displayed at Cremorne so that it could be inspected and gawped at in awe, by the public. However, on closer inspection by Charles, he considered it was not a write-off. Meanwhile, his busy season continued in *Nassau*, including one flight on 1 September when the gate takings were donated to Charles 'as a benefit for the loss of *Albion*.' That *Albion* emerged from the pile of rags, is confirmed by *The Globe* newspaper.[7]

'The *Albion* balloon, partially destroyed last year during a storm, on the flats at Cliffe, below Gravesend, has been restored during the winter [of 1845/46] by Mr and Mrs Green.'

The *Morning Post* described it as the 'new remodelled elegant *Albion*.'[8]

One of the remaining highlights of this eventful year, came at the Cremorne on 8 September 1845. *Nassau* was prepared for a voyage at 6.30 pm, with ten passengers, including Charles' wife and his son George. Prior to the main event, Charles laid on some tethered ascents. One of these involved a tethered ascent by a lady and gentleman, accompanied by a young leopard, the property of a Mr White, an animal trainer. The leopard was said to be 'of docile temperament,' but in order to overcome the potential problem of a wildcat going berserk in his car, Charles arranged for his spare, smaller car to be attached below the regular one. He would have control in the upper car while the big pussycat could do what it wanted in the car below! Watched in astonishment by 12,000 people, in the end, it all went off without incident and Charles could add another notch to his reputation.

The year closed with yet another reminder that Charles still yearned to have a go at crossing the Atlantic. The London correspondent of the *Boston Traveller* (USA) wrote:

> 'Mr Green, the aeronaut says that if a sufficient sum was secured for him, in England and America, to remunerate him for making the aerial voyage, he would go to Boston in the steamer and taking advantage of the westerly winds, would return to England in his balloon.'[9]

1846 was going to be an even busier year for Charles Green, but it did not kick off until the end of April. It did, however, confirm that *Albion* was back in service again.

If one wished to mark a great occasion in fine style, then there was still nothing to match a balloon for sheer spectacle. If, too, one wished to have the best aeronaut for such a celebration, then Charles Green was your man. This veteran of more than 300 ascents - but with many more still to come - returned for his last trip from Stamford on Thursday, 30 April 1846 - his 319th flight. There was to be a great festival at Burghley House in celebration of the coming of age of Lord Burghley, eldest son of the Marquis of Exeter and Charles Green was the star attraction at a grand dinner and ball.

'But for the amusement of those who did not wish to participate in the dinner or ball, Mr Charles Green was engaged to ascend in his balloon, the *Albion*, from the gas works in the town.'

The railway came into play again for the return to London following a solo trip from Bury St Edmunds to Lindsey, in *Albion* on 29 May 1846. The packed-up balloon and Charles were taken to Colchester where he caught the night train to London. Two weeks later, on 11 June, he was back in Suffolk again, making a solo trip in *Albion* from Ipswich to Bucklesham. This engagement was part of the celebrations for the grand opening of the Eastern Union Railway line from Ipswich to Colchester, the first line to open in Suffolk.

Back in London, Charles became involved in the festivities and entertainment surrounding the visit to England of Ibrahim Pacha, eldest son of Muhammad Ali, the ruler of Egypt and Sudan. Ibrahim Pacha was a General in his father's army and conducted successful campaigns all over the Middle East for many years. In failing health, Pacha embarked on a tour of Europe and in mid-1846 arrived in England where he was received with both respect and curiosity. Charles laid on an ascent in *Nassau* from the Cremorne on 29 June in celebration of the anniversary of Queen Victoria's coronation and the visit of Ibrahim Pacha. Charles' reputation was evidently known to Ibrahim Pacha, who insisted upon visiting the Cremorne to witness the start of this voyage. Charles, with eight passengers on board, lifted off at 8.00 pm and drifted across London. Passing over Buckingham Palace was the signal to crack the champagne and toast the health of HM The Queen; His Excellency Ibrahim Pacha and of course, many others. One of the passengers, Mr van Buren, was in excellent voice and suitably lubricated, gave a hearty rendition of '*God Save The Queen*' and led the singing of several popular airs, too. The landing was made at Stanford Rivers, Ongar, but as a consequence of the boisterous wind conditions, *Nassau* suffered an extensive rent in her fabric.

Speaking of the restorative powers of champagne, it was mentioned by the *Morning Post* of 18 August 1846 that, upon landing after a flight in *Nassau* from Cremorne to Southgate, near Barnet, the previous day 'champagne was then drunk and vehicles provided back to London.'

Charles was back on the road again, with events held in Bath and Bristol during July and Leeds, Exeter and Bridgewater in August. These venues could be reached from London by railway now and with engagements in London also interspersed among them, Charles could organise the travel quite easily. For example, trains first came to Bridgewater in 1841 with the opening of the initial section of the Bristol to Exeter railway (B&ER). Bridgewater was the terminus for a year, then the railway was first extended to Taunton in 1842 and then on to Exeter. Connecting to London via Bristol and the Great Western Railway, Bridgewater was about 193 miles from London.

Charles' son George assisted his father with both construction, repairs and the management of his flying programme but, for himself, he also constructed a new balloon of 36 feet diameter and 70 feet tall. He was keen to try out ballooning on the Continent and the press soon announced that George:

> 'Having just completed a new balloon, leaves London on Monday 27 July 1846 by the General Steam Navigation Company mail and steam ship *Princess Royal*, for Hamburg, for the purpose of ascending in the principal towns of Germany.'

August 1846 saw Charles and Henry Green go head-to-head in what were billed by the Cremorne as two-balloon Races between *Albion* and *Coronation*. This indicates that Charles' old *Coronation* balloon still existed - although clearly not used very often since its accident in September 1841. For these races Charles used *Coronation* and Henry used *Albion* and they took place on 16 and 24 August.

The season finished with quite a flourish, with the bizarre spectacle of *Nassau* being towed along the Thames and passed over bridges - complete with her passengers! Keen to squeeze in one more ascent, Mr Ellis, proprietor of the Cremorne, engaged Charles for 2 October 1846, but the Imperial Gas Company near the Gardens insisted it needed three days' notice to generate enough gas to inflate *Nassau*. Ellis, publicly committed to the event, organised inflation at the Vauxhall gas works, located between Vauxhall and Westminster bridges. Charles agreed that if this was not done, the balloon would never be filled in time to participate in the event - which would really make the punters very unhappy. Inflation completed at Vauxhall, *Nassau* and its car were placed on a barge, which was then towed by the *Starlight* steamer up river to Cremorne Gardens. The bridges had to be passed by allowing the balloon to rise from the barge and be man-handled, using her anchoring ropes and many sweating men, over Vauxhall, then Battersea bridge. It was a strange sight to behold until the Cremorne Gardens, which extended to the river, were reached safely. Charles Green, Mr van Buren and six other gentlemen were in the car for this extraordinary journey. Once they reached Cremorne's quay, *Nassau* was taken from the barge and hauled by brute force, still with the passengers aboard, into the Gardens. Here, in the middle of a heavy rain shower, they finally lifted-off and made a very uneventful flight to Leytonstone in Essex.

Chapter 13

Bombs Away! & The Brunswick Escapade

Charles Green had taken some business risks in his time but his latest venture was not one of the more successful ones; in fact, one might say: 'it bombed!'

The self-styled 'Captain' Samuel Alfred Warner (1793-1853) had a history of weird inventions involving things that made a BIG BANG! His background is obscure but he claimed to have had dealings with explosives while working for a London chemist in 1819. Allegedly, after service in Portugal in some unknown capacity for Pedro I of Brazil - who briefly ruled Portugal during 1826 as Dom Pedro IV - Warner returned to England and tried to sell his ideas for 'revolutionary secret military weapons' such as: 1. the 'Invisible Shell' and 2. the 'Long Range'. The former relates to an explosive under-water, mine-like device. However, it is the latter invention which involved Charles Green. Basically his 'Long Range' idea was for explosive projectiles (shells) to be dropped from un-manned balloons upon an enemy, at a distance of 5 or 6 miles - beyond the range of existing artillery methods. He pestered the British government about these inventions, but refused to reveal technical details until he was assured many thousands of pounds of public funds would be paid to him to trial and develop the secret weapons. The government was sceptical but did not actually tell him to 'get lost' and eventually he was told to 'put up or shut up.'

During 1846 he was allocated a relatively tiny sum to cover the cost of a trial of the 'Long Range.' Warner approached Charles Green to build for him a balloon that would be large enough to carry aloft 45 x 10lb projectiles, which were spherical, explosive artillery shells. The shells would be mounted on racks attached to an un-manned car beneath the balloon. The bombs would be released by delay-timer fuses lit at take-off. Different time-lengths could be arranged so that a certain quantity of shells might be dropped at different intervals. The shells would fall by gravity. Additionally, the shells themselves required time-delay fuses, all of which must have been a nightmare to sort out.

Charles calculated that, to meet Warner's specification, a balloon of 33 feet diameter with an 18,800 cubic-feet gas capacity was required. The cost of the silk was estimated at £300 and of course there would be other expenses. Warner obtained approval to spend up to £1,300 and two War Office commissioners, Lieutenant-Colonel Chalmer and Captain Chads of the Royal Engineers, were appointed to assess the viability of the invention from the trial. After some difficulty in finding a venue for the test - Spithead was one location mentioned - Warner came up with Haywood Park, a few miles north-west of Rugeley, on Cannock Chase in Staffordshire. The Lords Anglesey and Ingestre owned large tracts of land in the locality that were ideal for testing purposes.

Warner was instructed to arrange his invention so that fifteen shells dropped at 4 miles from the start point; the next fifteen shells dropped at 4½ miles and the final fifteen shells dropped at 5 miles. The first aiming point was to be a prominent oak tree, known as the Fair Oak and trial day was set for 28 November 1846.

On the day of the trial, Captain Chads and Lord Ingestre - the latter representing Warner's interests - took up position near the tree (brave - but was it wise?). Lieutenant-Colonel Chalmer and Lord Anglesey took their position a quarter-mile closer to Haywood Park. By 3.30 pm, nothing had happened. By 4.15 pm, Lord Anglesey was fed-up and trotted off towards home. Five minutes later, he was called back because the balloon was spotted by all parties - but still nothing seemed to happen. To the observers, the course of the balloon seemed to be very much off the mark. At one point there was thought to be 'a rushing noise,' heard in the distance to the east of them but, with darkness falling, it was too late to investigate the noise or look for evidence that the shells had done their work. Everyone agreed to meet next morning.

Searching proved fruitless, but it was established that the balloon had been recovered and taken into Rugeley. An account, published in the *Patent Journal & Inventors Magazine* describes what happened.

'About 4.00 pm, Lord Ingestre proposed to drive Captain Chads and Lieutenant-Colonel Chalmer in his chaise, through Rugeley, on their way back to *Beaudesert*, (the family seat of Henry William Paget, 1st Marquis of Anglesey) south of the town. Having ascertained that the balloon was at the Bell Inn, they stopped by to obtain information. On going into the town, they were met by a person called Brown whom Lord Ingestre appeared to know and were told by him that the balloon had fallen to earth half-a-mile from Rugeley last evening. Labourers who found the balloon were offered and accepted, a guinea from this person who claimed the balloon was his property. There was already some alarm in the town because nine of the shells and some fuse-powder, were found still attached to the car when it landed. There was also speculation - erroneous - that someone went up with the balloon and was killed. In view of this, the police took charge of it until Lord Ingestre and his party arrived on the scene. Lord Ingestre informed the police that he was a magistrate and there was nothing improper about the matter and to release the balloon to the person claiming it.

THE FLYING ADVENTURES OF CHARLES GREEN

This person then took Lord Ingestre and Captain Chads to a stable and showed them the balloon, explaining in detail and very knowledgably, about its ascent. When Lieutenant-Colonel Chalmer entered the stable he instantly recognised 'Mr Brown' as Charles Green, the famous aeronaut. Charles said it was his property and named *Albion* [sic]. Charles was passing himself off as 'Brown' in order to keep secret all proceedings about a balloon being in the district. Satisfied, Lord Ingestre said his gamekeepers would search for other projectiles and he and the commissioners were going to press on to *Beaudesert* for a meeting with Lord Anglesey, at which the whole matter would be discussed.'

The outcome was that Lord Ingestre (Warner's nominee) considered the experiment a failure, an opinion that Lieutenant-Colonel Chalmer and Captain Chads fully shared.

Several days later, Lord Anglesey's head-keeper found eighteen unexploded shells. Five fell within 100 yards of where the balloon came down. Eight more were found 3 miles from Haywood Park and five more turned up a mile from where the balloon started. There was evidence that some of the eighteen shells that had exploded on the ground penetrated up to 4 feet in the hard, gravelly soil.

Thus ended the experimental trial of the 'Long Range,' about which much public interest was roused and £1,300 of public money spent. The subsequent official report, containing a detailed description of events was considered, by those who read it, 'to be almost beyond credibility.'

While Warner was widely regarded as a charlatan, it has to be said that his idea had some merit. Dropping bombs from the air on the heads of a distant enemy was pretty forward thinking but, sadly, the idea was too advanced for its time. Technology and military thinking back in 1846 were just not ready for it. Balloons of that day lacked the directional freedom that would only materialise from the invention of the internal combustion engine - as powered dirigibles and aeroplanes would, in due course, demonstrate to the world. Captain Warner was harshly - but understandably - written off as a charlatan and his inventions consigned to the scrapheap of history, but it was not quite the end of the story. The matter reared its head again in the House of Commons in June 1847.

There was a debate in the House to determine whether to appoint a secret committee to examine the matter further. Robert Hollond, Charles' friend from his German voyage days, was now an MP (Hastings) and Charles had written to him to put him in the picture. Hollond said there ought to be an investigation by a committee, so that the matter would be proved as 'a gross imposition.' He contended that Captain Warner had not conducted the experiment in the way he said he would. Robert Hollond took the opportunity to defend Charles Green's view of the affair, quoting from his letter.

'Mr Green was called upon by a gentleman [Captain Warner] to prepare a balloon capable of carrying 400 to 500lbs weight, for which he was to receive the sum of

BOMBS AWAY!

£250 [≈ £21,300 in 2023]. Mr Green constructed the balloon and it transpired that it was for the purpose of Captain Warner's Long Range. The experiment, as far as Mr Green could judge, turned out a decided failure. He had not received payment for the balloon nor was any of his apparatus returned to him. Mr Green believed the whole subject was a gross deception upon the public and he hoped that a Select Committee should be appointed to enquire into the subject and that report would, no doubt, expose the whole deception.

Mr Green asked Mr Hollond to convey to the House that he was no party to the deception and that he regretted that his name was brought before the public in connection with such a [bad] business. Mr Green petitioned the House to order Captain Warner to restore his apparatus to him. As for the balloon experiment, Mr Hollond remarked that while dropping shells from balloons had long been talked of among aeronauts, he hoped the House would appoint a committee, as he felt perfectly satisfied that the Long Range was a deception.'

The concept of dropping bombs by air was not going to go away and in early-1849, press reports from Vienna claimed that Venice - under siege by the Austrians - was to be bombarded by balloons. Five balloons, each 23 feet in diameter and capable of carrying five bombs, were under construction at Treviso for this purpose. Ominously, too, the English aeronaut Henry Coxwell, during a ballooning tour of Germany in 1849, also demonstrated to and discussed with, his hosts in Berlin this method of waging war from the air.

It will be recalled that Charles said the balloon recovered after the experiment was named *Albion*. It may be that Charles used *Albion* and only partially inflated it to handle the altitude and payload required for the experiment. Charles also stated that 'it was so mutilated he could do nothing with it' and research certainly shows that Charles did not use *Albion* publicly after the date of the Long Range trial.

The demise of *Albion* appears to be confirmed by Charles' use of his new 30,000 cubic-feet capacity balloon called *Victoria* at public events, the first of which was from Cremorne Gardens to Little Waltham, Essex on 24 May 1847. This balloon, constructed with red and yellow striped silk from Sopers, could carry Charles and three passengers. Curiously, Mr Soper, the manufacturer of the silk, wrote to Charles only the previous week regretting that he would be unable to witness *Victoria's* maiden flight as he would be at his country house. He added that if Charles should come his way he was cordially invited to supper. By strange coincidence, *Victoria* flew over Mr Soper's farm, descending only a mile from his house. The travellers knocked on Mr Soper's door, reminded him of the offer of supper and were most hospitably entertained until it was time to catch the mail train from Chelmsford back to London.

The railway network burgeoning throughout Britain became important to Charles, helping him move around the country quickly; amply demonstrated, for example, after his successful trip from the cricket ground in Leicester on 30 June 1847. With the balloon track crossing the Midlands Railway then the Trent Valley Railway, it was convenient for a landing to be made just half-a-mile from Brandon station on the London & North Western Railway, which they rode into Rugby to await the mail train to Leicester. His ascent in *Victoria* from Old Vauxhall in Birmingham on 21 July saw him land at Lindley Hall, near Hinkley. He and the balloon were taken by chaise to Tamworth station on the Derby railway line, from where he travelled to Derby station and thence back to Birmingham. Back in Derby on 26 July for an ascent with *Victoria*, he landed at Willoughby-Waterleys, where the vicar conveyed both him and the balloon to Leicester station to catch a special train for Derby.

Charles had to be on his toes in July, since he was committed to an ascent from Cremorne in *Nassau* on 5 July, followed next day, 6 July, with an ascent in *Victoria* from Parker's Piece in Cambridge, in honour of the visit to the city by Queen Victoria and Prince Albert. Prince Albert was being installed as the Chancellor of Cambridge University and visited several colleges, while the Queen graced a huge Fete organised by the Cambridge Horticultural Society. In the evening there was a banquet for the Royal guests in Trinity College. Charles was late arriving in Cambridge from Cremorne but inflation was completed by 5.00 pm. Accompanied by his wife and Mr John Gedney of Redenhall near Harleston, the spectacle presented by the balloon suited the grand occasion and a safe flight was made to Bottisham.

Although several other aeronauts operated in London and the provinces, for Charles Green, 1847 continued to offer a varied diet of ascents. He still enjoyed the patronage of Cremorne Gardens, where his reputation attracted the curiosity of high-ranking dignitaries, such as Prince Louis Napoleon on 16 August. Charles took up the *Nassau* balloon, usually with full passenger loads - ten passengers on 19 July, for example - and interspersed these with engagements in other towns and cities, using his more-handy *Victoria* balloon, for example in Cardiff on 9 August and Nottingham on 19 August. He and Henry Green put on balloon races from Cremorne; Charles dropped monkeys, 'Jocko' and 'Garnerin,' by parachute and he renewed association with the Vauxhall Gardens for night ascents, during which he let off aerial firework displays. It is noticeable in subsequent years that Charles moved away from the Cremorne and more towards Vauxhall, probably because the newer aeronauts such as Gale and Gypson were being regularly engaged by Cremorne. It could also, though, have something to do with the fact that Mr Ellis, the proprietor of the Cremorne, was taken to court by Henry Green in December 1847 for non-payment of a £5 fee that Charles had agreed with Mr van Buren, assistant manager of Cremorne, in the absence of Mr Ellis. Charles was due to make an ascent in *Nassau* from Cremorne on 13 September, but due to bad weather he refused to fly. He was asked to make another attempt the next day, 14 September, but declined because he was due to make a flight in his smaller balloon 'somewhere in Wales'. He suggested that his brother Henry make the trip in *Nassau* at the Cremorne instead and that was duly agreed. Charles told Mr van Buren he usually paid Henry £5 to go up and when he asked him to pay Henry that sum, Mr Van Buren agreed. However, when Mr Ellis returned from his business trip to Paris, he countermanded Mr van Buren and refused to pay up. Charles and Henry took Ellis to court and at the hearing in the Palace Court on 3 December, won their case. It seems likely that Charles took umbrage over this incident and parted company with the Cremorne. The *Morning Advertiser* and *Daily News* newspapers reported that Charles told the court that he was due to make an ascent in Wales on or about the 14 September and that he made a subsequent ascent at Cremorne after that. Curiously, having actually made an ascent in Cardiff on 9 August, no further newspaper advertisements or articles have been found for any balloon ascents relating to Charles anywhere in the country between 6 September 1847 and 17 May 1848 - which, although not beyond the realms of possibility, would be a very unusual omission indeed on the part of the British press.

In 1848, as was his custom, Charles began his annual flying programme in May, first at Colchester on 17 May, then Beccles on 31 May. Around this period, among an increasing number of competitors, George Gale was operating at the Cremorne; John Hampton was flying in Ireland and Henry Coxwell was touring Belgium and Germany. Richard Gypson was still going strong and so too was Mrs Graham. There was even a new upstart named Richard Green - Charles made it clear that this fellow was no relation of his - operating a balloon called *Rainbow*, owned by William Wadman of Bristol - who made ascents at Bath; Bristol; Gloucester; Worcester and Lincoln in mid-1848.

Following his ascent from Windsor on 15 June, Charles landed at Mixbury in a seed-field owned by Mr Painter, who demanded five shillings for damage caused to his crop. Charles coughed up 'with indignation.' This was followed by ascents in *Victoria* at Derby; Oxford; Leicester and Bath, all of which were completed in complete safety. Things went awry though at Maidenhead on 1 August. The wind was particularly violent and buffeted *Victoria* during the inflation process. After the gas was shut off, the lower balloon valve detached itself and gas escaped rapidly. *Victoria* became unmanageable and the ascent was cancelled. Repairs were made in time for *Victoria* to appear in Aylesbury on 8 August without any further problems.

Charles continued his merry way round East Anglia with a successful ascent at Sudbury on 13 October, before moving on to Halsted for its Gala Day on 27 October. As the inflation of *Victoria* progressed, a raging storm blew in, causing the event to be postponed to the following day. In fact, the storm increased in ferocity, battering and rolling the balloon incessantly, threatening to sweep it away from its anchor-ropes, a ton-and-a-half of iron weights and the sweating efforts of thirty or forty powerful labourers. Inevitably, with the hurricane reaching a crescendo at 11.45 am again and again the balloon lifted and rolled then, with a sudden jerk, lost the men and ropes. The hoop snapped in two, pitching men and weights from the car into a heap on the ground. The netting ripped and the fabric spilled out, splitting it from top to bottom. Poor *Victoria* was done for! The demise of *Victoria* put an end to Charles' programme for that year and he set about doing repairs over the winter.

Charles Green and faithful *Victoria* were back in business by May 1849, starting his season at Colchester on 29 May, followed by High Wycombe on 5 June and 22 June saw him at Vauxhall Gardens, London for the first of his night ascents with fireworks. From now on, London newspapers, while carrying multiple advertisements for his ascents at London venues, seemed to have tired of actually reporting the subsequent flights although, since these were all pretty similar and flown without incident, they hardly made sparkling news. Consequently, most of his Vauxhall flights now have little or no detail beyond the advertised date. On the other hand, provincial newspapers, were still besotted with aerostation and continued to report such events in their own territory in great detail - and some London newspapers picked up those stories, too.

The summer of 1849 followed much the same pattern as previous years; Leicester on 27 June; Stowmarket, 6 July; Aylesbury, 11 July, interspersed with night ascents with firework displays at Vauxhall Gardens, all greatly assisted by railway travel. Despite this relatively mundane programme, July 1849 turned out to be an eventful month in more ways than one.

Newspapers across the country carried reports that one of the Green family disappeared over the Bristol Channel during a balloon flight from Cardiff. Great care was taken to make it clear that it was not the celebrated veteran aeronaut Charles Green, but was someone related to him.

Richard Green, standing in for William Wadman who fell ill, took off from Cardiff in *Rainbow* on 9 July. The balloon was found next morning on Godney Moor, near Glastonbury in Somerset but, despite items of clothing being found in the car, there was no sign of Mr Green - he had disappeared. A coastguard claimed to have seen the balloon near the surface of the sea with the car dragging through the water. Shortly afterwards, the balloon was seen to shoot up into the sky and drift off towards the Somerset coast. On 17 July, the body of a man, aged about 30-35, 5 feet 5 inches tall, with black full-whiskers and dark brown hair, was found by fishermen on a shoal between Flat Holm and Sand Bay, off Kewstoke, north of Weston-super-Mare. Unable to be positively identified due to decomposition, an inquest concluded from possessions found on it, the corpse was that of Richard Green. It was surmised that Mr Green had misjudged his ballast requirements and dropping into the sea, had decided to vacate the car and swim ashore but, overwhelmed by local rip-currents, was drowned in the process. Relieved of his own weight, ironically the balloon rose and was taken over land by an air current at a higher level. Richard Green was laid to rest in Kewstoke parish churchyard; the tenth aeronaut to lose his life since 1785 - and not the last. Aware of speculation, Charles wrote to several newspapers.

BOMBS AWAY!

'[*The Times* report] having induced many persons to imagine that the person lost was either my son or my brother, may I beg you to intimate that he was not of my family nor in any way related to me.'

The next fearful event was not long in coming and this time it did involve Charles. He was about to use up another of his nine lives but escape to live another day.

'Serious Accident to the *Nassau* Balloon' ran the headlines. Charles was back in London and billed to make an ascent in *Nassau* from Vauxhall Gardens on 25 July 1849. Due to a spell of bad weather, the trip had been postponed from the 23rd and the weather still had a stormy feel to it. The Gardens were crowded to watch Charles take on board a full passenger load of ten persons. He was accompanied in the car by his wife, Ann; his nephew William's wife; a Miss Green - un-related - a Miss Gascoyne; Richard Crawshay and Charles Thomas Pearce. Seated on the hoop and clinging to the ropes above their heads were four more gentlemen: Mr Stephens, Captain Ondre, Mr Ferrar and William Green.

Lift off was smooth and steady but, after heading into the sky between the Surrey Theatre and the Elephant and Castle Tavern, *Nassau* took a downward attitude so marked that it was in danger of crashing to the ground. It was as if gas was leaking from the balloon at a prodigious rate. Realising something was wrong, Charles emptied bags of sand over the side as fast as he could but while the rate of descent slowed, it did not stop. Passing over West Square on St George's Road - still sinking - it was clear that, unchecked, it would soon hit some buildings. Indeed, the car struck the house fronts of numbers 94 and 95 London Road with such force that three gentlemen on the hoop - Captain Ondre, Mr Ferrer and William Green - were catapulted from their perch on to the (fortunately) flat roof. The fourth, Mr Stephens, looked like falling but managed to hold on the rigging and regain his balance. In the car, Charles himself was only saved from an untimely end by the lightning-quick reaction of his wife, who grabbed hold of him as he staggered over the side. All the ladies helped pull him back in and crucially, recovered the valve-line released by the flying William, to whom it had been entrusted at take-off. Handing over this vital rope to Charles, he exclaimed: 'Thank Heaven, we are saved!'

Now relieved of the weight of three men, the balloon shot up into the clear sky and went on its serene way. Charles - coolness personified - took stock of the situation and promptly opened a bottle of sherry, presenting a glass to each of the ladies and gentlemen and taking a large draft to fortify himself. Toasts to the success of the trip and to 'absent friends' complete, the voyage continued for another hour. An easy descent was made half a mile from Erith church, near Purfleet, where a large crowd gathered to assist the travellers make a safe landing. The party, now eight in number of course, were conveyed to a local hotel for refreshment, returning in an omnibus to Vauxhall Gardens by 2.00 am next morning.

THE FLYING ADVENTURES OF CHARLES GREEN

There were some aches and pains taken home, too. When thrown against the edge of the car, Charles took a hefty thump in the chest which bruised his ribs and awakened an old rib injury he suffered in a balloon mishap some years earlier. He was quite sick and in some pain during the journey home. Charles' wife also seemed to be in a state of shock and had a nasty contusion on her face. Upon impact with the house, Miss Gascoyne fell against the grapnel, cutting her forehead slightly, while William's wife bruised one of her hands quite badly. As for the three 'flying' gentlemen, miraculously, they all escaped unharmed. 94 London Road lost 12 feet of coping stones and part of its chimney and similar damage was caused to the property next door.

When pressed by the newspapers for an explanation of the cause of the mishap, tactfully Charles blamed the loss of lift on 'the peculiar electrical state of the atmosphere.' However, it was actually due to William's mishandling of the valve-rope entrusted to him. Unwittingly, he was pulling on the rope, which caused the gas to escape. Having let go of the rope when he was thrown from the hoop, the valve closed, gas ceased to escape and the situation was saved - but the outcome could have been a lot worse.

Determined to show the world that he was fit and well and that the same went for his balloon, Charles quickly laid on another show for 1 August - and this time there would be no sitting on the hoop. He arranged to have two cars fixed to *Nassau*; the usual large car in its normal position and his original, smaller, car suspended below it - a double-decker. Charles controlled everything from the upper car and he was joined there by George Rush; Mr Ferrar; Miss Orme and Miss Forrest. In addition, he had two American circus celebrities with him: Young Hernandez, a well-known equestrian performer with Astley's Circus and Richard Risley Carlisle (known professionally as Richard Risley) a daring acrobat and athlete, who had recently opened an American Bar and bowling alley business concession in Vauxhall Gardens. In the lower car were Henry Green; Mr R. David and two un-named gentlemen; eleven travellers all-told. This time all went well and once at cruising altitude, the 'in-flight' refreshment began with Charles serving glasses of sherry to everyone, before a safe landing was made at 9.00 pm near Sydenham in Kent.

The following month saw Charles Green entertaining at the huge public gathering in Prince's Park, Liverpool, known as the Liverpool Fancy Fair. It was a grand fund-raising 'Philanthropic Festival' and flower show, staged under the joint auspices of the Mayor of Liverpool and the Chairman of the Mersey Docks & Harbour Board. Its objective was to raise funds to support the Liverpool North and Liverpool South Hospitals and by raising the sum of £9,593 (≈ £1 million in 2023), it was very successful. The event lasted from 8 to 10 August 1849 and Charles, assisted by his brother Henry, flew the coal-gas filled balloon *Royal Victoria* on 9 and 10 August.

Coal-gas was supplied to the balloon through a temporary 7 inch pipe tapped into a gas main running by the southern entrance to the Park. It was reported that

BOMBS AWAY!

around 30,000 cubic-feet of coal-gas, with a market value of £7.00 (≈ £720 in 2023), was supplied for each ascent. When filled, the balloon was anchored to half-a-ton of aggregate and steadied by the exertions of twenty labourers holding on to ropes.

Take-off was at 3.20 pm on Thursday, 9 August and Charles was accompanied by his brother Henry and Councillor Fisher. There was disappointment for another aspiring passenger: Mr Luff of Murray Street who, due to lack of lifting power in the balloon, was asked to vacate his seat in the car. In overcast weather, *Victoria* climbed away to the south-east, then veered south towards Runcorn. Passing through the clouds, the travellers encountered heavy rain, hail and even snow, accompanied by thunder and flashes of lightning. For Charles and Henry these phenomena were nothing new but the experience must have been quite alarming for Councillor Fisher. At first, *Victoria* tracked across the Mersey towards the coast of Wales, but a change in the air currents sent her over Rock Ferry then south towards Chester. Due to the inclement weather and being soon out of sight of spectators on the ground, Charles decided to bring *Victoria* down to a safe landing near Sutton, between Ellesmere Port and the northern outskirts of Chester.

The second day brought much better weather and this time, Charles was accompanied by the brothers Robert and William Horsfall, who paid 15 guineas each for the privilege. It was reported that a Doctor Cripps was most anxious to take a flight and offered Charles £20 to secure a seat, but he refused to 'bump' any of his passengers. Refreshed by a tankard of porter, handed to him as he stood in the car, Charles stowed a few more bottles of porter on board, then took to the skies at 6.00 pm. Climbing to about 4,000 feet, the air current took *Victoria* towards Knotty Ash and Prescot; above the London & North-West railway line to Knowsley Park. Here, Charles began a descent to land safely at 6.45 pm near Knowsley Hall, the seat of the Earl of Derby. Servants from the Hall lent a hand to steady the collapsing balloon and His Lordship's steward invited the travellers to the Hall for refreshment. However, the brothers Horsfall, having made prior arrangements with a Mr Pemberton, who lived in a mansion close by, declined the offer and the three travellers were wined and dined by Mr Pemberton. They returned to Liverpool by 10.00 pm that night.

Charles and Henry went on to Leeds for a flight on 14 August, followed by a trip from Ashton-under-Lyne gas works as part of the celebrations for Dukinfield Wakes Week, the local textile trade's annual holiday 'bash'. Charles then had one engagement back in London on 22 August before taking up an invitation from George Rush to visit him in Norfolk so that the pair of them could make an ascent from Norwich.

Rush was keen to try out his new acquisition: an aneroid barometer which, although it did not perform perfectly during the flight, his barometer and thermometer recordings were published afterwards in the Annual Report of the British Association for the Advancement of Science. It was at 7.00 pm on Tuesday, 4 September 1849, when their balloon was seen rapidly descending from a considerable altitude in the vicinity of West Newton, near King's Lynn. Curious local inhabitants were drawn like moths to follow the monster being borne along by the wind and with the assistance of several strong harvest-men, the balloon finally came to earth in a meadow farmed by a Mr Griggs, in the picturesque village of Appleton, adjacent to the modern Royal Sandringham Estate.

Having set out in 1845 in HMS *Erebus* and HMS *Terror*, Sir John Franklin and his Arctic expedition had gone missing at some point in 1846 or 1847, during his quest to discover the fabled north-west sea passage, north of Canada. Subsequently, several further expeditions set out to try to find and rescue Franklin's party. One such attempt was a private effort, raised in 1850 by Lady Franklin and known as 'the branch expedition', which planned to assist vessels under the command of Captain Austin, that were despatched by the British government. It used the *Prince Albert*, a 90 ton clipper under the command of Commander Charles Forsyth RN, who was tasked to search around the Regent Inlet, an area which could not be examined by Austin's larger vessels.

During February 1850, Charles Green was approached by Lady Franklin to provide her expedition with some small balloons for aerial signalling and message distribution purposes. The object of this mass-message distribution idea was to print instructions pertinent to the rescue and hope that one might be picked up by the lost souls. It was on 11 March that Charles arranged a practical demonstration of his design and invited Lady Franklin, his friend Robert Hollond MP and others to visit him at his home in Tufnell Park Road, Holloway to witness the experiment. The balloons - made to Charles' high-grade, oiled-silk specification - were of small dimensions, about 5 or 6 feet in diameter, containing just 30 cubic-feet of hydrogen - a gas that Charles manufactured himself. He also made a portable small-scale hydrogen gas generator unit to offer to the expedition. The balloons could be filled in minutes; were capable of remaining airborne for twelve hours and depending on the wind, could travel downwind a distance of 500 miles. The key feature was that the balloons could carry aloft signals or printed messages in the form of slips of silk and paper. Packets of these slips - and small parachutes with larger containers - could be dropped at intervals by the judicious use of a slow-match fuse to control their regular release. The message packets and burning fuse were protected from rain or dew by a waterproof conical cover.

The demonstration presented one of these balloons, loaded with thirty-two suspended packets containing a total of roughly 3,000 silk and paper message slips; one packet to be released every five minutes. The balloon was released and heading south-east, soon the packets could be seen being released at short intervals and their contents fluttering and being dispersed on the breeze. Later, Charles received word that message slips had been picked up in Chichester and on the 18 March, he received a letter from the mayor of St Denis in Normandy that he, too, had found some message slips on 12 March. The balloon was reported to have fallen to earth on the Bay of Biscay coast. Lady Franklin, convinced by the demonstration, asked Charles to provide nine balloons and a portable gas generator to her expedition, which he duly obliged. *Prince Albert*, with Charles Green's balloons on board, set sail on 5 June 1850 but, like all the rescue attempts, failed to find the missing men.

Charles was airborne again on 29 June 1850 with George Rush when they met with an accident that put both men's lives in peril, but from which they emerged, thankfully, unharmed. The trip from Vauxhall Gardens, London in *Nassau* was intended to allow George Rush to test the performance of his Mason's Hygrometer at a high altitude. A hygrometer - sometimes referred to as a 'wet and dry bulb thermometer' - is a two-column adaption of a thermometer, from which measurement readings are the basis of calculating the amount of moisture in the air. One thermometer bulb is wrapped in a fabric wick while the other bulb is left uncovered. The wick is kept moist by soaking up water from a tiny reservoir. The difference between the readings is used to give an accurate calculation of humidity. The earliest examples of this device were made by John Abraham Mason, hence its generic name, but later models such as that acquired by George Rush, were manufactured by other instrument makers.

Taking off at 7.50 pm all went well, with the balloon passing through several layers of cloud until it reached about 20,000 feet. The temperature fell to 20 degrees F and having been above the clouds for half-an-hour, Charles felt it prudent to start his descent. When the balloon emerged below cloud, they found themselves breezing along over water above Sea Reach and heading towards Nore Sands in the Thames estuary. Seeing there was no option but to ditch in the sea, Charles opened the valve and brought the car gently onto the water. It splashed down about 2 miles north of Sheerness but the wind then caught the balloon and with the deflated fabric taking the form of an open umbrella, dragged the car through the water, rotating constantly and rapidly outpacing boats racing to their aid. Charles, struggling to keep his head above water and stay in the car, threw out the grapnel which took hold on the sandy bottom and brought their progress to a halt.

A barge arrived first and its crew launched a small boat to rescue Charles and George. At this point the balloon threatened to make off again, but now HM Revenue cutter *Fly* (Lieutenant Girling) swooped in, snagged her with a grapnel and the crew fired a volley of musket shots into *Nassau* to release the remaining gas. *Nassau* obligingly collapsed and was hauled aboard the barge. George Rush was put aboard a fishing boat and Charles on the barge, then both returned to Gravesend on the next morning tide and on to London later that day. Charles suffered minor injuries to his head and face - but they were both alive! It was September before Charles felt fit enough to take to the air again; after all, he was 65 and getting a bit old for such exertions. He finished his season with some uneventful night ascents from Vauxhall gardens.

The Duke of Brunswick and Charles Green had crossed swords back in 1836 when Charles had refused to take the Duke aloft. It would seem, however, that the

Duke did not hold the grudge because, in 1851, he turned to Charles to take him out of the country in rather unusual circumstances.

Not noted for benevolence towards his subjects in the German state of Brunswick and having accumulated vast wealth allegedly at their expense, Karl II, Duke of Braunschweig-Wolfenbüttel was so despised that, shortly after he returned from a trip to Paris in 1830, he was deposed by a revolution and told to pack his bags for good. Settling in England, he led a privileged, ostentatious life-style in high society circles and was never far from the public limelight. The Duke came into sharp national focus in 1849, when he took grave exception to an article about himself that appeared in a London newspaper. He considered it to be libellous and sued the publisher. The odd thing about the incident is that the article was first published in 1830 and was way outside the prevailing time limit for taking such action. The story goes that he instructed his servant to buy a copy of the original newspaper from an archive source, then asked the publisher to directly supply him with a copy, too. Upon receipt of the second copy, he claimed it was a re-publication of the offending article and he was therefore entitled to sue. He took the publisher to court in the now famous 'multiple-publication rule' case - and in Brunswick versus Harmer at the Queen's Bench in November 1849, won his action. This was a landmark case which went on to govern the conduct of libel cases in the English courts - with increasing controversy - for nearly two centuries, until it was superseded by the Defamation Act of 2013.

There were rumours of a whiff of perjury in this affair and although it is not proposed to dwell on that here, it is noted that, in an article in *The Newfoundlander* of 7 April 1853, it was stated:

'Outlawry has been proclaimed against the Duke of Brunswick for encouraging a person to commit perjury in an action against *The Despatch*, the Duke having absconded from London.'

Charles Green enters the picture in March 1851, when his services and that of the *Nassau* balloon were engaged by the Duke to make a long-distance voyage to the Continent. It seems that the Duke made no secret of his intention to fly to the Continent since newspapers certainly reported it widely. Take-off from Vauxhall Gardens, London was planned for noon on 4 March and a vast array of provisions preceded his grand entrance, so a long journey was also contemplated. The Duke intended to live well, too, as hams, fowls, pheasants, partridges, bread, chocolate, coffee together with a Soyer's cooking stove, were packed on board and Charles loaded 13cwt of ballast and his trail-rope floatation gear. The reason for the journey by air was that the Duke claimed he suffered greatly from sea-sickness and wishing to travel across the Channel, had resigned himself to doing it by balloon. It might be speculated that, with such an array of provisions, did he need all that to simply reach

France - or did he really intend to make a spectacular aerial return to his estranged Duchy of Brunswick and snatch back what he believed was his rightful position? In fact, neither option came to pass because it was clear that, at altitude, the winds were dead against a Channel crossing and after just two hours in the air, Charles landed at Gravesend. The Duke returned to London to await more favourable conditions, while Charles remained with the problem of how to get the Duke across the Channel.

Nearly a month elapsed before Charles felt confident to make another attempt at a Channel crossing. He reckoned he stood the best chance by taking the handier *Victoria* down to Hastings and starting from there and for several days prior to 31 March, Charles was seen preparing the balloon near the gasworks. The Duke of Brunswick arrived quietly in the town, staying *incognito* at the Victoria Hotel in St Leonard's. Occasionally he was seen riding with some friends; described as a romantic-looking gentleman, with coal-black whiskers and moustache, and tactfully referred to by the local press as 'Mr Smith.'

Interestingly, while Charles attended Hastings gas works, he lodged close by with Mr and Mrs William Ellis of 42 St Andrews Terrace and it was in their house that he was recorded - as: 'aeronaut' and 'visitor' - for the national census, counted overnight 29/30 April 1851. Ann, Charles' wife, was recorded by the census at their home: '2 Belgrave Villa, Upper Holloway' as 'married, age 54, husband: aeronaut.' Also recorded with Ann was her sister-in-law Mary Smallbone: widow age 69 and Joseph Nyman, age 46, watchmaker: visitor.

31 April dawned fine and with a stiff breeze blowing from between north and north-west, Charles decided it was time to go. Inflation was complete by 1.00 pm and Charles with the Duke dressed for adverse weather in an oilskin suit and leather cap, was airborne at 1.20 pm. The balloon track across the Channel was erratic due to encountering different air currents and changes in buoyancy and at one stage, about mid-channel, it was becalmed for a time. Eventually they reached the French coast south of Boulogne and left a broad sandy beach behind; Charles seeking a level, inhabited area with the prospect of help on hand to make a safe landing. Spotting habitation and many people running towards them, with the Duke bellowing instructions to the peasantry from his exalted position above them, Charles lowered the grapnel and brought *Victoria* down to a gentle grounding near the village of Neufchatel. The voyage had taken 5 hours and they were 10 miles south-west of Boulogne with a convenient station on the Boulogne-Amiens railway a mere half-mile away. Leaving Charles to organise the recovery, the Duke took his leave, hired a carriage to the station and caught a train almost immediately, *en route* for Paris. That was the last Charles - or, for that matter, anyone else in England - saw of the Duke of Brunswick, who spent the rest of his years in Paris and finally Geneva, where he was able to continue the high-life, untroubled by the issue of perjury.

Chapter 14

Happy Landings

In February 1852, reports appeared in newspapers across the land that: 'Charles Green, The Veteran Aeronaut intends to retire from the occupation of balloon-flyer at the end of the forthcoming season'. It was reported that he had made 489 ascents thus far and hoped to reach 500. Charles was now 67 years of age and enjoying such national-treasure status, that many people expressed relief.

'We are very glad (for his own sake) that our old adventurous navigator is bringing his aerial voyages to a close.'[1]

Dicing with death for over thirty years, he had used up his nine lives and seen many aeronauts try to emulate him - some of whom were still around; some had faded into oblivion and some had died pursuing this profession. There was always a new generation of aeronauts riding on his coat-tails; the stage for aerostation itself was now global and the dual prospect of navigable air vehicles and air travel was not far off. But, there was still life in The Old Ethereal Pilot - Henry Mayhew's name for him - yet.

Vauxhall Gardens, London opened for the season on Whit Monday, 31 May 1852 and Charles made the first of what was advertised as 'a series of ten farewell flights in *Royal Nassau.*' On 2 June he made a rare ascent from a provincial town: The Cricket Ground, Leicester; billed as 'a celebration of the laying of the foundation stone of the new Temperance Hall.' Charles could hardly be described as an advocate of temperance, but a job is a job after all! It will, however, be as the pilot engaged privately for a programme of four scientific research flights with *Nassau*, organised by the Kew Committee of the Council of the British Association for the Advancement of Science, for which he will be particularly remembered in 1852.

Mr Wardell, lessee of Vauxhall Gardens, made the site available free of charge for all four flights. The car of the balloon was equipped with duplicate sets of high-quality, precision barometer, thermometer and hygrometer instruments, in the care of John Welsh, superintendent of Kew Observatory and Richard Nicklin an assistant at the Observatory, who were to make the observations and ascent with Charles. At 3.50 pm on 17 August, *Nassau* took to the sky for the first trip, which achieved an altitude of 19,500 feet and was a great success in respect of the scientific observations. Upon his safe return to earth, John Welsh wrote:

'The main object of these aerostatic expeditions is the determination of the laws of change in the temperature and humidity as we rise in the atmosphere. Other experiments and observations are not lost sight of, but it is proposed to attempt at first only what it is probable can be satisfactorily executed - it being of more use to do one thing well, than many things imperfectly. Such subjects as atmospheric electricity and (less probably) magnetism, may be taken up when the observers shall have become familiarised with their work. Specimens of air will be taken at different elevations for analysis. The aerial data will be analysed in conjunction with voluntary observations taken during the same time at stations on the ground. [Thirty-four people across the UK submitted data.].

The Kew committee has been particularly fortunate in obtaining the zealous co-operation of Mr Green. His great experience and well-known ability and caution afford a guarantee that the risks attending these expeditions will be reduced to a minimum. The confidence which his dextrous management of the immense but beautiful balloon cannot fail to inspire and will contribute much to that calmness in the observer which is so necessary in the presence of unusual phenomena.'[2]

A safe landing, with all instruments intact, was made at Swavesey, in Cambridgeshire, after flying 60 miles in 1½ hours.

The second 'Kew' flight in *Nassau* took place on 27 August, this time with John Welsh, Richard Nicklin and the instrument maker Patrick Adie on board with Charles. The famous photographer, John Jabez Edwin Mayall took what has become a well-known Daguerreotype photograph of the four voyagers prior to this second trip. Take off from Vauxhall was at 4.44 pm and a successful flight - during which the balloon reached an altitude of 19,200 feet - ended safely at Latimer, 6 miles south of Boxmoor station near Hemel Hempstead, at 7.35 pm. His next flight with *Nassau* from Vauxhall was somewhat more bizarre, when Charles took a portion of a military band into the air. This strange ascent was witnessed by the Maharajah of Coorg, who no doubt appreciated the mellow brass band sounds wafting from on high.

There was no great ceremony attending his 500th flight and indeed several flights were claimed by both Charles and the newspapers to be that landmark event. The first of these came on 2 September 1852, when Charles repeated the feat of taking part of the Garden entertainment band, billed as 'Music in The Clouds; ten performers with their instruments,' up with *Nassau*. The *London Daily News* reported this as 'Mr Green's 500th ascent, if the placards are trustworthy - and his last.' His next flight - technically his 501st - was a night flight from Vauxhall on 6 September. *Nassau* carried ten passengers, six of whom were lucky winners in a seat lottery and Charles told his passengers this was his 500th ascent. Yet again, on the much-quoted night flight with Henry Mayhew from Vauxhall on 8 September - nominally his 502nd - this, too, was reported by the press as his 500th ascent. This ascent was followed by another 'lottery' flight on 13 September and in a letter from one of the passengers to *The Sun*,[3] was stated to be his 503rd ascent - which is sequentially correct.

One of the most detailed personal accounts by a passenger on any flight with Charles Green (apart from the Weilburg flight), is that of Henry Mayhew after the *Nassau* flight of 8 September 1852. Mayhew (1812-1887), an English journalist, social researcher and reformer, playwright and co-founder and editor of *Punch* magazine, waxed lyrical about the apprehension, exhilaration, *bonhomie* and sheer joy of:

> 'floating through the endless realms of space, drinking in the pure thin air of the skies, sailing almost among the stars, free as the lark at heavens' gate; enjoying a brief half-hour, at least a foretaste of that Elysian destiny which is the hope of all. To see, to think and to feel thus was surely worth some little risk and this it was that led me to peril my bones in the car of the balloon.'[4]

This flight was advertised as the 500th ascent and was a celebration evening laid on by the lessee of Vauxhall Gardens, for the financial benefit of Charles. Six cannons, accompanied by a cacophony of cheering and applause, roared out as the great *Nassau* rose majestically into the sky with Charles and eight passengers on board. All went well but, in the darkness that greeted the landing, it needed all of Charles' steely authority to keep everyone safe, as Henry Mayhew recalled. Instructed to sit tight at the bottom of the car it was still a jarring impact as the basket hit the ground on Pirbright Common, near Guildford.

'For heavens' sake, hold fast! shouted Mr Green, as the car pounded along the ground, rolling this way and that, to the roar of discharging gas. 'Sit still all of you, I say!' roared our pilot, as he saw someone trying to clamber out. It was a swamp into which we fell and water was seeping into the car as we shifted into a ditch. Obediently, we sat still until, to our delight, some hundred drab-smocked countrymen appeared as if by magic, held the car firmly and one after another we were extricated from our seats; unharmed.'

The third 'Kew' flight took place on 21 October, with only John Welsh accompanying Charles this time, but the altitude reached was just 12,640 feet. The final 'Kew' flight was made on 10 November, again with just John Welsh making observations and after reaching an altitude of 23,000 feet, they landed safely near the village of Acrise, a few miles from Folkestone. Both men commented that they experienced some breathing discomfort and 'a heaviness in the head.' A report of the observations and analyses was eventually published by John Welsh in *Philosophical Transactions*, Journal of The Royal Society.[5]

Onset of winter and then John Welsh's ill-health, prevented Charles Green being involved in any further such flights. Their mantle was taken over - in a longer series of similar flights during the 1860s sponsored by the British Association - by Henry Coxwell and James Glaisher, the latter being allowed to use Welsh's instruments; Welsh having died in the meantime. It has sometimes been written that Henry Coxwell used Green's *Nassau* for these experiments, but that is incorrect since, having been unable to find a balloon that in his opinion was large enough to facilitate the high altitudes contemplated, he constructed an entirely new balloon for the purpose.

Meanwhile, 1853 saw Charles showing no sign of retiring. Far from it, he undertook another season at Vauxhall, where the popularity of seat-lotteries remained undiminished and his trademark ascents drew large crowds. Uncertainty with his flight numbers still be-devilled his final score, too. Sequentially, his ascent on 5 September 1853 worked out at #507 but, according to a letter written by one of his passengers, Charles Paternoster and published in the *Morning Advertiser*, it was #510. His 513th trip from Surrey Zoological Gardens on Whit Monday, 5 June 1854 and 514th from Brecknock Arms Gardens, Camden Road, London on 6 June (#514 as per *Morning Advertiser*), both with *Victoria*, then restore a sequence, although several more advertised flights with *Nassau* during July and August 1854 cannot be verified by subsequent newspaper reports.

Even at this late stage of his career, Charles' expert opinion was sought on many occasions, such as at the inquest into the death of Monsieur Henri Latour, who died while attempting a parachute descent from a balloon piloted by Mr Adams from the Cremorne Gardens on 27 June 1854. The parachute was of an unusual design (again!) and Charles gave the opinion that some ropes used in a weird, treadle-operated propulsion system, ought to have been braided instead of twisted. That might have stopped them twisting-up and preventing the canopy from opening properly.

Charles does not appear to have made any ascents during 1854 or 1855 and his final flight - his 518th by his counting - is believed to have taken place at Vauxhall Gardens, London on 8 September 1856. The Gardens were to re-open for a series of ten galas organised by Mr Wardell and top billing for the first of these went to Joseph J. Oddy Taylor, described as 'successor to Mr Green' and a lottery for five seats in *Nassau*. The advertisement claimed 'the veteran Green has consented to accompany the aerial voyagers.'[6] The ascent was described by *The Sun (London)* as 'magnificent,' but did not confirm - or deny - Charles' presence on board and no detailed report of the ascent has been found. However, shortly afterwards the *Cheltenham Journal*[7] published an article by the Reverend John Richardson, in which he said he had been at Vauxhall Gardens and:

> 'met Mr Bacon and the celebrated surgeon, Mr Lister, both of whom were about to take a trip with the veteran Green.'

The article included quotations from the conversation both passengers had with Mr Green during the course of that flight. This seems to confirm Charles made the flight and that it also appears to be the last time he was airborne. There is evidence that Charles attempted one more flight in 1859 and indeed would have made it, had it not been for an accident prior to take off that caused significant damage to *Nassau* and caused him to abort the flight. This incident relates to an attempt to make the first of a new series of scientific flights under the auspices of the Royal Astronomical Society and The British Association, from Wolverhampton gas works on 15 August 1859. James Glaisher, now Meteorological Assistant at Kew Observatory, had briefed passenger Mr S.H. Eaton on how and what observations were to be made. Unfortunately, the balloon was tossed around incessantly by a strong wind funnelling through a nearby railway viaduct. At the crucial point, a huge gust ripped the fabric and put an end to the attempt. Further successful attempts would be made during the 1860s by James Glaisher himself, piloted aloft by Henry Coxwell, in the latter's new balloon.

In respect of his own project to undertake research flights for the British Association, Coxwell wrote:

> 'I undertook to provide a suitable balloon for a five mile [altitude] ascent. Previous high ascents [by Welsh and Green] were conducted in the *Nassau* balloon. It was supposed that, owing to [its] age and its behaviour at a previous trial, Green's balloon was unequal to fresh duties... all these drawbacks led to the acceptance of my offer [to build an entirely new balloon for the project].'[8]

As for *Nassau*, well, she was repaired and flown a few times by Charles' son George. The final fate of *Victoria* is uncertain but some indication arose on 23 July 1857, when a case was heard in Bloomsbury County Court: Scotcher versus Tingey, involving the law of auctions and conditions of sale at such. On 15 May 1857 at the Pantechnicon sale room, the plaintiff Mr Scotcher, a piano maker, bid £20 for the purchase of what was described in the catalogue as 'The *Royal Nassau* Balloon.' Thinking he was on to an absolute bargain, Mr Scotcher put in his bid and was successful. He then put an advertisement in *The Times* on 19 May, indicating his *Royal Nassau* was now for sale or hire. Naturally, Charles had something to say about this and wrote to Mr Scotcher, pointing out that he, Charles Green, was the owner of *Nassau*; it was most certainly still in his possession and Mr Scotcher should withdraw his offensive advertisement immediately. It transpired that the balloon which Mr Scotcher had bought was named *Victoria*. Considering himself deceived by the owner of the Pantechnicon, Mr Scotcher took him to court and won his case for the return of his £20. It is not known what then happened to *Victoria*.

Nassau was back in the news in 1859 in yet another court case, this time in Fairbank versus Green on 1 February 1859, before the Queen's Bench. It will be recalled that Charles had had dealings with Joseph Taylor, whom he allowed to pilot *Nassau* back in September 1856. In 1857, George junior took *Nassau* and his own balloon, *Le Continent*, with Joseph Taylor to Russia where they made a number of successful flights from St Petersburg. Joseph Taylor - drawing on some ideas patented during the 1830s - claimed to have invented a screw-propeller and steering mechanism that would revolutionise balloon travel. Since George's ambition was to fly from St Petersburg to London, he agreed to what became known as the Russian Expedition, in order to put Taylor's apparatus to the ultimate test. On behalf of George and Charles Green, an order was placed with Mr Fairbank to manufacture the apparatus to Taylor's specification. The experiment did not succeed. Fairbank was not paid and took the Greens to court to recover his money.

In their court defence, Charles and his son said they had no faith in the apparatus - it was their opinion that no apparatus could be constructed that was capable of propelling and steering a balloon and therefore that they would not and did not, give the order. They also deposed that they sold the balloon (*Nassau*) to Taylor for a sum of £250, payable in instalments out of the profit it was hoped would result from the ascents. Furthermore, the balloon was to be restored to them if the venture was unsuccessful, or if the conditions of the agreement were not carried out. They also deposed that Taylor was not the inventor of the apparatus. The jury found in favour of the plaintiff for the full amount and Charles had to cough-up £21. It seems that *Nassau* therefore reverted to Charles' ownership once again but there is no evidence of it making any further flights, at least prior to Charles death in 1870.

In respect of the fate of the *Nassau* balloon; it was certainly seen in Charles' possession in October 1868. The French aeronaut Gaston Tissandier wrote that one of his acquaintances, another French aeronaut, Wilfrid de Fonvielle, was in London and sent him a letter in which Fonvielle said he had visited Charles 'at Aerial Villa in Upper Holloway'. In 1868 Charles resided at 51 Tufnell Park Road, Holloway. The name 'Aerial Villa' is not recorded on the 1861 census form; merely shown as No.51. It is possible that Charles used the name informally after 1861. Fonvielle said he 'discovered this elegant little house, pleasantly situated on a hill among groups of houses and trees.' He was cordially received and in the dining room, over a glass of wine, Charles showed him a large portfolio that he said: 'contained the account of all my aerial travels that have been published and all the letters written to me upon the subject. It would require an entire lifetime to peruse them and put in order.' Charles went on to say he had: 'made over 600 [*sic*] aerial excursions and [had carried] as many as 700 persons in the car of my balloon.' Fonvielle told Tissandier that Charles then took him outside to the end of a narrow court and opened the door of an outhouse. Inside was, packed away, the *Nassau* balloon. Fonvielle said the old aeronaut became quite emotional as he stood before the famous balloon that had carried him on his aerial adventures. Charles touched the car with something like reverence and with a tear in his eye, said: 'here is my car which, like its old pilot, now reposes quietly, after a long and active career. And there is the tissue of the *Nassau* itself, poor old balloon; I love it like a child.' Shaking him by the hand, he wished Fonvielle every success with his own ventures, then took him back inside the house, where he and the Frenchman conversed in quiet conviviality well into the night; about past aerial adventures made; those wished for and what the future might hold.[9]

Wilfrid de Fonvielle noted:

> 'the celebrated *Nassau* balloon became the property of Henry Coxwell in 1869; Charles Green wishing his successor to have it before his death.' Its varnish was blackened with age, like an old painting; Coxwell completely restored the silk and varnished it afresh. He ascended with it in 1873, seeking to prove the 'eastern air current' theory; concluding as a result that 'no such current could be relied on.'[10]

Another report states:

> '*Nassau* balloon was purchased by Henry Coxwell in July 1869 and underwent restoration during the following winter. Fresh silk for repairs was bought from H. Soper, Spital Square, at 18 shillings per yard. *Nassau* will soon be available for further expeditions. Despite his age, Charles Green expressed the wish to accompany Coxwell on his first trip in the renovated balloon, but died before it was ready.'[11]

It was on 18 June 1873 that Henry Coxwell made his first trip in the rejuvenated *Nassau*, at the annual Yorkshire Gala in York. He flew five passengers from York to Huby, just 11 miles distant, before returning to York by train. There is newspaper evidence that Coxwell flew *Nassau* from Hornsey on 25 September 1873 and again on 5 June 1875 from Crystal Palace. Thereafter, *Nassau* fades from the limelight. In August 1888 it was reported that several balloons were stored in Coxwell's workshop in Seaford, Sussex: 'Green's famous old balloon *Nassau* is also here laid up in packed condition.'[12] After Coxwell's death in 1890, several of his balloons were auctioned off together with many other artefacts, including 'grapnels and the car from *Nassau*'.[13]

Another of the myths surrounding Charles Green, concerns his association with the Aeronautical Society of Great Britain, founded in 1866. He is often said to be 'a founding member' of the Society, but this is not strictly correct. A single page document dated 17 February 1839 and written at Highgate by Charles, proposed an 'Aeronautic Fraternity' with aims not unlike those espoused by the Aeronautical Society many years later. Charles signed the document as 'President' and the other signatories were F. (?) Green, William Westcott, Edward Spencer, Jacob Henry Burn and J. (?) Green.[14] However, nothing further seems to have emerged as a result of that meeting.

HAPPY LANDINGS

Although Charles showed interest in the Aeronautical Society's activities, his name does not appear in any of the official minutes of the Society in the years 1866 to 1870 where, amongst other business, the names of members being proposed and admitted are noted. In a list of members published in the second annual report of the Society, covering the years 1866 and 1867, Charles' name is also missing. However, there is evidence of Charles attending two meetings. The first of these was the first general meeting of the Society, held in the Society of Arts in London on 27 June 1866, but Charles did not speak. Contributing to a general discussion about the Laws of Flight, the meteorologist and treasurer/council member of the Society, James Glaisher said:

> 'It is well known that for the last three or four years the balloon has been the means of enabling me to take observations in the higher regions of the atmosphere. Now, any gentleman who has been in the position of myself and my friend Mr Charles Green, the hero of 500 ascents, who I am glad to see present here this evening (cheers), will know that when we are 5 miles high and engaged in these experiments, we are in no easy mind...'[15]

The second occasion was at a general Aeronautical Society meeting held on 17 April 1867, during which Francis Herbert Wenham, a Society council member, contributed to a discussion about the use and merits of aerial screws and mentions Charles who, again, did not speak, but was obviously present.

> 'Our friend Mr Green, the aeronaut, has just handed me this model to illustrate the effect of two superposed [sic] screws. It is a very well-made piece of clockwork, which runs for several minutes by a wound-up spring, and was adapted to raise and lower and propel a small balloon some years ago at the Polytechnic Institution. Now, you will observe that, with one screw only, it produces a strong current of air; but, as Mr Green has just shown me, by superposing another screw, the current is destroyed.'[16]

No other written references by the Society to Charles Green have been found prior to his death.

Charles Green, this Grand Old Man of the Air suffered heart failure and passed away quietly in his home at 51 Tufnell Park Road, on 26 March 1870, aged 85. An inquest was held by the deputy coroner, Doctor W. Hardwicke, at the *Hercules Tavern*, [504] Holloway Road, London with an account of proceedings published in the *Islington Gazette* of Friday, 1 April 1870. It is most revealing and contains information not found in any other newspapers of the time. In addition to family relatives, Mrs Jane Green (third) wife of the deceased attended the inquest.

THE FLYING ADVENTURES OF CHARLES GREEN

Mrs Green said her husband enjoyed excellent health and had been out and about every day during the past week, except for the day he died. She recalled that in the afternoon of Saturday, 26 March, while she was in the garden, Charles was in the parlour drinking champagne. He had a couple of glasses then called out to her to come and join him for a drink, but soon afterwards said he felt unwell. With the help of their servant Catherine Henderson, Charles was taken upstairs and put to bed. He then asked for some gruel with a little laudanum in it but while this was being prepared downstairs Charles rang the bedroom bell violently. Mrs Green went back to him and he complained of being very cold and asked for something to put round his shoulders and to send for Mr Pierpoint, a surgeon who lived at 1 Tufnell Park Road, as quickly as possible. Mrs Green sent the servant for the doctor but Charles passed out and within five minutes he was dead.

When questioned by Mr Ricketts, solicitor for some of the relatives of the deceased, Jane Green gave the following information.

'Mrs Green said her maiden name was Shaw and that she was married to Mr Green at St Mary's Church, Islington, five or six years ago but she could not recollect the date [it was 1865]. She knew the deceased had left a will but she had never seen what was in it. Mrs Green had never lived in the house with him, until a fortnight prior to his death, because his circumstances had greatly altered of late years. Mr Green, she said, was a peculiar man. [Neither of these answers were elaborated upon]. She had always visited him three or four times a week since her marriage and Mrs Green said she had been living at her own house, 3 Stanhope Terrace, Regent's Park. She knew the house in Tufnell Park was owned by Charles but did not know he also owned a considerable amount of other property as well. She did not know he had £3,000 (≈ £309,000 in 2023. Some reports state: £3,600) in Consols [an investment in Consolidated Annuities, a government-issued security] and thought there was only about £160. [At this point the newspaper report stated, also without elaboration:] It may be remarked that the witness was considerably the junior of the deceased.'

About this latter acerbic remark; records suggest that Jane Green was born in 1818. This would, when she married Charles in 1865, put her age at 47 years and his at 80 years. In 1870, she was 52 years old when Charles died aged 85; indeed, quite a difference – and maybe one that accounted for the rather pointed questioning at the inquest by a solicitor acting for the rest of the Green family? Whatever the respective motives, Charles always had an eye for the ladies. Indeed, he had told Fonvielle:

> 'I have [flown] 120 ladies. The ladies have always shown courage in this respect. If you wish balloons to become popular in France, begin by taking women in your balloons; men will be sure to follow.'

HAPPY LANDINGS

Since his only son George died in 1864; having - it is assumed - now inherited an undisclosed amount of Charles' estate, there is evidence that widow Jane Green, when aged 55, married George Edward Stanyon, gentleman, aged 32, in Kentish Town parish church on 2 September 1874. That wedding, too, was witnessed by her father: Isaac Culling, farmer. It is believed Jane, then of 160 Albany Court, St Pancras, died in March 1896.

Giving evidence to the coroner, Thomas Pierpoint MRCS, surgeon, said he attended Charles at 6.30 pm that evening and found him dead. Having conducted a *post mortem*, he found the deceased generally healthy, but his heart-valves were ossified and fatty, which in his opinion had produced the condition of syncope that was the cause of death. The jury returned a verdict of 'death by natural causes.' Such was his reputation that Charles' death and inquest was reported in the world's press.[17]

Charles Green was laid to rest in Highgate (Eastern) cemetery; grave number 17325 and burial number 37568. His memorial plinth, capped by a hemisphere with a 'netting' design, representing a balloon, is somewhat overgrown but, in a photograph taken in 2021, still bears the name 'Charles Green' with the word 'Aeronaut' just discernible beneath. A word of caution. This tomb should not be confused with that of Charles Green Spencer, god-son of Charles Green, named by his father Edward Spencer in honour of his great friend the aeronaut Charles Green. The Spencer tomb - also with a depiction of a balloon - is in Highgate (Western) cemetery.

Having been born within months of Lunardi's first balloon flight in England Charles Green, pilot of the skies, indeed rose above all his contemporaries, to straddle the golden age of Georgian and Victorian aeronautics like a true Colossus.

Appendix 1

List of Claimed and Verifiable Ascents by Charles Green

Numbers in **bold** are those quoted in advertisements or newspaper reports. <u>Underlined</u> items relate to unexplained gaps in the numbering sequence.

Ascent Number	Date	Ascent	Descent
1	19 July 1821	Green Park, London	South Mimms
2	1 Aug 1821	Belvedere Gardens	Barking
3	25 Aug 1821	Portsea	Langstone
4	6 Sept 1821	Portsea	Frimley
5	2 Oct 1821	Brighton	In sea off Cuckmere
6	30 July 1822	Cheltenham	Salperton
7	3 June 1823	Mermaid, Hackney	Romford
8	14 June 1823	Oxford	Henley
9	1 August 1823	Reading	North Mimms
10	5 Sept 1823	Leeds	Haxey, Gainsborough
11	19 April 1824	Halifax	Hornby Castle, Bedale
12	26 April 1824	Leeds	Thurner
<u>13</u>	Not found.		
14	18 May 1824	Leamington Spa	Milton Malsor
15	Not found.		
16	25 June 1824	Coventry	Willoughby
17	8 July 1824	Northampton	Soham, Cambs
18	26 July 1824	Leicester	Haselor, (Warks)
19	5 August 1824	Warwick #1	Gilmorten/Lutterworth
20	23 August 1824	Shrewsbury	Monkhopton
21	9 Sept 1824	Warwick #2	Rugby
22	17 Sept 1824	Wolverhampton	Dunston Heath, Penkridge
<u>23</u>	Not found.		
24	25 Oct 1824	Portsea	Heyshott, near Midhurst
25	9 Nov 1824	Chichester	Henfield, W Sussex

LIST OF CLAIMED AND VERIFIABLE ASCENTS

Ascent Number	Date	Ascent	Descent
26–27	Not found.		
28	9 April 1825	Eagle Tavern, London	Ewell
29	11 May 1825	Newcastle; Nun's Field	Newbegin House; Ponteland Road
30	23 May 1825	Newcastle	Low Elswick
31	30 May 1825	Newcastle	Tontine Inn, Potto
32	9 June 1825	Leeds	Askham Richard
33	16 June 1825	Stockton	Acklam
34	Not found.		
35	2 July 1825	Stamford	Thorney, near Peterborough
36	27 July 1825	Leicester	Atherstone
37	6 August 1825	Worcester	Beauchamp Lodge, Highnam, Glos
38	16 August 1825	Kendal	Close to Kendal
39	30 Aug 1825	Kendal	Appleby
40	17 Sept 1825	York	Pickering
41	27 Sept 1825	York	Osgodby, near Selby
42	11 Oct 1825	Carlisle	Gilsland
43	18 Oct 1825	Richmond	Yarm
44	24 Oct 1825	Blackburn	Braithwell, near Maltby
45–47	Not found.		
48	28 March 1826	Eagle Tavern, City Road, London	Rainham
49	30 March 1826	Eagle Tavern, City Road, London	Sevenoaks
50	18 April 1826	Golden Eagle, Mile End, London	Enfield Chase
51	16 May 1826	Eagle Tavern, City Road, London	St Mary Cray, Kent
52	31 May 1826	Hertford	South Mimms
53	8 June 1826	Boston, Lincs	Allington, Sleaford
54	21 June 1826	King's Lynn	Southery
55	21 July 1826	Vauxhall, London	Richmond
56	28 July 1826	Vauxhall, London	Merton
57	4 August 1826	Louth	Partney, near Spilsby
58	14 August 1826	Vauxhall, London	Foots Cray
59	30 August 1826	Boston	Manby
60	11 Sept 1826	Stamford	Whittlesea
61	3 Oct 1826	Hanley, Staffs	Ashbourne
62	19 Oct 1826	Newcastle-under Lyme #1	Nantwich

THE FLYING ADVENTURES OF CHARLES GREEN

Ascent Number	Date	Ascent	Descent
63	26 Oct 1826	Newcastle-under-Lyme #2	Abbots Bromley
64-65	Not found.		
66	17 April 1827	Golden Eagle, Mile End, London	Fulham
67	8 May 1827	White Conduit Gardens, London	Bedfont
68	18 May 1827	Newbury #1	Crowmarsh, Wallingford
69	24 May 1827	Newbury #2	Guildford
70	5 June 1827	Ashton-under-Lyne #1	Hatfield Moss, Thorne, Yorks
71	9 June 1827	Ashton-under-Lyne #2	Chapel-en-le-Frith
72	18 June 1827	Stockport #1	Wentworth, Rotherham
73	25 June 1827	Macclesfield #1	Lincoln
74	3 July 1827	Macclesfield #2	Branston, Lincoln
75	9 July 1827	Stockport #2	Welbeck Abbey, Worksop
76	27 July 1827	Warrington #1	Bolton
77	1 August 1827	Warrington #2	Kearsley Moor, Bolton
78	Not found.		
79	10 August 1827	Manchester Vauxhall Gardens	Worksop
80	27 August 1827	Burnley	Fairfield, Buxton
81	4 Sept 1827	Doncaster	Woodthorpe, Sheffield
82	10 Sept 1827	Gainsborough	Burringham, Scunthorpe
83	Not found.		
84	24 Sept 1827	Hull	Foston-on-the-Wolds, Driffield
85	3 Oct 1827	Liverpool	Eton, Liverpool
86	19 Oct 1827	Cambridge	Chatteris
87	19 Nov 1827	Eagle Tavern, City Road, London	Barnard Park, Islington
88-92	Not found.		
93	7 May 1828	Boston	Gosberton
94	14 May 1828	Boston	Sleaford
95-97	Not found.		
98	9 July 1828	Swan Inn, Stratford, London	?
99	29 July 1828	Eagle Tavern, City Road, London	Beckenham
100	30 July 1828	Beckenham	Bromley Common
101	26 Aug 1828	Canterbury #1	Chart, Ashford

LIST OF CLAIMED AND VERIFIABLE ASCENTS

Ascent Number	Date	Ascent	Descent
102	2 Sept 1828	Canterbury #2	Bonnington, near Ashford
103	10 Sept 1828	Dover	Eastry near Sandwich
104	28 Oct 1828	Ludlow #2	Burrington, 6 miles W of Ludlow
105-114	Not found.		
115	19 May 1829	Barnwell, Cambridge	Wellingborough
116	21 July 1829	Portsea #2	Appledram
117	27 July 1829	Southampton #1	Compton, Winchester
118	6 August 1829	Southampton #2	Lee near Romsey
119-148	Not found.		
149	26 May 1830	Peterborough #1	Littleport
150	5 June 1830	Peterborough #2	Moulton Chapel, Spalding
151	5 July 1830	Lincoln #1	Scrivelsby, Horncastle
152	13 July 1830	Lincoln #2	Rothwell
153-159	Not found.		
160	9 Oct 1830	Dewsbury #2	Leeds
161-189	Not found.		
190	23 June 1831	Norwich #1	Oby, near Acle
191	2 July 1831	Norwich #2	Hemblington near Blofield
192	1 August 1831	New London Bridge	Charlwood
193	15 August 1831	Vauxhall, London	Parsons Green, Fulham
194	22 August 1831	Vauxhall, London	Thornton Heath, Croydon
195	24 August 1831	Vauxhall, London	near Croydon
196	8 Sept 1831	Green Park, London	?
197	16 May 1832	Barnwell, Cambridge	Fowlmere
198	8 July 1833	Southampton	?
xxx	1834	**No ascents made.**	
199	25 May 1835	Surrey Zoological Gdns	Brentwood
200	20 July 1835	Surrey Zoological Gdns	Greenwich Park
201	22 July 1835	Surrey Zoological Gdns	Staines
202	Not found.		
203	13 August 1835	Vauxhall, London	Wandsworth
204	17 August 1835	Vauxhall, London	? towards the West
205	27 August 1835	Vauxhall, London	Uxbridge
206	Not found.		
207	12 Sept 1835	Vauxhall, London	?
208	17 Sept 1835	Vauxhall, London	near King's Lynn
209	6 Oct 1835	Uxbridge	Braintree
210	23 Oct 1835	Bury St Edmunds	Hoxne, Diss

THE FLYING ADVENTURES OF CHARLES GREEN

Ascent Number	Date	Ascent	Descent
211	Not found.		
212	25 May 1836	Surrey Zoological Gdns	Neston Park, Guildford
213	24 May 1836	Surrey Zoological Gdns	Charlwood, Horley
214	5 July 1836	Vauxhall, London	Hertford Common
215	Not found.		
216	23 July 1836	Vauxhall, London	St Paul's Cray
217	2 August 1836	Vauxhall, London	Farningham
218	9 August 1836	Vauxhall, London	Crawley
219	16 August 1836	Vauxhall, London	Plaistow Marshes
220	30 August 1836	Vauxhall, London	Romford
221	9 Sept 1836	Vauxhall, London	Cliffe, Kent
222	21 Sept 1836	Vauxhall, London	Beckenham, Kent
223	27 Sept 1836	Vauxhall, London	Writtle, near Chelmsford
224	9 Oct 1836	Vauxhall, London	Uxbridge
225	17 Oct 1836	Vauxhall, London	Leighton Buzzard
226	7/8 Nov 1836	Vauxhall, London	Weilburg, Germany
227	19 Dec 1836	Paris #1	Vitry, France
228	9 Jan 1837	Paris #2	Claye-Souilly, France
229	15 May 1837	Vauxhall, London	Nutfield, near Redhill
230	16 May 1837	Vauxhall, London	Charlwood Park, Horley
231	30 May 1837	Vauxhall, London	Wormshill, Kent
232	16 June 1837	Vauxhall, London	Offley Hole, near Hitchin
233	23 June 1837	Vauxhall, London	Westcroft Park, Chobham
234	3 July 1837	Cheltenham	Ashton Keynes near South Cerney
235	24 July 1837	Vauxhall, London	Offham, Town Malling, near Maidstone
236	9 August 1837	Vauxhall, London	Laleham, Staines
237	14 August 1837	Vauxhall, London	Osterley Park, Hounslow
238	21 August 1837	Vauxhall, London	High Ongar, Essex
239	25 August 1837	Vauxhall, London	Enfield Chase
240	4 Sept 1837	Vauxhall, London	Blackheath
241	11 Sept 1837	Vauxhall, London	Little Hadham, Bishop's Stortford
242	15 Sept 1837	Vauxhall, London	West Thurrock, Purfleet
243	20 Sept 1837	Vauxhall, London	Roxeth, Harrow-on-the-Hill
244	22 Sept 1837	Vauxhall, London	Uxbridge
245	12 Oct 1837	Surrey Zoological Gardens	?

LIST OF CLAIMED AND VERIFIABLE ASCENTS

Ascent Number	Date	Ascent	Descent
246	16 October 1837	Salford, Manchester #1	Poynton, near Hazel Grove
247	23 October 1837	Salford, Manchester #2	Wintersett, 5 miles SE Wakefield
248	4 November 1837	Salford, Manchester #3	Offerton, Stockport
249	Not found.		
250	25 June 1838	Vauxhall, London	Denham Court, near Uxbridge
251	28 June 1838	Midsummer Green, Cambridge	Fulbourn
252	2 July 1838	Vauxhall, London	? Essex
253	10 July 1838	Vauxhall, London	Sandon, Chelmsford
254	17 July 1838	Vauxhall, London	Near Kelvedon, Essex
255	24 July 1838	Vauxhall, London	Oxted, Surrey
256	7 August 1838	Vauxhall, London	Near Rochester
257	13 August 1838	Vauxhall, London	Farnborough
258	17 August 1838	Vauxhall, London	Charlton, Kent
259	21 August 1838	Vauxhall, London	?
260	24 August 1838	Vauxhall, London	Beckingham, Kent
261	28 August 1838	Vauxhall, London	Waltham Cross, Herts
262	4 Sept 1838	Vauxhall, London	Debden, 3 miles South of Saffron Walden
263	7 Sept 1838	Vauxhall, London	?
264	10 Sept 1838	Vauxhall, London	Southover, near Lewes
265	14 Sept 1838	Vauxhall, London	Romford/Chelmsford area?
266	18 Sept 1838	Vauxhall, London	Between Bedfont and Hounslow
267	2 Oct 1838	Vauxhall, London	Bishop's Waltham, near Fareham
268	8 Oct 1838	Vauxhall, London	?
269	25 April 1839	Cheltenham	Hazeley Heath, near Winchfield, Hants
270	8 July 1839	Vauxhall, London	Toppesfield, Castle Hedingham near Braintree
271	15 July 1839	Vauxhall, London	Rawreth, Rayleigh
272	14 August 1839	Stafford House, Chiswick	Totteridge/Whetstone
273	5 Sept 1839	Vauxhall, London	?
274	16 Oct 1839	Norwich	Trunch, near Mundesley
275	17 August 1840	Cremorne, London	Rainham, Essex
276	24 August 1840	Norwich	Metton

THE FLYING ADVENTURES OF CHARLES GREEN

Ascent Number	Date	Ascent	Descent
277	6 Oct 1840	Stepney, London	Mereworth, near Tonbridge
278	12 July 1841	Vauxhall, London	Hextable, near Dartford
279	26 July 1841	Vauxhall, London	Farningham, Kent
280	30 July 1841	Vauxhall, London	?
281	9 August 1841	Vauxhall, London	near Barking
282	23 August 1841	Vauxhall, London	East Ham Marshes
283	30 August 1841	Vauxhall, London	Navestock, near Brentwood
xxx	28 September 1841	Hull	X *Coronation* damaged before take-off
284	27 June 1842	Albert Saloon, London	Dartford
285	12 August 1842	Weymouth	Bere Regis, Dorset
286	5 September 1842	Vauxhall, London	?
287	9 September 1842	Vauxhall, London	?
288	17 July 1843	Birmingham	Coleshill
289	1 August 1843	Cremorne, London	Skreen's Park, near Chelmsford
290	11 August 1843	Stepney, London	Cuckfield, Sussex
291	17 August 1843	Hove, Brighton	Patcham
292	2 September 1843	Belfast #1	Craigavad House, near Belfast
293	9 September 1843	Belfast #2	Near Belfast
294	25 September 1844	Stepney, London	Horton, near Epsom
295	5 May 1845	Vauxhall, London	?
296-299	Not found.		
300	23 June 1845	Albert Saloon, London	St Paul's Cray, Kent
301	25 June 1845	Cremorne, London	Dagenham
302	7 July 1845	Albert Saloon, London	Essex
303	14 July 1845	Cremorne, London	Edenbridge, Kent
304	28 July 1845	Cremorne, London	Tottenham Marshes
305	4 August 1845	Vauxhall, London	Ponders End, Enfield
306	7 August 1845	Cremorne, London	Farningham, Kent
307	11 August 1845	Albert Saloon, London	Kidderborough, Woolwich Common
308	12 August 1845	Vauxhall, London	Beckenham, Kent
309	18 August 1845	Cremorne, London	Harrow
310	20 August 1845	Vauxhall, London	Hoo peninsula, Kent
311	25 August 1845	Cremorne, London	High Beech/Waltham Abbey
312	27 August 1845	Cremorne, London	Beddington Park
313	1 September 1845	Cremorne, London	near Epsom
314	8 September 1845	Cremorne, London	Shepherd's Bush

LIST OF CLAIMED AND VERIFIABLE ASCENTS

Ascent Number	Date	Ascent	Descent
315	22 September 1845	Vauxhall, London	Plumstead Marsh
316-318	Not found		
319	30 April 1846	Stamford	Oxney, Peterborough
320	Not found		
321	5 May 1846	Ipswich	Otley, near Ipswich
322	18 May 1846	Albert Saloon, London	High Ongar
323	29 May 1846	Bury St Edmunds	Lindsey, South of Bury
324	1 June 1846	Cremorne, London	Denham Park, Bucks
325	11 June 1846	Ipswich	Bucklesham, 4 miles East of Ipswich
326	15 June 1846	Cremorne, London	?
327	24 June 1846	Leicester	Cranoe, Northants
328	29 June 1846	Cremorne, London	Stanford Rivers, Ongar
329	6 July 1846	Bath	near Trowbridge
330	20 July 1846	Cremorne, London	Leyton, Essex
331	22 July 1846	Bristol	Doynton, Glos
332-333	Not found.		
334	3 August 1846	Cremorne, London	Walthamstow
335	5 August 1846	Vauxhall, London	Richmond
336	7 August 1846	Leeds	Calverley Carr, near Bradford
337	10 August 1846	Exeter	Rockbeare, East of Exeter
338	13 August 1846	Bridgewater	?
339	17 August 1846	Cremorne, London	Southgate, Edmonton
340	24 August 1846	Cremorne, London	Thames Ditton
341	31 August 1846	Cremorne, London	Penge Common, near Norwood
342	7 September 1846	Cremorne, London	Hazel Green, Hendon
343	21 September 1846	Cremorne, London	towards Putney?
344	2 October 1846	Cremorne, London	Leytonstone
345	5 April 1847	Cremorne, London	Mottingham, Kent
346-348	Not found.		
349	24 May 1847	Cremorne, London	Little Waltham, near Chelmsford
350	1 June 1847	Southampton	Lymington
351	7 June 1847	Cremorne, London	Wenington Level, near Rainham
352-353	Not found.		
354	10 June 1847	Salisbury	Lyndhurst
355-356	Not found.		

THE FLYING ADVENTURES OF CHARLES GREEN

Ascent Number	Date	Ascent	Descent
357	21 June 1847	Cremorne, London	?
358	30 June 1847	Leicester	Brandon, near Coventry
359	Not found.		
360	5 July 1847	Cremorne, London	Edgeware
361	6 July 1847	Cambridge	Bottisham
362	19 July 1847	Cremorne, London	near Hounslow?
363	21 July 1847	Birmingham (Vauxhall)	Lindley Hall, near Hinkley
364	26 July 1847	Derby	Willoughby Waterleys, near Bruntingthorpe
365	2 August 1847	Cremorne, London	Purley
366-368	Not found.		
369	9 August 1847	Cardiff	Nailsea, near Bristol
370	16 August 1847	Cremorne, London	?
371	19 August 1847	Nottingham	Staunton Harold
372	23 August 1847	Cremorne, London	Epsom
373	30 August 1847	Cremorne, London	Bexley
374	6 September 1847	Vauxhall, London	?
xxx	14 September 1847	Cremorne, London	?
375-394	Not found.		
395	17 May 1848	Colchester	Diss
396	31 May 1848	Beccles	Somerleyton
397	15 June 1848	Windsor	Mixbury, near Brackley
398	26 June 1848	Derby	Shipley, near Heanor
399	5 July 1848	Oxford	Steane Park, near Brackley
400	12 July 1848	Leicester	Burbage, near Hinckley
401	Not found.		
(402)	1 August 1848	Maidenhead	No flight, due to bad weather conditions and valve damage. #402 was reported in press as scheduled for 1 August 1848
403	26 July 1848	Bath	Beckhampton Down, near Marlborough
404	8 August 1848	Aylesbury	Horton, near Cheddington, Bucks
405	25 August 1848	Needham Market	Campsea Ashe Park, Suffolk
406	8 September 1848	Stowmarket	Darsham, near Yoxford
407	Not found.		
408	13 October 1848	Sudbury	Aythorpe Roding, Suffolk
(409)	27 October 1848	Halstead	No flight. *Victoria* badly torn. Advertised as #409

LIST OF CLAIMED AND VERIFIABLE ASCENTS

Ascent Number	Date	Ascent	Descent
409	29 May 1849	Colchester	Fingeringhoe Marsh, Wivenhoe
410	5 June 1849	High Wycombe	Farnham
411	22 June 1849	Vauxhall	?
412	27 June 1849	Leicester	Ramsey Hurn, near Whittlesey
413	6 July 1849	Stowmarket	Southolt Plough, near Eye
414-415	Not found.		
416	11 July 1849	Aylesbury	Crowsley Park, Oxon
xxx	13 July 1849	Vauxhall, London	? Advertised, but no press reports. See #414
417	25 July 1849	Vauxhall, London	Purfleet
xxx	27 July 1849	Vauxhall, London	Advertised, but no press reports. See #415
418	1 August 1849	Vauxhall, London	Sydenham
419	3 August 1849	Vauxhall, London	?
420	9 August 1849	Liverpool	Ellesmere Port
421	10 August 1849	Liverpool	Earl Derby's Park
422	14 August 1849	Leeds, White Cloth Hall	near York
423	17 August 1849	Vauxhall, London	? As CG was up North, this flight possibly cancelled
424	20 August 1849	Ashton-u-Lyne	Wortley, near Sheffield
425	22 August 1849	Vauxhall. London	?
426-430	Not found.		
431	4 September 1849	Norwich	Appleton, near Sandringham
432	7 September 1849	Vauxhall, London	? Advertised, but no press report found
433	10 September 1849	Derby	Elmton, near Bolsover
434	11 October 1849	Blisworth, Northants	Tredington, near Shipston-on-Stour
435	22 June 1850	Vauxhall, London	St Paul's Cray, Kent
436	29 June 1850	Vauxhall, London	Into the Thames off Gravesend
437	5 July 1850	Vauxhall, London	?
438	10 July 1850	Leicester	Ravenstone, near Olney
439	23 July 1850	Aston-under-Lyne	Barton Cross, near Preston
440	31 July 1850	Vauxhall, London	Norwood
441	9 August 1850	Vauxhall, London	?
442-445	Not found.		

Ascent Number	Date	Ascent	Descent
446	16 August 1850	Vauxhall, London	? Advertised in *Morning Post* as #446 but no flight information found
447	20 August 1850	Ashton-u-Lyne	Graizelound, Haxey
xxx	22 August 1850	Blisworth, Northants	No flight, *Victoria* damaged during inflation
448	26 August 1850	Vauxhall, London	?
449	4 September 1850	Vauxhall, London	? Night ascent, no report found
450	11 September 1850	Vauxhall, London	? Night ascent, no report found
451	16 September 1850	St Helena Gardens, Rotherhithe, London	? Night ascent, no report found
452	20 September 1850	Vauxhall, London	? Night ascent, no report found
453	4 March 1851	Vauxhall, London	Hastings
454	31 March 1851	Hastings	Neufchatel, France
455	5 May 1851	Vauxhall, London	?
456	27 May 1851	Colchester	Berechurch
457-459	Not found.		
460	23 June 1851	Vauxhall, London	?
461-482	Not found.		
483	29 August 1851	Vauxhall, London	Croome, near Croydon
484	1 September 1851	Vauxhall, London	?
485	8 September 1851	Vauxhall, London	Surrey County Lunatic Asylum, Wandsworth
486	9 September 1851	Surrey County Lunatic Asylum, Wandsworth	Wantage Downs
487	12 September 1851	Vauxhall, London	?
488	15 September 1851	Vauxhall, London	?
489	23 September 1851	Dulwich London	Dorking. CG stated he had made 489 ascents to date
490	31 May 1852	Vauxhall, London	?
491	2 June 1852	Cricket Ground, Leicester	Honington, near Grantham
492	14 June 1852	Vauxhall. London	?
493	18 June 1852	Vauxhall, London	?
494	9 July 1852	Vauxhall, London	?
495	28 July 1852	Vauxhall, London	?
496	17 August 1852	Vauxhall, London	Swavesey, Cambs

LIST OF CLAIMED AND VERIFIABLE ASCENTS

Ascent Number	Date	Ascent	Descent
497	18 August 1852	Vauxhall, London	Deptford
498	27 August 1852	Vauxhall, London	Latimer, near Hemel Hempstead
499	30 August 1852	Vauxhall, London	?
500	2 September 1852	Vauxhall, London	?
501	6 September 1852	Vauxhall, London	Bromley, Kent
502	8 September 1852	Vauxhall, London	Pirbright Common, near Guildford
503	13 September 1852	Vauxhall, London	Cuckfield, near Crawley
504	21 October 1852	Vauxhall, London	?
505	10 November 1852	Vauxhall, London	Acrise, near Folkestone
506-508	Not found.		
509	29 August 1853	Vauxhall, London	Brentwood
510	5 September 1853	Vauxhall, London	Wimbledon Common. CG told passengers #510
511	12 September 1853	Vauxhall, London	Bricket Wood, Herts
512	16 May 1854	Vauxhall, London	?
513	5 June 1854	Surrey Zoological Gardens	Mitcham, Surrey
514	6 June 1854	Brecknock Gardens, London	Near Epsom racecourse
515	3 July 1854	Vauxhall, London	?
516	17 July 1854	Vauxhall, London	?
517	24 July 1854	Vauxhall, London	?
518	8 September 1856	Vauxhall, London	?

Appendix 2

Charles Green's Passenger List

(754 persons identified)

30 July 1822	Samuel Griffith
14 June 1823	Isaac Sparrow
1 August 1823	Henry Simonds
25 June 1824	Henry Brookes
5 August 1824	Harriet Bryant
17 Sept 1824	Edward Clarke
25 Oct 1824	Lieutenant Gandy, Royal Engineers
9 April 1825	George Green (brother)
11 May 1825	George Green (brother)
23 May 1825	George Green (brother)
30 May 1825	George Green (brother)
9 June 1825	Sophia Stocks
2 July 1825	Sophia Stocks
27 July 1825	Sophia Stocks
30 Aug 1825	Miss Dawson
24 Oct 1825	Mr C. Radcliffe
28 March 1826	George Green (brother)
30 March 1826	George (son) & William Henry (brother)
18 April 1826	Charles Thomas Hill
16 May 1826	Mr Barham
31 May 1826	George (brother)
21 June 1826	George (brother)
21 July 1826	George (son) & Mr Whittaker
28 July 1826	Mr Barham & Mr Walter Cave
14 August 1826	Mr Clarke & Mr Hitches
30 August 1826	Henry Brooke Jr
11 Sept 1826	Octavius Simpson
3 Oct 1826	Rev B. Vale
26 Oct 1826	P.E. Wedgwood
17 April 1827	Mr Fox & Mr Mercer (some reports say Mr Beckett)
18 May 1827	George (son)
24 May 1827	Henry Simonds
5 June 1827	Henry Backhouse
9 June 1827	William Astley & Mr Gee
18 June 1827	Mr Gee
25 June 1827	George (son) & Mr Grafton

CHARLES GREEN'S PASSENGER LIST

9 July 1827	George (son)
27 July 1827	George (son) & Captain Leigh
1 August 1827	George (son) & William Heath
10 August 1827	T.W. Strapps & Mr A.H. Philips
27 August 1827	George (son) & Mr Radcliffe
4 Sept 1827	Mr Hodgkins
10 Sept 1827	Thomas Hinton
24 Sept 1827	Mr Hill & Mr Rees-Davies
19 Oct 1827	Mr Scott
19 Nov 1827	George (brother)
7 May 1828	John Willerton
14 May 1828	John Willerton & Henry Brooke junior
9 July 1828	Professor Hemming
26 Aug 1828	Charles Beer & George Cramp
2 Sept 1828	George (son) & Mrs Robinson
10 Sept 1828	George Pearne
28 Oct 1828	George (son)
19 May 1829	2 x un-named passengers from Cambridge University
6 August 1829	George (son) & Mr Whicher (or Witcher)
5 June 1830	George (son)
5 July 1830	George (son)
13 July 1830	George (son) & Mr J.B. Cuttill
9 Oct 1830	Mr Webster & Mr Brown
23 June 1831	Richard Crawshay
2 July 1831	Alderman John Marshall
1 August 1831	Richard Crawshay
15 August 1831	George (son)
22 August 1831	George (son) & Mr Adams
8 Sept 1831	George (son)
25 May 1835	Jacopo Monkey & (possibly) Mr Jephson
22 July 1835	Mr Jephson
27 August 1835	Mr Vivian
12 Sept 1835	Lord Dudley Stuart
17 Sept 1835	Mr Butler
6 Oct 1835	G. Harman
23 Oct 1835	Mr Gocher & Mr Crawshay junior
25 May 1836	Edward Spencer
24 May 1836	Richard Crawshay
23 July 1836	Mrs Ann Green (CG's wife)
2 August 1836	Lord Clanricarde
9 August 1836	Charles Wrottesley
16 August 1836	W. Hodges
30 August 1836	Mrs Evans

9 September 1836. *Royal Vauxhall* first flight.
Captain Currie; believed to be Army officer Robert William Currie of 3rd Dragoon Guards and a 'frequent flyer' with Charles Green and other contemporary aeronauts.
James Green, CG's youngest brother.

THE FLYING ADVENTURES OF CHARLES GREEN

Mrs Ann Green, CG's wife.
Miss Mary Ann(e) Green, Charles' niece.
Edwin Gye, son of Vauxhall proprietor
Robert Charles Hildyard, barrister (later QC, MP)
Robert Hollond. Desperate to make this momentous flight, Hollond took his seat only because he proffered such a large sum of money that Thomas Hughes (the proprietor's other son) was persuaded by his father to vacate his seat.
William Hughes, son of Vauxhall proprietor

21 September 1836. *Royal Vauxhall.*
Mr John Adams, of St Martin's Lane.
Robert Burnett, 21 Park Crescent, Marylebone.
Edward William Cocks, painter and scenic artist-in-residence at Vauxhall Gardens.
Captain Robert William Currie.
Mrs Green, CG's wife Ann.
Thomas Hughes, son of proprietor.
William Hughes, son of proprietor.
Edward Spencer, solicitor and friend of Charles Green.
George Rush.
Mr Woodroffe.
The Hon Mr Young.

27 September 1836. *Royal Vauxhall.*
John Adams.
An un-named 'gentleman with connections to the Gardens.' It is believed this was the ill-fated Robert Cocking, a commercial artist and budding parachutist.
Mr Delafield: believed to be Joseph Delafield, a brewer in Long Acre, London.
Charles' brother; not named but believed to be James Green.
William Hughes, son of proprietor.
Thomas Hughes, son of proprietor.
Thomas Monck Mason.
Edward Spencer.

9 October 1836. *Royal Vauxhall.*
Miss Anderson; a few reports say Miss Harrison.
Mr Back.
Charles' brother, un-named, but believed to be James Green.
Captain Ogle of The Guards.
The Hon William Talbot.
The Hon Frances Gabriella Talbot, Countess of the Austrian Empire. Some newspapers reported this lady as: Madame Fanny Gabrielle, Baroness de Talbot.
Mr Woodroffe.

17 October 1836. *Royal Vauxhall.*
John Adams.
C. Gye.
Frederick Gye: not known whether this is Gye senior or junior.
Robert Edward Hollond.
Edward Holloway.

CHARLES GREEN'S PASSENGER LIST

Thomas Monck Mason.
Edward Spencer.
James Williams.

7 November 1836. (To Germany). *Royal Vauxhall/Nassau.*
Robert Hollond.
Thomas Monck Mason.

19 December 1836. (In Paris). *Royal Vauxhall/Nassau.*
Joseph Louis Gay-Lussac, the famous scientist and aeronaut from the French Academy of Sciences.
Richard Hughes, joint proprietor of the *Vauxhall* balloon.
Monsieur Pilté, a director of the French Gas Company.
Mrs Roscoe: said to be an English lady who paid £25 for her seat.
Lord Yarmouth: believed to be Richard Seymour Conway, a society playboy resident in Paris.

9 January 1837. (In Paris). *Royal Vauxhall/Nassau.*
Monsieur Geniste.
Captain Rees Howell Gronow, a former Welsh Guards officer, who became a writer and resided in Paris after 1825.
Edwin Gye, son of Frederick Gye.
Monsieur Alexandre de Piré, son of Lieutenant General Le Conte de Piré.
Monsieur A. De Seguin de la Salle.
'An unidentified American gentleman.' (It is believed this gentleman was actually Monsieur Pierre M. Jullien).
Count Zichy, an Austrian aristocrat.

15 May 1837. *Royal Vauxhall/Nassau.*
Edwin Gye, son of proprietor of Vauxhall Gardens.
Richard Hughes junior, son of proprietor of Vauxhall Gardens.
William Hughes, son of proprietor of Vauxhall Gardens.
Captain Frederick Polhill, MP for Bedford and former officer in the King's Dragoon Guards.
Robert Rouse, a resident of Highgate.
Edward Spencer.

16 May 1837. *Royal Vauxhall/Nassau.*
Richard Hughes junior, son of proprietor of Vauxhall Gardens.
Thomas Hughes, son of proprietor of Vauxhall Gardens.
Mr J. Hume.
Baron von Kreusser (not Baron Maltitz, as widely reported).
Captain Frederick Polhill MP.
Mr Marr.
George Rush.
Mr Charles Taylor, former superintendent of the gas works in Manchester.

30 May 1837. *Royal Vauxhall/Nassau.*
Robert Hollond.
Mr S. Hughes.
Mr T. Hughes.

THE FLYING ADVENTURES OF CHARLES GREEN

Mr Lambert.
George Rush.
Mr Woodroffe.

16 June 1837. *Royal Vauxhall/Nassau.*
R.B. Barnes.
Captain Carnegie.
T.L. Crommelin.
Mr Laing.
J. Reynolds.
Edward Spencer.
H. Tracey.

23 June 1837. *Royal Vauxhall/Nassau.*
John Bush(e).
Lord Walter Butler.
Robert Hildyard.
Captain Leicester.
T. Power.
Captain Tollemache.
Captain Wilmot-Horton.

3 July 1837. *Royal Vauxhall/Nassau.*
Mr Brunsden, of Cheltenham.
Richard Hughes, proprietor of Vauxhall Gardens, London.
R. Jearrad junior, son of R. W. Jearrad, an architect in Cheltenham.
Mr S. Moss, chemist of Cheltenham.
Thomas Spinney, gas works manager.

24 July 1837. (Cockings Parachute ascent). *Royal Vauxhall/Nassau.*
Edward Spencer

21 August 1837. *Royal Vauxhall/Nassau.*
Captain Blakesley.
Joseph William Carttar, coroner for West Kent, who presided at the inquest of Robert Cocking.
Mr Finch, this may be the surgeon who gave evidence at the inquest of Robert Cocking.
Richard Hughes junior.
Captain Polhill MP.
Doctor J.P. Simon MD, a French medical and scientific gentleman.

23 October 1837. *Royal Vauxhall/Nassau.*
Mr Green, proprietor of the Rainbow Tavern and coffee rooms, on corner of Spring Gardens and Market Street, Manchester; no relation to CG.
Richard Hughes junior.
Mr James Lord junior, of Broad Street, Pendleton.
Mr Sloan, a performer at the Queen's Theatre, Manchester.
Mr James Veysey, proprietor of the Brown Bull Inn on Chapel Street, Salford.

CHARLES GREEN'S PASSENGER LIST

4 November 1837. *Royal Vauxhall/Nassau.*
Miss Ann Brougham, daughter of a builder in Hardman Street, Manchester.
Mr John Chadwick, superintendent of the Salford Gas Works.
Lieutenant Colonel Sir Michael Creagh, an officer of the 86th Regiment.
Mr Green, of the Rainbow Tavern, Manchester, his second trip.
William Hughes, a son of the proprietor of Vauxhall Gardens.
Mr Mansfield, a chemist of Bury Street, Salford.
Mr Sloan, of the Queen's Theatre, Manchester, his second trip.

25 June 1838. *Royal Vauxhall/Nassau.*
Mr Bord.
W. Hughes.
Edward Spencer.
Mr Wight.

2 July 1838. *Royal Vauxhall/Nassau.*
Mrs Green, CG's wife Ann.
Edwin Gye, son of the proprietor.
Richard Hughes junior.
Mr Mercer.
George Rush.

10 July 1838. *Royal Vauxhall/Nassau.*
Captain Carnegie.
Monsieur le Comte Kalling, of the Swedish Embassy.
Lieutenant Tryon, Royal Navy.
Mr Power MP.
Mrs Webb.
Mr Wrottesley, son of Sir John Wrottesley, MP for Staffordshire.
An unidentified gentleman (possibly Mr Parbury).

17 July 1838. *Royal Vauxhall/Nassau.*
Captain Carnegie.
Mr Gye.
Mr Hughes.
Mr Power MP.
Mr Tennyson.
Two unidentified gentlemen.

24 July 1838. *Royal Vauxhall/Nassau.*
Miss Crawshay.
Mr Crawshay.
Mr Fitzroy.
Richard Hughes junior.
William Albert, Mons le Comte de Neipperg, an Austrian nobleman.
George Rush.
Miss Waters.

THE FLYING ADVENTURES OF CHARLES GREEN

31 July 1838. *Royal Vauxhall/Nassau.*
Mr Crawshay.
Mr Chichester.
Two unidentified gentlemen.

7 August 1838. *Royal Vauxhall/Nassau.*
Six unidentified passengers.

13 August 1838. *Royal Vauxhall/Nassau.*
Mr Barclay.
Mr Barrett.
Mr Boyd.
Mr Connell.
Mr Thomas Green, Charles Green's father.
R. Hughes.
Edward Spencer.

17 August 1838. *Coronation* balloon.
Mrs Green, CG's wife Ann.

21 August 1838. *Coronation.*
One unidentified gentleman.

24 August 1838. *Coronation.*
No passengers taken.

28 August 1838. *Royal Vauxhall/Nassau.*
W. Hughes.
One unidentified lady.
Mr Tucker.

4 September 1838. *Royal Vauxhall/Nassau.*
Edward Spencer.
George Rush.

7 September 1838. *Royal Vauxhall/Nassau.*
Believed no passengers taken.

10 September 1838. *Royal Vauxhall/Nassau.*
George Rush.

14 September 1838. *Royal Vauxhall/Nassau.*
Lieutenant Archibald William, Viscount Drumlanrig, of 2nd Regiment, Life Guards.
An unidentified officer of 2nd Regiment, Life Guards.
Richard Hughes junior.
Mrs Green, presumed to be CG's wife Ann.
Mr Green senior, CG's father Thomas.
Thomas Hughes.

CHARLES GREEN'S PASSENGER LIST

Mr Poole, an author.
Edward Spencer.

18 September 1838. *Royal Vauxhall/Nassau.*
R. Hughes.
W. Hughes.
Colonel Sir Charles Dance Webb, of 2nd Regiment, Life Guards.

2 October 1838. *Royal Vauxhall/Nassau.*
Mr B. Boyd.
Mr F. Dalley (or Dulley).
Frederick Gye junior.
Mr Howard.
Mr J. Thomas.
Captain J. Webb (or Mr R. Webb in some newspapers).

8 October 1838. *Royal Vauxhall/Nassau.*
Advertised ascent, but unconfirmed and no passenger information.

25 April 1839. *Royal Vauxhall/Nassau.*
R. Hughes junior.
George Rush.

8 July 1839. *Royal Vauxhall/Nassau.*
Mr Corrie.
Mr Duff.
Mr Fielding.
Mr W. Hughes.
Sir C. Kent.
Mr Wellesley.

15 July 1839. *Royal Vauxhall/Nassau.*
Richard Crawshay.
David Dulley.
W. Gye.
An unidentified Lady.
Edward Spencer.

14 August 1839. *Coronation.*
Mr Dulley.

5 September 1839. *Coronation.*
No passengers.

16 October 1839. *Coronation.*
Richard Crawshay.

17 August 1840. *Coronation.*
Richard Graves MacDonnell.

THE FLYING ADVENTURES OF CHARLES GREEN

24 August 1840. *Royal Vauxhall/Nassau.*
W. Andrews.
Nicholas Bacon
Richard Crawshay.
Edward Crawshay, son
Frederick Crawshay, son
W. Shalders.

6 October 1840. *Royal Vauxhall/Nassau.*
Thomas Monck Mason.
Two unidentified Naval officers.

12 July 1841. *Royal Vauxhall/Nassau.*
Captain R.W. Currie.
Mr Davidson.
David Dulley.
Mrs Green, CG's daughter-in-law,
Mr Hepworth.
Captain Dudley Ward, younger brother of Lord Ward.

26 July 1841. *Royal Vauxhall/Nassau.*
Mr Adams.
Captain R.W. Currie.
Mr G. Green, believed to be CG's son George.
Mr Leche of Cardom Park, Cheshire.
Henry Soper.
Captain Dudley Ward.
The Hon Mortimer West.

30 July 1841. *Royal Vauxhall/Nassau.*
Captain R.W. Currie.
Thomas Monck Mason.
Mr Sotherby junior.
CG's brother, unidentified.
CG's son, George.
One unidentified gentleman.

9 August 1841. 'in one of his smaller balloons.'
No passengers.

23 August 1841. *Royal Vauxhall/Nassau.*
Captain R.W. Currie.
Mr G.H. Davidson.
Mr Dulley.
Mrs Green, not known which one.
CG's father, Thomas Green.
Thomas Moates.
Henry Soper.

CHARLES GREEN'S PASSENGER LIST

30 August 1841. *Royal Vauxhall/Nassau*.
Captain R.W. Currie, his 33rd balloon ascent (not all with CG).
Mr Dulley
Mrs Joanna Forrest, a portrait painter from Bloomsbury.
Dr Locock.
One unidentified gentleman.

27 June 1842. *Albion*.
No passengers.

12 August 1842. *Albion*.
Captain R.W. Currie, his 36th balloon ascent.

17 July 1843. *Royal Vauxhall/Nassau*.
Captain R.W. Currie.
J. Barwell.
H. Jeffries.
W. Welch.

1 August 1843. *Albion*.
Captain R.W. Currie, his 41st ascent.

11 August 1843. *Albion*.
Alfred Bradley.

17 August 1843. *Albion*.
Alfred Bradley.

2 September 1843, *Albion*.
No passengers.

9 September 1843. *Albion*.
Mr Montgomery.

25 September 1844. *Albion*.
Edward Curry.
Mr J. Reynolds Pugh junior.

5 May 1845. *Albion*.
No passengers.

23 June 1845. *Albion*.
W. Selwyn Morris, a surgeon from Wye, Kent.

26 June 1845. *Royal Vauxhall/Nassau*.
Joseph Charles, of Fleet Street.
George Green, CG's son.
William Green, CG's nephew.

THE FLYING ADVENTURES OF CHARLES GREEN

W. Selwyn Morris.
Captain Simpson.
Henry Williams, of Pentonville.

7 July 1845, *Albion*.
Mr Brading junior, son of proprietor of Albert Saloon.
Thomas Green, CG's father.

14 July 1845, *Albion*.
Mr T.E. Bass, of Peckham.

28 July 1845. *Royal Vauxhall/Nassau*.
Mr T.E. Bass.
Mrs T.E. Bass.
Lord G. Beresford
Mrs Green, CG's wife Ann.
Mr W. Green, CG's nephew.
Mr David Littlejohn, proprietor of Cremorne Gardens.
Mr Thomas Matthews, celebrity clown from Drury Lane Theatre.
Unidentified officer of the Life Guards.
Mr Williams, 'who painted the balloon.'
Mr Wyman.
2 unidentified gentlemen.

4 August 1845. *Albion*.
No passengers taken.

7 August 1845. *Albion*.
No passengers taken.

11 August 1845. *Albion*.
Henry Brading, proprietor of the Albert Saloon.
Mrs Brading, his wife, formerly Mrs Ismay, an actress.

12 August 1845. *Albion*.
Mrs Green, CG's wife.

18 August 1845. *Albion*.
No passengers taken.

20 August 1845. *Albion*.
No passengers taken.
Albion badly damaged.

25 August 1845. *Royal Vauxhall/Nassau*.
George Green, CG's son.
Henry Green, CG's brother. Some newspapers state 'T. Green.'
W. Green, believed to be CG's nephew William.

CHARLES GREEN'S PASSENGER LIST

Mr Littlejohn.
Edward Spencer.
Mr Williams.
One unidentified gentleman.

27 August 1845. *Coronation*.
The Hon G. Vansittart, nephew of Lord Bexley.

1 September 1845. *Royal Vauxhall/Nassau*.
Mr Butler, an undertaker of Faringdon Street.
Colonel Charles.
W. Green, believed to be William, CG's nephew.
Dr Henry.
Mr C.N. Kirkham.
Mr Granville Mansell.
Mr Moss, of Leadenhall Street.
Two unidentified gentlemen.

8 September 1845. *Royal Vauxhall/Nassau*.
Mr Bass.
Mrs Bass.
Mr Denton.
G. Green, believed to be George, CG's son.
Mrs Green, CG's wife.
Mr Hardwicke, a magistrate.
Mr J.A. Layard, of the Ceylon Rifles.
Mr David Littlejohn.
Captain G. Sprigg, Royal Navy.
Mr Salter, of Piazzas, Covent Garden.

22 September 1845. *Royal Vauxhall/Nassau*.
Mr J. Finch junior, of Liverpool.
W. Green.
Mr Laws.
Mr David Littlejohn.
Mr C. Stewart, of Great Yarmouth.
Mr Wymer.
Mr Walset.
Three unidentified gentlemen.

30 April 1846. *Albion*.
Mr Jones, Stamford gas works manager.

5 May 1846. *Albion*.
No passengers taken.

18 May 1846. *Albion*.
Henry Green, brother.

29 May 1846. *Albion*.
No passengers taken.

1 June 1846. *Albion*.
CG's brother, believed to be Henry.

11 June 1846. *Albion*.
No passengers taken.

15 June 1846. *Albion*?
One unidentified gentleman.
'Jocko,' a monkey.

24 June 1846. *Royal Vauxhall/Nassau*.
CG's brother, un-named.
William Moore, chemist.
Alfred Padley, of Bulwell Hall, Nottingham.
Mr Padley's servant, unidentified.
Mr Prosser, superintendent of Leicester lunatic asylum.
Mr H. Stallard, surgeon.
Mr Williams, CG's brother-in-law.

29 June 1846. *Royal Vauxhall/Nassau*.
Mr J. Armstrong, of the College of Civil Engineers, Putney.
Mr G.H. Davidson, publisher of the well-known *Music for the Millions*.
Mr J.J. Fryer, of Kensington.
Mr G. Lawton, of Ditchley Park, Essex.
Mr Powell, of Benson, Oxfordshire.
Mr Sargent, of Fleet Street.
Edward Spencer, solicitor and friend of CG.
Mr van Buren, of Cremorne Gardens.

6 July 1846. *Albion*?
No passengers taken.

20 July 1846. *Royal Vauxhall/Nassau*.
Hon R. Clifton.
Mr Davidson.
Mrs Davidson.
Ambrose Goddard.
George Green, CG's son.
Mrs Green, believed to be CG's wife.
Mr J. Snow.
Edward Spencer.
Mr van Buren.
Mr Williams.

22 July 1846. *Albion*.
Mr Wall, a stonemason of Easton

CHARLES GREEN'S PASSENGER LIST

3 August 1846. *Royal Vauxhall/Nassau*.
Mr Bee.
Mr Bee's friend.
Mr Burton?
Mr James Ellis, lessee of the Cremorne Gardens.
Ebenezer Landells, wood engraver, Illustrator and magazine proprietor.
Edward Spencer
Mr van Buren.
Four unidentified gentlemen.

5 August 1846. *Coronation*.
No passengers taken.

7 August 1846. *Albion*.
No passengers taken.

10 August 1846. *Albion*?
John Benham, clockmaker of Cullompton.

13 August 1846. no details reported.

17 August 1846.
Eleven passengers; two ladies and nine gentlemen all unidentified.

24 August 1846. *Coronation* and *Albion*.
Captain Davies in *Coronation*.
No passengers in *Albion*.

31 August 1846. *Royal Vauxhall/Nassau*.
CG's brother, believed to be Henry.
Miss Dixie.
Mrs Green, believed to be CG's wife.
Mr Hoole.
Miss Lowe.
Mr Pond.
Edward Spencer.
Mr van Buren.
Mrs van Buren.
Two unidentified gentlemen.

7 September 1846. *Royal Vauxhall/Nassau*.
Madame Corri, a trainer of performing animals.
Mr van Buren.
Mrs van Buren.
Mr Williams.
Mrs Williams.
Six unidentified persons.

THE FLYING ADVENTURES OF CHARLES GREEN

21 September 1846. *Royal Vauxhall/Nassau.*
Eight unidentified passengers, no details reported.

2 October 1846. *Royal Vauxhall/Nassau.*
Mr van Buren.
Six unidentified persons.

5 April 1847. *Royal Vauxhall/Nassau.*
Mr James Ellis, lessee of Cremorne Gardens.
Edward Spencer.
Mr van Buren.
Nine unidentified persons.

24 May 1847. *Victoria.*
Arthur Pratt Barlow.
Mr Hoole, 'a friend of CG.'
Herr Koenig, a musician who played his cornet during the trip.

1 June 1847. *Victoria.*
Major Greenwood, son of Colonel Greenwood.
Mr Green's 'assistant,' unidentified.
Miss Longford, of Portland Street, Southampton.

7 June 1847. *Royal Vauxhall/Nassau.*
Charles William Shirley Brooks, writer.
Mr Davidson, of the Garrick Club.
Mr Drew.
Mr Ibbotson.
Maurice Johnson, of Spalding, Lincolnshire, a friend of Edward Spencer.
John Lee, writer.
Morris Power.
Albert Smith, writer.
Edward Spencer.
Mr P. Thompson of Guy's Hospital.

10 June 1847. *Balloon unidentified.*
Mr Wadman, of Bristol.

21 June 1847. *Victoria.*
No passengers reported, but two monkeys dropped by separate parachutes.

30 June 1847. *Victoria.*
Mr J. Hildyard.
John Moxon, of High Street, Leicester.

5 July 1847. *Royal Vauxhall/Nassau.*
One unidentified gentleman 'connected with the daily journals.'
Mr Davidson, 'the popular solicitor and theatrical amateur.'

CHARLES GREEN'S PASSENGER LIST

Mr van Buren.
Seven other unidentified gentlemen.

6 July 1847. *Victoria*.
John Gedney, of Redenhall, near Harleston, Norfolk.
Mrs Green, CG's wife.

19 July 1847. *Royal Vauxhall/Nassau*.
Lindsey Antrobus, possibly Hugh Lindsay Antrobus, an Army officer
Captain Henry Percival de Bathe, Scots Fusilier Guards.
CG's brother, unidentified.
Captain F. Crest, Grenadier Guards.
Windsor Heneage.
James Little.
Hugh McCalmont, possibly Hugh McCalmont Cairns, barrister.
Mr Rein, some newspapers state 'Dr Fresch.'
Mr Spencer, possibly Edward Spencer.
Mr Williams, possibly CG's brother-in-law.

21 July 1847. *Victoria*.
Two unidentified gentlemen from Birmingham.

26 July 1847. *Victoria*.
John Foxcroft, of Nottingham.
Arthur Holmes, of Derby.

2 August 1847. *Royal Vauxhall/Nassau*.
Captain Bradford, Grenadier Guards.
James Carnegie, Grenadier Guards.
John Hilder, possibly John Hildyard?
Captain the Hon Charles Lindsay, Grenadier Guards.
Captain Henry Montresor, Grenadier Guards.
Mr Newton.
Sir Edward Poore, Scots Fusiliers.

9 August 1847. *Victoria*.
One unidentified gentleman relative of CG.

16 August 1847. balloon not known.
No passenger information found.

19 August 1847. *Victoria*.
Captain Forster, 4th Royal Irish Dragoon Guards.
Mr Foxcroft, solicitor of Nottingham.

23 August 1847. *Coronation*.
No passengers taken.

THE FLYING ADVENTURES OF CHARLES GREEN

30 August 1847. ?
Two monkeys, 'Jocko' and 'Garnerin.'
No other passenger information.

6 September 1847. possibly in *Victoria*.
One other unidentified 'aeronaut.'

14 September 1847. ?
Two monkeys, 'Jocko' and 'Garnerin.'
No other passenger information.

17 May 1848. *Victoria*.
No passengers taken.

31 May 1848, *Victoria*.
Robert Oswald of Shaddingfield House, Beccles.

15 June 1848. *Victoria*.
Mr Bellis of Maidenhead.

26 June 1848. *Victoria*.
Henry Peet, of the Derby Silk Mills.

5 July 1848. *Victoria*.
Mr Milner of Merton College and said to be a relative of Lord John Russell.
Hon. Mr Wrottesley, fellow of All Soul's College and son of MP for Staffordshire.

12 July 1848. *Victoria*.
Richard Crawshay, reported as making his 9th ascent.
Alfred Payne.
Arthur Frederick Payne, sons of Henry Payne of The Newarke.

26 July 1848. *Victoria*.
Mr Brooks, a stonemason of Henrietta Walk, Bath.

8 August 1848. *Victoria*.
Richard H. Howard, gas works manager from Aylesbury.
An unidentified relation of CG referred to as 'his assistant.'

25 August 1848. *Victoria*.
Mr W. Gross, of Bury St Edmunds.
Joseph Paul, of Thorpe Abbotts.

8 September 1848. *Victoria*.
Joseph Paul (#2).
Thomas Peck, of Wetheringsett, Suffolk.

13 October 1848. *Victoria*.
Robert Spooner, of Bulmer, Sudbury.
Mr Surridge, of Halstead.

CHARLES GREEN'S PASSENGER LIST

29 May 1849. *Victoria*.
William A. Burgess
Charles Page, cattle dealer of Great Horkesley, Essex.

5 June 1849. *Victoria*.
No passengers taken.

22 June 1849. ?
No passenger information.

27 June 1849. *Victoria*.
Captain Cheslyn, of Leicester.
George Rush, of Elsenham Hall.

6 July 1849. possibly *Victoria*.
Miss Cully (or Culley), daughter of Stowmarket gas works manager.

11 July 1849. *Victoria*.
No passengers taken.

13 July 1849. *Victoria*.
No passenger information.

25 July 1849. *Royal Vauxhall/Nassau*, accident just after take-off
Richard Crawshay.
Mr Ferrar (or Farmer, or Faunce), current treasurer of Vauxhall Gardens.
Miss Gascoyne.
Mrs Green, CG's wife.
William Green, nephew of CG.
Mrs William Green.
Miss Green, daughter of a Mr T. Green; no relation to CG.
Captain Ondre.
Charles Thomas Pearce, of Park Road, Regent's Park; 'patentee of the Electric Light'.
Mr Stephens.

27 July 1849. ?
No flight or passenger information found.

1 August 1849. *Royal Vauxhall/Nassau*.
Upper car:
Richard Risley Carlisle, a celebrated American circus athlete/acrobat, professionally known as Richard Risley.
Mr Ferrar, of Vauxhall Gardens, his second trip.
Miss Forrest.
Young Hernandez, a celebrated American circus equestrian performer, age 17.
Miss Orme.
George Rush.
Lower car:

THE FLYING ADVENTURES OF CHARLES GREEN

Mr R. David.
Henry Green, CG's brother.
Two unidentified gentlemen.

3 August 1849. advertised as *Royal Vauxhall/Nassau*.
No flight or passenger information found.

9 August 1849. *Victoria*.
Councillor Fisher.
Henry Green, CG's brother.

10 August 1849. *Victoria*.
Robert Horsfall,
William Horsfall, sons of a former mayor of Liverpool.

14 August 1849. *Victoria*.
Henry Green.

17 August 1849. *Victoria*.
No passenger information found.

20 August 1849. *Victoria*.
Captain Ross, of 90th Regiment.

22 August 1849. *Victoria*.
No passenger information found.

4 September 1849. possibly *Victoria*.
George Rush.

7 September 1849. *Victoria*.
No passenger information found.

10 September 1849. *Victoria*.
No passengers taken.

11 October 1849. *Victoria*.
George Rush, his 14th flight with CG.

22 June 1850. *Royal Vauxhall/Nassau*.
George Rush.

29 June 1850. *Royal Vauxhall/Nassau*.
George Rush.

5 July 1850. *Victoria*.
No passenger information found.

CHARLES GREEN'S PASSENGER LIST

10 July 1850. *Victoria*.
George Rush.

23 July 1850. *Victoria*.
Isaac Watt Boulton, a railway engineer of Ashton-u-Lyne.

9 August 1850. possibly *Victoria*.
No flight or passenger information found.

16 August 1850, possibly *Victoria*.
No flight or passenger information found.

20 August 1850. *Victoria*.
Isaac Watts Boulton.

26 August 1850. *Coronation*.
No flight or passenger information found.

29 June 1850. *Royal Vauxhall/Nassau*.
George Rush.

4 September 1850. *?*
No flight or passenger information found.

11 September 1850. *?*
No flight or passenger information found.

16 September 1850. *?*
No flight or passenger information found.

20 September 1850. *?*
No flight or passenger information found.

4 March 1851. *Royal Vauxhall/Nassau*.
Duke of Brunswick.

31 March 1851. *Victoria*.
Duke of Brunswick.

5 May 1851. *Royal Vauxhall/Nassau*.
No flight or passenger information found.

27 May 1851, *Victoria*.
Adolphus G. Burgess.

23 June 1851. *Royal Vauxhall/Nassau*.
No flight or passenger information found.

THE FLYING ADVENTURES OF CHARLES GREEN

29 August 1851.
No flight or passenger information found.

1 September 1851. *Royal Vauxhall/Nassau.*
No flight or passenger information found.
'Accompanied by a number of members of the Army and Navy.'

8 September 1851. *Royal Vauxhall/Nassau?*
Four unidentified military officers.

9 September 1851. *Royal Vauxhall/Nassau.*
Same four unidentified military officers.

12 September 1851. *?*
No flight or passenger information found.

15 September 1851. *Royal Vauxhall/Nassau?*
No flight information found.
Full load, (say ten) since several passengers sat on hoop.

23 September 1851. *Royal Vauxhall/Nassau.*
Five unidentified passengers.

31 May 1852. *Royal Vauxhall/Nassau.*
No flight or passenger information found.

2 June 1852, *Victoria.*
CG's brother, unidentified.

14 June 1852. *Royal Vauxhall/Nassau.*
No flight or passenger information found.

18 June 1852. *Royal Vauxhall/Nassau.*
No flight or passenger information found.

9 July 1852. *Royal Vauxhall/Nassau?*
No flight or passenger information found.

28 July 1852. *?*
No flight or passenger information found.

17 August 1852. *Royal Vauxhall/Nassau.*
Richard Nicklin, of Kew Observatory.
John Welsh, of Kew Observatory.

18 August 1852. *Royal Vauxhall/Nassau.*
One lady and eight gentlemen, unidentified.

CHARLES GREEN'S PASSENGER LIST

27 August 1852. *Royal Vauxhall/Nassau.*
Patrick Adie, instrument maker of 395 The Strand, London.
Richard Nicklin.
John Welsh.

30 August 1852. *Royal Vauxhall/Nassau.*
No flight information found.
'A portion of a military brass band taken into the air.'

2 September 1852. *Royal Vauxhall/Nassau.*
No flight information found.
Ten members of a brass band performed in the air.

6 September 1852. *Royal Vauxhall/Nassau.*
J.W. Clayton, of 13th Dragoons, on hoop.
Charles Paternoster, of Southwark, on hoop.
Two unidentified officers of the Dragoons, on hoop.
Six other unidentified persons in the car.

8 September 1852. *Royal Vauxhall/Nassau.*
W. Little.
James Macswinney
Henry Mayhew.
Horace Mayhew.
E. Watkins.
Three other unidentified gentlemen.

13 September 1852. *Royal Vauxhall/Nassau.*
Dr Goodeve, of 2 Kensington Place Gardens, London.
Charles Hufnagle, United States consul in Calcutta.
G. Moulson, of Clapham.
Septimus Parrott, of Clapham Common.
George Stevens, of Vauxhall.
J. Tell Topham.

21 October 1852. *Royal Vauxhall/Nassau.*
John Welsh, of Kew Observatory.

10 November 1852. *Royal Vauxhall/Nassau.*
John Welsh.

29 August 1853. *Royal Vauxhall/Nassau.*
William Green, CG's nephew.
Six other unidentified passengers

5 September 1853. *Royal Vauxhall/Nassau.*
George Davis Gibbs, an artist.
William Green.

THE FLYING ADVENTURES OF CHARLES GREEN

Charles Paternoster.
Four other unidentified passengers.

12 September 1853. *Royal Vauxhall/Nassau.*
William Green.
Eight other unidentified passengers.

16 May 1854. *Royal Vauxhall/Nassau.*
A 'private party' of unidentified gentlemen.
No flight or passenger information found.

5 June 1854. *Victoria.*
No passengers taken.

6 June 1854. *Victoria?*
Charles Paternoster.
No flight information found.

3 July 1854. *Royal Vauxhall/Nassau.*
Seat lottery.
No flight or passenger information found.

17 July 1854, *Royal Vauxhall/Nassau.*
Seat lottery.
No flight or passenger information found.

24 July 1854. *Royal Vauxhall/Nassau.*
Seat lottery.
No flight or passenger information found.

8 September 1856. *Royal Vauxhall/Nassau.*
Charles Green, aeronaut, as passenger to pilot Joseph J. Oddy Taylor.
Mr Bacon.
Dr Lister, a surgeon.
No flight information found.

Endnotes

Chapter 1
1. Bacon, J.M., *Dominion of The Air*, Cassell & Co, London; 1902, pages 23-30.
2. Cyril Bowdler Henry: 1962, via David E. Coke: vauxhallhistory.org.
3. Volume 1: 1892.
4. *Derbyshire Courier*, 15 September 1849, page 2.
5. *Islington Gazette*, 1 April 1870, page 2.
6. *The Aeronauts*: Alan Sutton: 1985; Gloucester.
7. Cavallo, *History & Practise of Aerostation*, pages 233-235.
8. Using the Bank of England's on-line inflation calculator: bankofengland.co.uk/monetary-policy/inflation/inflation-calculator.

Chapter 2
1. *The Literary Chronicle & Weekly Review for 1821*: London, page 490.

Chapter 3
1. via David Arnold; 2014.
2. *London Evening Standard*: 27 February 1836.
3. *Morning Post*: 27 February 1836.

Chapter 9
1. *Essex Standard* :10 Oct 1835.

Chapter 10
1. *Globe*: 6 July 1836, page 2.
2. e.g. *Globe*; *Sun*; *Morning Post*: all 7 July 1836.
3. *Morning Advertiser*: 21 Sept 1836.
4. *Sun*, London: 31 October 1836.

Chapter 11
1. *Morning Post, et al*: 4 Oct 1837, page 3.

Chapter 12
1. David E. Coke; vauxhallhistory.org: 2018.
2. e.g. *Morning Post*: 18 November 1839.
3. *Bell's Weekly Messenger*: 15 March 1840, page 6.
4. *The Literary World*, No.54: 4 April 1840.

5. British-history.ac.uk and footnote 340.
6. See also a letter in *Kentish Gazette*: 23 April 1844, page 3.
7. *The Globe*: 21 April 1846.
8. *Morning Post*: 18 May 1846.
9. *Manchester Times*: 22 November 1845, page 8.

Chapter 14

1. *Lady's Own Paper*: 21 August 1852, page 11.
2. *The Athenaeum*, Journal of Literature, Science and the Fine Arts: London; 1852.
3. *The Sun*: 14 Oct 1852.
4. *In the Clouds or, some Account of a Balloon Trip with Mr Green*; Mayhew; 1852.
5. *Philosophical Transactions*, Journal of The Royal Society, Vol 143: 31 Dec 1853.
6. *Morning Advertiser*: 4 September 1856.
7. *Cheltenham Journal*: 27 September 1856.
8. *My Life and Ballooning Experiences*, Volume 2, page 189.
9. Tissandier, *Travels in the Air*, 1871, pages 329-341 and Fonvielle, *Adventures in the Air*, 1877, page 168.
10. *Adventures in the Air*, page 169.
11. *Daily News*: 15 April 1870.
12. *Penny Illustrated Paper*: 25 August 1888, page 6.
13. *Surrey Gazette*: 25 May 1900, page 4.
14. Trinity College, Cambridge archive ref: Crewe MS/8/f.23r.
15. Aeronautical Society First Annual Report, 1866, page 45.
16. Aeronautical Society Second Annual Report, 1867, page 29.
17. e.g. *New York Herald*: 11 April 1870, page 2.

Bibliography

Anderson, Katherine, *Predicting the Weather; Victorians and the science of Meteorology*, (University of Chicago Press, USA, 2005).
Axon, William E.A., editor, *Annals of Manchester*, (?, 1886).
Bacon, J.M., *The Dominion of the Air*, (Cassel & Co, London, 1902).
Cavallo, T., *History and Practice of Aerostation*, (?, London, 1785).
Coke, David & Borg, Alan, *Vauxhall Gardens, A History*, (Paul Mellon, London, 2011).
Coxwell, Henry, *My Life and Balloon Experiences, Vols 1 & 2*, (W.H. Allen, London, 1887 & 1889).
Cunningham, Hugh, *Leisure in the Industrial Revolution 1780-1880*, (Croom Helm, London, 1980).
Davies, Mark, *King of All Balloons*, (Amberley, Stroud, 2018).
De Fonvielle, Wilfrid, *Adventures in the Air*, (E. Stanford, London, 1877).
Dollfus, Charles & Bourke, Henri, *Histoire de L'Aeronautique*, (L'Illustration, Paris; 1942, p 63, via Federation Aeronautique Internationale [FAI] Hall of Fame, 1999).
Glaisher, James, editor, *Travels in the Air*, (Richard Bentley, London, 1871).
Goodrum, Alastair, *Balloons, Bleriots and Barnstormers*, (The History Press, Stroud, 2009).
Hayward, Arthur L., *The Dickens Encyclopedia*, (George Routledge, Abingdon, 1924).
Hodgson J.E., *The History of Aeronautics in Great Britain*, (Oxford University Press, London, 1924).
Holmes, Richard, *Falling Upwards*, (William Collins, London, 2013).
Holmes, Scanlon & Nibleth, *Higher Education in a Changing World*, (Routledge, London, 1971/72).
Kotar S.L., & Gessler J.E., *Ballooning, A History 1782-1900*, (McFarland, Jefferson NC, USA & London, 2011).
Layton-Jones, Katy & Lee, Robert, *Places of Health and Amusement, Liverpool's Historic Parks & Gardens*, (English Heritage, Swindon, 2008).
Livermore, Seward W, *Early Commercial & Consular Relations in the East Indies*, (University of California, USA, 1946).
Macdonald, Lee T., *Kew Observatory and the Evolution of Science*, (University of Pittsburgh, USA, 2018).
Mackie, Charles, *Norfolk Annals, Volume 1*, (Norfolk Chronicle, Norwich, 1901).
Mason, Monck, *Account of the late aeronautical expedition from London to Weilburg*, (F.C. Westley, London,1836).
Mason, Monck, *Aeronautica*, (F.C. Westley, London, 1838).
Matthew, H.C.G., & Harrison, Brian, editors, *Oxford Dictionary of National Biography*. (Oxford University Press, London, 2004, and updates).
Minckelers, M, *Memoire sur l'air inflammable, tiré de différentes substances*, (?, Louvain, 1784).

Montgomery, Henry H., *The History of Kennington and its Neighbourhood*, (H.S. Gold, London, 1889).
Mondey, D., & Taylor, M.J.H., *The Guiness Book of Aircraft Facts and Feats*, (Guiness Publishing, London, 1988).
Rolt, L.T.C., *The Aeronauts*, (Alan Sutton, Gloucester, 1985).
Rush, George, *Great Heights - from Vauxhall*, (W.H. Jones, London, 1851).
Strange, W., *Figaro in London, Volume V*, (?, London: 1836).
Sweet, Jack William, *More Somerset Tales*, (Amberley, Stroud, 2017).
Tissandier, Gaston, *Travels in the Air*, (R. Bentley, London, 1871).
Wise, John, *A System of Aeronautics*, (Joseph A. Speel, USA, 1850).
Wroth, Warwick, *Cremorne & the Later London Gardens*, (Elliot Stock, London, 1907).

Annual Reports of the Aeronautical Society of Great Britain for 1866 and 1867; from *Aerial Locomotion* (Cassel, Petter & Galpin, London, 1868).
British Art Studies.ac.uk: *gasworks/ballooning*.
Elements of Meteorology, 3rd Edition. Journal of Royal Institution of Great Britain, Vol 12.
Stanmore Tourist Board, *The Hollonds of Stanmore Hall*, (?).

Index

Names

Adie, Patrick, 173
Airy, George Biddel, 136
Anglesey, Lord, 159-60

Bacon, John Mackenzie, 1
Bell, Henry, 54
Bibra, Baron de, 126
Black, Joseph, 2
Bowles, George, 84
Branson, Richard, 146
Broadmeadow, Simeon, 73
Brooke, Henry, 78
Brookes, Henry, 39-40
Brunswick, Duke of, 111, 169-71
Bryant, Harriet, 44-5
Burghley, Lord, 155

Carttar, Joseph William, 136
Cavallo, Tiberius, 8
Cavendish, Henry, 2
Cayley, Sir George, 130
Chads, Captain, 159-60
Chalmer, Lieutenant-Colonel, 159-60
Cheesman, Francis, 22
Clear, Captain, 22-3
Cocking, Robert, 6, 119, 131-37, 142
Cocks, E.W., 129
Coxwell, Henry, 3, 6, 20, 161, 163, 175-78
Crawshay, Richard, 93-4, 145-48, 165
Culling, Isaac, 5, 181
Culling, Jane, 5
Currie, Captain Robert William, 115, 141, 148, 150
Cuttill, J.B., 91

Davy, Sir Humphrey, 76, 122
de Fonvielle, Wilfred, 177-78
Depuis-Delcourt, Jean-Francois, 121
Duncombe, Thomas Slingsby, 73
Dyke, Percy Holt, 72, 110
Dymoke, Champion, 91

Ellis, Mr & Mrs William, 171

Finch, Frederick Charles, 136
Franklin, Sir John, 168-69
Frewen-Turner, Thomas, 92

Gandy, Lieutenant, 47-8, 50
Gay-Lussac, Joseph Louis, 2, 19, 128
Glaisher, James, 3, 20, 175-76, 179
Glover, Ann, 5
Graham, George & Margaret, 10, 61, 89, 94, 120, 137, 141-42, 163
Green, Richard, 163-64
Griffith, Samuel Young, 24-6
Gulson, Edward, 38-9
Gye, Frederick, 76, 101, 119, 121, 127, 131-32, 134, 137, 144

Hampton, John, 145, 149, 163
Harris, Thomas, 51-2, 60
Hollond, Robert, 92, 115-16, 118-20, 122, 126-27, 129, 160-61, 168
Hope, James, 95
Hughes, Richard, 76, 101, 119, 127, 144
Hunt, Henry, 27
Hunter, Christopher Thomas Agrippa, 75

Ingestre, Lord, 159-60

Jones, Thomas, 143

Lamley, Charles, 25
Latour, Henri, 175
Lindstrand, Per, 146
Lister, Anne, 36
Lunardi, Vincente, 6, 58, 181

Macintosh, Charles, 105-107
Mantell, Gideon, 21
Mason, John Abraham, 169
Mason, Thomas Monck, 118-21, 124-26, 129, 148
Matthew, Thomas, 152
Mayall, John Jabez Edwin, 173
Mayhew, Henry, 172, 174
Millbank, William, 148
Minckelers, Jan Pieter, 8
Montgomery, Reverend Francis, 38
Mounsey, Major, 68

Napoleon, Prince Louis, 162
Nicholson, John, 36
Nicholson, Renton, 151
Nicklin, Richard, 172-73

Onthett, John, 17, 65

Pacha, Ibrahim, 155-56
Peck, John, 74-5
Pierpoint, Thomas, 180-81
Pope, Martha, 5
Preen, Baron de, 126
Pulleine, Colonel Percy Henry, 36
Purland, Theodosius, 2-3

Random, Charles, 147
Riddell, Colonel, 24
Rush, George, 6, 98, 142-45, 166-67, 169
Russell, James, 152

Seares, Thomas, 136-37
Shaw, Jane, 5, 180
Simonds, Henry, 31-3
Simpson, Christopher Herbert, 99
Simpson, Octavius, 79-80
Simpson, Thomas Bartlett, 147
Sparrow, Isaac Earlysman, 29-30
Spencer, Edward, 105-108, 125, 130-37, 142, 178, 181
Spinney, Thomas, 24, 26, 130
Stanyon, George Edward, 181
Stocks, Sophia, 51, 56-62
Stuart, Lord Dudley, 100

Taylor, Charles, 139
Taylor, Joseph J. Oddy, 175, 177
Tissandier, Gaston, 177

van Amburgh, Mr, 98, 143-44
van Buren, Mr, 156-57, 162-63

Wadman, William, 163-64
Warner, Samuel Alfred, 158-61
Webb, William, 43
Welby, Thomas Earle, 74-5
Welsh, John, 172-76
Wenham, Francis Herbert, 179
Widdicombe, John, 108
Willerton, John, 81
Wrottesley, Charles, 110-11

Places

Atherstone, 60, 89

Barnet, 14, 73, 156
Barnsley, 92
Beckenham, 83-4, 117
Belfast, 151
Blackburn, 70
Boston, 73-5, 77-8, 80-2, 91
Bradford, 36
Braintree, 104

Brentwood, 97
Bridgewater, 156
Brighton, 21-4, 47, 88, 130, 143, 151

Cambridge, 41, 86, 89, 92, 95, 120, 141, 162
Cannock Chase, 159
Cardiff, 162-64
Carlisle, 67-70, 76
Chelmsford, 87, 92, 104, 118, 141, 148, 161

INDEX

Cheltenham, 23-6, 62-3, 130-31, 144-45, 175
Chesterfield, 82, 87, 99
Chester-le-Street, 55
Chichester, 48-9, 168
Colchester, 87, 155, 163-64
Coventry, 8, 37, 38-40, 42, 45, 82, 89, 95
Croydon, 51, 94

Daventry, 38
Derby, 5, 76, 87, 151, 162-63
Devizes, 87-8
Dewsbury, 89, 92
Downham Market, 75, 103
Dublin, 139, 149
Dundee, 92
Dunfermline, 92
Durham, 53, 55-7

Ely, 41
Exeter, 82, 156

Folkestone, 174

Gainsborough, 34
Gloucester, 24, 63, 163
Gosberton, 80-1
Grantham, 74-5
Gravesend, 116, 153-54, 169, 171
Guildford, 18, 108, 144, 174

Halifax, 35-6, 49
Hastings, 119-20, 160, 171
Hertford, 73, 108
Hitchin, 130
Huddersfield, 70
Hull, 69, 149

Ilford, 16, 112
Ipswich, 82, 89, 155

Kendal, 57, 63-4
Kettering, 41
King's Lynn, 75, 102-103, 168
Koblenz, Germany, 125, 127

Leamington, 37-8, 43
Leeds, 34-6, 53, 56-7, 92, 156, 167
Leicester, 39, 42-3, 53, 59-61, 162-64, 172

Leighton Buzzard, 118
Liverpool, 83, 139, 144, 166-67
Louth, 78
Ludlow, 86
Lutterworth, 45
Lyons, France, 113

Manchester, 95, 138
Mansfield, 5, 92

Neufchatel, France, 171
New York, USA, 146
Newcastle, 52-7, 92
Newhaven, 23
Northampton, 25, 38, 40-1, 44, 82
Norwich, 10, 92-3, 135, 145-46, 148, 167
Nuneaton, 42

Otley, 36
Oxford, 29-30, 163

Paris, France, 19, 119-28, 140, 146, 153, 163, 170-71
Perth, 92
Peterborough, 59, 79, 88-9
Plymouth, 144
Portsea, 3, 16-18, 47-8, 50, 65, 87-8
Preston, 64, 67-8, 82

Reading, 31-3
Richmond, 50, 67, 69-70, 77
Rochdale, 70
Romford, 26, 28, 77, 112
Rotherham, 70
Rugby, 45, 162

Selby, 67
Sevenoaks, 71
Shibden, 36
Shrewsbury, 45-7, 49
Southampton, 88, 96, 145, 150-51
St Denis, France, 168
St Petersburg, Russia, 177
Stamford, 52-3, 57-9, 78-80, 82, 155
Stockton, 53, 55, 57, 69
Stratford-on-Avon, 43
Stroud, 96

Tewkesbury, 24, 62-3
Thionville, France, 127
Turkdean, 25

Uxbridge, 100, 104, 118, 141

Wakefield, 92, 139
Walthamstow, 100-102
Warwick, 43-5

Weilburg, Germany, 19, 125-26, 174
Wellingborough, 86
Wigan, 82
Wijk-aan-Zee, Holland, 35
Wolverhampton, 82, 176
Worcester, 24, 53, 61-3, 163

Yarm, 69-70
York, 53, 57, 64-8, 178